*The Raj,
the Indian Mutiny,
and the Kingdom of Oudh
1801–1859*

The Raj, the Indian Mutiny and the Kingdom of Oudh 1801–1859

JOHN PEMBLE
Research Fellow, University of Leicester

Rutherford · Madison · Teaneck
FAIRLEIGH DICKINSON UNIVERSITY PRESS

First American edition © 1977 published by
Associated University Press, Inc.,
Cranbury, N.J. 08512

copyright © 1977 John Pemble

Library of Congress Catalog Card Number: 76–55892
ISBN 0–8386–2092–2
Printed in Great Britain

All rights reserved

For
A.K.

CONTENTS

Acknowledgements	ix
List of Plates	x
List of Maps	xi

PART ONE: THE CITY

I	3
II	33
III	48
IV	89

PART TWO: THE PLAIN

V	119
VI	144

PART THREE: THE CATASTROPHE

VII	165
VIII	205
IX	233

PART FOUR: EPITAPH FOR A PRINCELY STATE

X	249

Appendices	258
Notes	264
Bibliography	285
Index	294

ACKNOWLEDGEMENTS

My overriding debt is to the University of Leicester, for providing the Research Fellowship that made the writing of this book possible. I wish to thank also the Trustees of both this book possible, and to the History Department at Leicester, for its generous hospitality during three years. I wish to thank also the Trustees of both the Twenty-Seven Foundation and the Dame Lillian Penson Memorial Fund, for awards which enabled me to undertake a research trip to Delhi and Lucknow.

Many colleagues at Leicester were kind enough to allow me to pick their brains, most notably Peter Graves, who translated from the German for me, and Clive Dewey and Peter Musgrave, who were never too busy to answer questions and offer suggestions but who, I must hasten to add, are in no way responsible for the views I have put forward, some of which, I am sure, must fail to meet with their agreement. Dr Desmond Henry read my comments on Sleeman and made suggestions for which I am most grateful. I was lucky enough to secure the expert professional services of David Orme, who drew the maps, and June Lee, who typed the copy.

I am beholden to the authorities at the India Office Library and Records, London, for permission to consult and quote from materials in their charge. Similar privileges were granted to me in the National Archives of India, New Delhi, and the Tagore Library, University of Lucknow, for which I wish to record my thanks. Of the many people who were glad to help me in Lucknow I wish to thank especially 'A.P.', for good comradeship and swift transportation to unlikely places, and Reggie Jones and his friends at La Martinière College, whose courtesy and amiability have ensured that my memories of that fascinating institution will always be among my most pleasant.

Leicester, October 1976   J.P.

LIST OF PLATES

appearing between pages 148 and 149

Nawab Ghazi-ud-din Haidar and Major Baillie, *circa* 1814.

The Residency, Lucknow, before the Mutiny.

Dilkusha Chateau, Lucknow.

Constantia (La Martiniere) after bombardment by Sir Colin Campbell, March 1858.

Rumi Darwaza, Lucknow, before the Mutiny.

The Chattar Manzil and Farhatbakhsh Palaces, Lucknow, *circa* 1880.

Part of the Quaisarbugh, Lucknow, showing the dome of the tomb of Saadat Ali Khan.

Reception of Lord Hardinge by Wajid Ali Shah.

MAPS

1 India, *circa* 1830   2
2 Oudh, *post* 1801   118
3 Lucknow, at the time of the Mutiny   164

PART ONE: THE CITY

Je t'aime, O capitale infame! Courtisanes
Et bandits, tels souvent vous offrez des plaisirs
Que ne comprennent pas les vulgaires profanes.

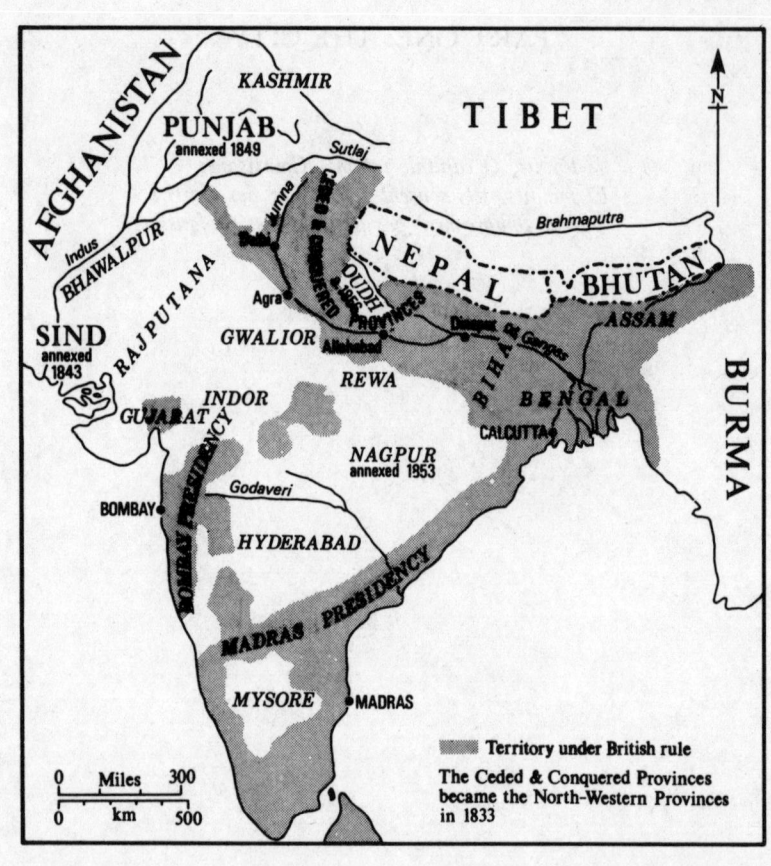

1 India, *circa* 1830

I

One day in March 1858 William Russell, correspondent of *The Times,* heaved his sixteen-stone bulk to the top of Dilkusha château to admire the view. Facing west, he saw to his right the curving Gomti river, whose passage across the flat and fertile landscape was boldly marked in yellow bands of silt. To the front he looked down on groves and orchards of cypress, mango, orange, pomegranate, guava, custard apple, peach, nectarine, apricot and date palm – acre after acre of dark green foliage, spreading almost to the rim of the limpid sky. In the distance, scattered domes, towers and parapets, fretted and curved, painted and gilded, broke the surface of vegetation and caught the sunlight like ornamental galleons becalmed. This was the city of Lucknow, than which even the much-travelled Russell thought that Earth had not anything to show more fair. 'Not Rome, not Athens, not Constantinople; not any city I have ever seen', he wrote, 'appears to me so striking and so beautiful as this.'

At this time Lucknow had a population of about half a million, which made it one of the largest towns in India. With Calcutta, Bombay and Benares, it ranked as one of the metropolitan wonders of the British Raj. Native poets praised it as The Heavenly City (*Akhtarnagar*), and later it was to feature as the fair Nucklow in Kipling's *Kim*.

It was a city of gardens, palaces, mosques, bazaars and spacious suburbs, renowned above all for its art, its letters and its luxurious living. There was nothing in its reputation or its aspect to suggest war or strife, heroes or martyrs. It had thrown up no frowning bastions, and it had bred no race of warriors. Yet destiny had reserved for it the leading role in a violent drama. Even as Russell was admiring the distant vista of its pinnacles and rooftops, preparations were under weigh which were to turn Lucknow into a place of bloodshed and devastation; and its name lives in the annals of the Raj as the scene of one of the most celebrated sieges in its history. In

1857 and 1858 the British were engaged in a desperate struggle to crush the revolt known as the Indian Mutiny, and Lucknow was one of the most important of the rebel strongholds. Russell was visiting the city not as an idle tourist, but as a war correspondent, in the train of an avenging army. Behind this agony of Lucknow lay a long and intriguing story, whose main components were the interacting and conflicting interests of a Muslim aristocracy, a Hindu peasantry and the Christian rulers of Britain's Indian empire.

Lucknow was one of the most recent acquisitions of the British. Until 1856 it had been the capital of a nominally independent prince, who bore the title of King of Oudh.[1] Like all his forebears, this prince was a Muslim, and his capital had become a major Islamic centre. Only about forty percent of its inhabitants were Muslims, but evidences of Islam were everywhere. The skyline was crowded with cupolas and minarets, and in the thoroughfares women were heavily veiled. Street-corner faquirs preached impromptu for alms and muezzins calling the faithful to prayer started nasal echoes among mosques and tombs. 'In no place in India', wrote Emma Roberts, who visited Lucknow in the 1830s, 'can there be a more vivid realization of the visions conjured up by a perusal of the splendid fictions of the *Arabian Nights.*'

The royal family of Oudh was the most modern of the Muslim dynasties in India. It dated only from 1720, when Saadat Khan, a Persian adventurer from Khurasan, was made governor of the province (*subah*) of Oudh in reward for military services rendered to the Emperor of India. Until 1819 these rulers were not, in theory, monarchs. Saadat Khan had been only *nazim* (governor) of the province; and although his successor obtained the tital *nawab* from the Emperor in Delhi, which gave him viceregal status, he had no claim to sovereignty. He wielded only a delegated authority. In 1748 the Nawab was created *wazir* (or Vizier), which means minister, of the Emperor; and thereafter the ruler of Oudh was known as the Nawab Vizier. In practice the titles, like the authority they designated, were hereditary; but in theory they were enjoyed only during the pleasure of the Emperor, to whom the Oudh rulers paid allegiance and in whose name they struck coins. A *nazar,* or gift of tribute, was sent yearly to Delhi, and princes of the Imperial family were paid ostentatious deference. Two of these princes resided in Lucknow during the early decades of the nineteenth century on pensions provided by the Nawab, and etiquette prescribed that whenever the latter met one of them in the street he must either dismount or cause the elephant on which he was riding to kneel in homage.

It is a wonder that these tokens of obeisance lasted so long, for even as early as Saadat Khan's appointment to Oudh the Emperor in Delhi was a mere king of shreds and patches, without power of coercion. The Imperial hegemony in India had been a fruit of slow growth and swift decay. Five dynasties of Muslim sultans, mostly Turks and Afghans from central Asia, had ruled in Delhi since 1206; but only the most powerful of the sixth, or Mughal dynasty, [2] in the seventeenth century, had been real emperors of India. The Emperor Aurangzeb, who died in 1707, was the last to exercise imperial authority. Success had begot decadence and decadence had begot weakness. Effeminacy, cupidity and treachery tainted the Muslim aristocracy of Delhi; provincial governors asserted their independence; and religious factiousness divided the Muslim community. The empire thus fell a swift victim to the dangers that were besetting it from within and without. Predatory monarchs from Afghanistan and Persia invaded India and raided Delhi on several occasions during the first half of the eighteenth century, and subject Hindus moved in to take the pickings with new-found martial vigour. The Muslims had made many conversions in Sind, north-western India and eastern Bengal; but elsewhere in the subcontinent the population had remained Hindu. The traditional warriors of Hindu society, the Rajputs, had been demoralised and dispersed by the extensive successes of the Muslims in northern India; but other groups and races were not wanting to sustain the military traditions of their faith. Most notable in this respect were the Sikhs and the Mahrattas. The Sikhs, a turbanned, bearded sect of reformed Hindus, turned themselves into a martial élite and took advantage of Imperial weakness to extend their sway over the Punjab; while the Mahrattas, a warlike people from the southwest, undertook expeditions of conquest which made them masters of most of central India and custodians of Delhi and its Imperial figurehead. By the end of the eighteenth century all seemed set fair for a Hindu empire in the place of the old Muslim one; but the course of history took an unexpected twist, and in the event the successors of the Mughals were not Indians at all, but Europeans. A power had arisen in the east which challenged and subdued the Hindu candidates for empire. This was the British East India Company, whose agents came to India to trade in the seventeenth century and ended as the rulers of a vast empire in the nineteenth. The transformation was the result rather of political circumstances than of premeditated ambition. During the eighteenth century Indian history was a struggle for power in which British neutrality was impossible, given the participation of hostile parties such as the French and the native dynasties of Mysore and Bengal. Following the example of the French, who had introduced Western military techniques into the subcontinent, the Company protected its interests by furnishing its own allies and protégés with European-trained native troops (*sepoys*), and acquired territorial possessions and political hegemony largely as a corollary of this military sponsorship. In the prevailing economic and political circumstances territory was the only sure mode of payment, so military subsidies often became converted into grants of land; while the native princes, by relying on hired assistance and neglecting their own resources, became in effect not only the paymasters but the prisoners of the British military machine. The wealth and influence they acquired in this way enabled the British, under the imperialist Governor-General Lord Wellesley (brother of the Duke of Wellington), to challenge the Mahrattas to a final struggle for supremacy. The contest opened in 1803 and continued, after an interlude of uneasy truce, under the aegis of the Marquis of Hastings in 1817. By the following year British paramountcy was assured over the whole of India, excluding Sind and the Punjab, and the Mughal Emperor was the pensioned puppet of an infidel trading corporation.

The East India Company, acting as trustee of the British Crown, now ruled directly an area of some half a million square miles, made up mainly of the Gangetic plain and delta in the north (the Bengal Presidency) and the Deccan, the appendix of the subcontinent, in the south (the Presidencies of Madras and Bombay). It exercised besides powers of supervision and protection over the native rulers of central India and Rajputana. These rulers retained nominal control over their domestic affairs; but the subsidiary system ensured that they were militarily impotent and diplomatically isolated. To each court a British Resident was appointed, who controlled the subsidiary force and kept an eagle eye on all the transactions of the princely protégé.

The Mughals retained their high-sounding titles and their throne until 1858, when his part in the Indian Mutiny finally sent the last of the dynasty into inglorious exile; but the great increase in British power and influence meant that Calcutta, the capital of the East India Company's dominions, became the real focus of political power in India after 1805. The Emperor's domain, stretching no farther than the walls of the Red Fort in Delhi, was a pathetic vestige of the great empire of his ancestors, and the fiction of his supremacy was gradually demolished as his nominal vassals discontinued their symbols of allegiance. In theory the East India Company ruled the provinces of Bengal, Bihar and Orissa as his fiscal agent, or *diwan*; but it stopped sending pecuniary tribute to Delhi in 1770 and in 1835 replaced the Emperor's image on its coinage with that of the British monarch. The British Governors-General recognised the Emperor only as King of Delhi, and refused to meet him under any conditions of etiquette that suggested their inferior status. In 1819 the Nawab Vizier of Oudh, one of the Emperor's most important native vassals, likewise rejected his nominal master. In April of that year he issued coins struck in his own name, and on 9 October had himself crowned King of his territories.

The ceremony was conducted with great pomp and ostentation; but as a gesture of independence it had no meaning. The Nawab of Oudh was no longer a free agent, for he, like the princes of Hyderabad, Mysore, Nagpur, Baroda, Cochin and Travencore, was already enmeshed in the web of the British subsidiary system.

The Nawabs had mortgaged their independence in the usual way: first seeking British military assistance (against the Rohillas, in 1773), and then finding that as the Subsidiary Force usurped the functions and resources of their own army, this declined drastically in efficiency and left them helpless dependents of Calcutta. Within the space of thirty years they had had to give up half their territories to pay for the essential but unwelcome favour of protection. In 1772 they had lost the fort of Chunar to the East India Company. In 1775 they had made over the districts of Benares and Ghazipur as part of a defence treaty; and in 1798 the fortress of Allahabad, previously bought from the British, had also been ceded. Meanwhile the cash subsidy had been progressively increased, and in 1801 the Governor-General, Lord Wellesley, had commuted it for the province of Rohilkhand and the remainder of the old province of Allahabad, to prevent default. In the territories that remained to them the Nawabs enjoyed only emasculated authority. Emancipation from Delhi had been followed closely by subjection to Calcutta, and the signs of tutelage to the one replaced by signs of tutelage to the other. In 1773 the Nawab had resigned control of his foreign policy to the British and a British Resident had been appointed to his court. During the rule of Warren Hastings in British India (1772-85) this individual had become the real master of the province. In 1798 British interference had been taken to the point of dethroning one Nawab and replacing him by another. The Governor-General, Sir John Shore, had decided to remove Wazir Ali from the throne, ostensibly because he was believed not to be the true son of Asaf-ud-daula, but in reality because he promised to be an intractable ally whereas the rival claimant, Saadat Ali Khan (brother of Asaf), offered attractive terms as the condition of his elevation. Thereafter, the validity of a succession was always reckoned to depend upon its recognition by the British authorities.

It was largely as a result of encouragement from the Governor-General that the Nawab decided to assume the title of King in 1819. In 1816 there had been anti-British riots among the Muslim population of Bareilly in Rohilkhand, and these had awakened Governor-General Lord Hastings to the effects which an appeal to Muslim religious susceptibilities might have on British authority in the north. The probability of such an appeal was increased by the anti-British animosity of Prince Jahangir, third in the line of succession to the Mughal throne. It was in order to drive a wedge of resentment between the courts of Delhi and Oudh, and thus obviate the possibility of an anti-British alliance, that Lord Hastings humoured the Nawab's disposition to renounce his traditional allegiance and proclaim himself sovereign of his domains.[3] The British inspiration behind the coronation ceremony of October 1819 was reflected in a curious way, for the court musicians signalled the crowning of the new monarch not with some oriental anthem, but with *God Save the King*.[4]

As Kings, the rulers of Oudh were granted a royal salute of twenty-one guns; but this was the only concession made by the British to their new dignity. They remained deprived of the power of making peace and war, and Ghazi-ud-din's attempts to assert his monarchical status were brusquely disallowed. He tried in vain to make European officers stand in his presence, to ban their umbrellas and palanquins (the symbols of royalty in India) from the inner courtyard of his palace, and to alter the mode of his reception of the Resident.[5] The British in Lucknow continued to treat the ruler as they had ever done: always with less than deference, and often with familiarity or contempt. No hint of superior status was permitted in his relations with the Governor-General, and when Lord Hardinge visited Lucknow in 1847 the King was required to wear English patent leather shoes to receive him. Indian shoes had been strictly forbidden, since keeping them on would have implied the superior rank of the King. This incident was mentioned by Kamal-ud-din, of the Lucknow observatory staff, in his history of Oudh, and the King was so sensitive about it that he retaliated by abolishing both the observatory and all the private printing presses in Lucknow.[6] This convention concerning shoes was a source of perennial friction, and it explains why in all court portraiture featuring a European in company with the monarch the artist has contrived to keep their feet hidden. The Calcutta authorities maintained a jealous vigilance over the titles assumed by the

King, and immediately objected to those that they deemed too pretentious or extravagant. Two of the titles adopted by Ghazi-ud-din in 1819 were *shah-e-zaman* ('King of the Age') and *padshah-e-ghazi* ('Imperial Crusader'). The British prohibited both. The first was a title traditionally held by the Emperor of Delhi and, they explained, 'we felt strong objection to any measure which might give colour to a supposition of our concurrence in the elevation of a rival King of India, opposed to the King of Delhi, inasmuch as such procedure might be construed into a wanton oppression of a dignified though unfortunate family'. The title of *ghazi* they could not allow, since 'its direct purport would imply inherent principles of difference between the King [as a Muslim] and the British Government [as "infidels"] involving eventual rupture'. The title *shah-e-zaman* was finally permitted on the condition that it was qualified by the rider *padshah-e-awadh* ('King of Oudh'), though the latter never in fact appeared on the King's coins. This tedious dispute was revived in 1827 when, on his accession, Nasir-ud-din adopted the title *shah jahan* ('King of the Universe'), which had been that of one of the most illustrious of the Mughal Emperors. 'We could not approve', reported the Calcutta government, 'the disposition thus manifested by the Court of Oudh to persevere in appropriating the Imperial style and titles'. The Governor-General refused to accept correspondence from the King which bore his new seal, and after two years the objectionable title quietly disappeared from the Oudh coinage.[7]

The Kings of Oudh were thus never real kings. Their royalty was of the nature of private fantasy – humoured to a limited extent by the British, but without consequence for anyone but themselves. All its trappings were symbols without meaning. Few even among the population of Oudh were disposed to take it seriously, and his subjects continued to refer to their prince as 'the Nawab'.[8]

But if the British connection made royalty a sham and destroyed political independence, it also created conditions ideal for cultural and commercial efflorescence. It provided security – attested by the fact that Lucknow is the only major Muslim city in north India that has never been walled – and it diverted the energies and wealth of the aristocracy and court from war and internecine struggles to pleasure activities and the arts of peace. Thus Lucknow grew and thrived while Delhi languished and all but died. Here alone did Muslim architecture, which had given northern India some of its greatest man-made glories, continue as a living art. The buildings of Lucknow were being erected while those of Delhi were falling into ruin.

As a metropolis, Lucknow dated only from 1780. Before that it was a prosperous Muslim settlement surrounding a citadel – 'an irregular dirty town'[9] on the undulating ground beside the river Gomti. It was little used by the first three Nawabs, who preferred to reside either near the corridors of power in Delhi or in the reputedly healthier air of Faizabad, though Safdar Jung, who chose not only to live but also to be buried in Delhi, did build a modern fort on the site of the old citadel. This he called Machhi Bhawan ('Fish House') after the fish on his escutcheon.[10] It was the fourth Nawab, Asaf-ud-daula (1775-97), who finally moved the court from Faizabad to Lucknow. He built himself a palace called Daulat Khana ('House of Prosperity') on the banks of the Gomti just west of the Machhi Bhawan and, according to a contemporary chronicler, proceeded to expend a million rupees a year in a 'building mania'. The Chowk Bazaar and a stone bridge were built to encourage settlement and commerce, and a new urban nucleus developed, absorbing, it is said, the sites of fifty-two villages and rendering many long-settled subjects homeless. Under Asaf's successors the town expanded towards the east, following the court, which moved first to Farhatbakhsh ('Pleasure-giving') palace, and then to the Chattar Manzil ('Umbrella Palace') and finally to the Qaisarbagh. In 1843 a second permanent bridge was built, further downstream from the stone one. This was 'an iron bridge of three arches, two hundred paces in length'. Its parts had arrived from England thirty years before, together with an engineer called Jessop, who was sent to supervise their assembly; but Saadat Ali Khan, the Nawab who had ordered the bridge, died shortly after its arrival and construction was delayed until the reign of his nephew, Amjad Ali Shah.[11] The most ambitious engineering project of the Nawabs, a canal designed to make Lucknow accessible by water from the Ganges, by linking that river with the Gomti, was a failure. The work was conceived by the Nawab Nasir-ud-din (1827-37), but confided to incapable hands. The line of the canal was marked out and partly excavated – to a depth of 40 feet in some places – but the basic surveying had been faulty and as planned the canal would have been incapable of carrying the waters of the Ganges, which lay higher than those of the Gomti, any further east than 16 miles. In 1833 the services of a British engineer were sought and obtained; but funds ran out before he had rectified the mistakes and the canal has remained unfinished from that day to this. [12]

Lucknow architecture cannot satisfy a taste formed by the finest buildings of the Mughals. The Nawabs, for all their wealth, did not have access to the marble which the Mughal builders had brought, at vast expense, from Rajputana; and by the time it reached Lucknow, the Mughal style was already showing signs of debasement. It had attained its zenith under the Emperor Shah Jahan (1627-58), in whose buildings at Delhi and Agra the Hindu features (short, square pillars, bracket capitals and horizontal architraves) so often incorporated into earlier Indo-Saracenic architecture have either disappeared or been subordinated, and the Islamic pointed arch, dome and minaret dominate, blended into a rare and haunting harmony. But with the banishment of the massive ruggedness of the pre-Mughal styles, the way had been opened to excessive refinement and ornamentation, and these are precisely the faults that mar most of the buildings of Shah Jahan, so precarious was the perfection achieved in the Taj Mahal. The ribbed domes, striped elongated minarets, foiled arches and fretted parapets of the Jama Masjid (Friday Mosque) in Delhi are unmistakable harbingers of decadence; decadence that was finally to declare itself in the awkward proportions, garrotted dome and profusion of plaster masquerading as marble of the eighteenth-century tomb of Safdar Jung. The best examples of the Lucknow provincial style bear the stigmata of congenital weakness and everywhere in the city the beautiful Islamic pointed arch, combining suggestions of both elegance and strength, has degenerated into the baroque multi-foiled arcature. But such religious edifices as the Bara (Great) Imambara, with its adjacent mosque, and the tombs of the Nawab Saadat Ali Khan and his consort are, in proportions if not in detail, as fine as anything produced by the contemporary metropolitan school. The dome of the tomb of Saadat Ali Khan probably deserves to rank amongst the best examples of the motif in India. Its hemispherical form suggests a reaction against the Persian type of narrow-necked, bulging dome made fashionable by the later Mughals, and a return to the nobility of the provincial style of Bijapur or the pre-Mughal styles of Hindustan. Lacking marble and stone, the Nawabs of Lucknow used brick, concrete and stucco (*chunam*), and achieved in these materials buildings of great constructive ingenuity and durability. The hall of Asaf-ud-daula's Bara Imambara is 50 feet high, 162 feet long and 53 feet wide, and is covered by unsupported concrete vaulting unique in its extent. Even generally hostile observers used to admit its impressiveness. The Lucknow stucco, made from the calcareous deposits of ancient lake beds, gave an effect of great chasteness when not covered with surface distemper, and its toughness was fully attested in 1858, when the plastered walls of the building called Sikandarbagh proved indestructible by nine-pound cannon shot and yielded to the British eighteen-pounders only after more than an hour's bombardment. The city's most ambitious piece of purely ornamental architecture is the Rumi Darwaza, a triumphal arch of brick and coloured stucco built beside the Gomti by Asaf-ud-daula. It was supposed to be an imitation of one of the gateways of Constantinople (Rum). It consists of an ogee'd portal 60 feet high surmounted by an elaborate lantern, with flanking curtain walls pierced with cusped windows and terminated by octagonal bastions. It is perhaps over-florid, and it suffers by comparison with the most successful exercise of the genre, the magnificent sandstone and marble Buland Darwaza ('Lofty Portal') of the Emperor Akbar at Fatehpur Sikhri. But it is impressively situated and is – or rather was – well proportioned. Originally there was a slender column on each side of the central arch and imaginary lines drawn from the tip of each to the base of the other intersected at the apex of the small arched opening in the back wall of the main portal.

Until the death of Ghazi-ud-din (1827), the best traditions of Indo-Muslim architecture were emulated, if not equalled; but thereafter the religious, like the domestic architecture of Lucknow began to reflect the peculiar cultural climate of the city. It changed from art to artifice as the inspiration behind it became less architectonic and more decorative. Ornamentation and colour took precedence over line and the play of light and shadow. Thus buildings like the Husainabad Imambara and the Jama Masjid are adorned with a riot of mouldings and crude colouring that suggest either naïve exuberance or calculated defiance of every canon of aesthetics and craftsmanship.

After the decline of Delhi, only in Lucknow was that tradition of courtly opulence maintained that had made Muslim India a byword throughout the world. No oriental despot ever lived more luxuriously than Asaf-ud-daula, the most extravagant of his house. The marriage of his putative son, Wazir Ali, was celebrated in 1795 with an ostentation that even the great Mughals would have been hard put to surpass.

About seven at night [wrote an English guest] the bridegroom Wazir Ali, the young Nawab, appeared loaded so absurdly with jewels that he could scarcely stagger under the weight. We then mounted our elephants to proceed to a rich and extensive garden, which was about a mile off. The procession was grand beyond conception. It consisted of about 1,200 elephants richly caparisoned and drawn up in a regular line like a regiment of soldiers; about 100 of the elephants which were in the centre had castles, called *howdahs*, lashed on their backs, which were covered with silver. In the centre was the Nawab mounted on an uncommonly large elephant, covered with cloth of gold and a rich *howdah* covered with gold and studded with precious stones ... On both sides of the road ... were raised artificial sceneries of bamboo work very high, representing bastions, arches, minarets and towers, covered with lights in lamps, which made a grand and sublime display; and on each side of the procession, in front of the line of elephants, were dancing girls richly dressed [and] carried on platforms supported by men called bearers, who danced as we went along. All these platforms were covered with gold and silver cloths; and there were two girls and two musicians on each platform. The number of these platforms was about a hundred on each side of the procession. All the ground from the tents to the garden, over which we moved along, was *enlaid* with fireworks, and at every step the elephants took the ground burst before us and threw up artificial stars in the heavens ... In the centre of the garden was a large edifice, to which we ascended, and were introduced into a grand saloon adorned with innumerable girandoles and pendant lustres of English manufacture, lighted with wax candles. Here we had an elegant and sumptuous collation of European and native dishes, with wines, fruits and sweetmeats; at the same time above a hundred dancing girls sang their sprightly airs and danced their native dances ... The whole expense of this marriage feast, which was repeated three successive nights in the same manner ... cost above £300,000.[13]

When Asaf went on a hunting expedition he was reported by the same authority to be accompanied by

10,000 soldiers, 1,000 cavalry and near 150 pieces of cannon; 1,500 elephants, 3,000 carts or hackeries, and an innumerable train of camels, horses and bullocks; great numbers of rutts, or covered carriages for women, drawn by oxen, which were filled with the Nawab's ladies; many large and small boats carried on carts drawn by 50, 40 and 30 oxen each; tigers, leopards and hawks, fighting cocks, fighting quails and nightingales; pigeons, dancing women and boys, singers, players, buffoons and mountebanks.

Even when exaggeration is allowed for, this indicates a style of life which would have been unthinkable anywhere else in India at the time. Luxury crafts were fostered by the prodigality of the court. The Chowk Bazaar, and later the quarters called Hazratganj and Aminabad, became colonies of high-class merchants dealing in jewelry, cloth of gold and silver, pottery, the type of embossed embroidery known as *cikan*, embroidered shoes, enamel ware, silver *étuis* decorated with filigree motifs and, perhaps most celebrated of all, attar (*itr*) or perfume essence, one drop of which would scent a garment for years. Lucknow became renowned for its attars of *gulab* (rose), *khas* (vetiver), *motiya* (lily) and *chameli* (jasmine); and the far-famed *hina* or henna, an attar of lowsonia flowers whose blood-red colour made it a favourite symbol in poetry, was perfected according to a secret formula by the perfumier Asghar Ali of Chowk.

This wealth, and the security of Lucknow, exercised a powerful attraction on the poets, musicians, scholars and professional men who had hitherto subsisted on the bounty of the Mughal court. When Delhi could no longer support them, they made their way almost *en masse* to Lucknow, which soon became the centre of the most urbane, literate and brilliant society in India. Lucknow was thus the inheritor of the role once filled by Delhi as the focus of Muslim culture, learning and fashion in the subcontinent.

The city's reputation as a seat of Muslim scholarship dated from the end of the seventeenth century, when the Farhangi Mahal ('Scientific Academy') was founded. The renown of the *ulema,* or doctors, of this seminary, for Arabic, philosophy, mathematics (including astronomy), rhetoric, jurisprudence, exegesis of the Koran, Islamic tradition and Islamic mysticism spread beyond India to Bokhara, Herat and Kabul. The Nawabs further enhanced the prestige of Lucknow by encouraging poetry and letters. They collected a splendid library, and Asaf-ud-daula, Ghazi-ud-din and Wajid Ali Shah themselves wrote poetry, the first and last with real talent. Ghazi-ud-din's verses were bad, but he acquired something of a reputation as a lexicographer by compiling a seven-volume dictionary of Persian. The royal taste for poetry spread to all levels of society. The *mushaira,* or literary symposium, at which poets recited their new verses to audiences of friends and patrons, flourished in Lucknow long after it had become extinct in Delhi. The capital of the Nawabs was especially renowned for its Urdu literature. It became something of an Urdu Parnassus. The language had originated as a sort of *lingua franca,* a cross between the Persian spoken by the Muslim solidery and élite of northern India and the dialects (especially East Punjabi and Brajbasha) spoken by the subject Hindu population. The word 'urdu' itself is a Mongol one, meaning military camp; and it had been in the camp bazaars and, later, in the quarters of the native wives of the Muslim colonists, that the language for which it became the name developed. It was used as a literary language in Delhi in the eighteenth century, but the Mughal court language remained Persian and few poets reckoned themselves qualified for the title who did not compose in that language as well as in Urdu. Ghalib, possibly the greatest Urdu poet of the century, always evinced a snobbish predilection for Persian, and affected to regard his own Urdu verses as of little merit. In Lucknow, on the other hand, Urdu was the court language and the principal medium of literary expression.[14] It was taken in hand by lexicographers and prosodists and transformed from a fluid patois into a formal language with rules of grammar and diction. 'Lakhnavi' usage became the criterion of correctness and good taste and the Muslim citizens of the town became, and have remained, renowned for the elegance and sophistication of their Urdu. This is not to say that Persian influences were wanting. On the contrary, Persian was still an indispensable accomplishment for all educated men, and Lakhnavi Urdu became strongly impregnated with a Persian flavour. Not only vocabulary, but syntax – which is essentially Hindi in the more colloquial or 'Hindustani' form of Urdu – became modified by Persian importations. The language, nevertheless, remained Urdu; and it was here that it first really came into its own as one of the most rich and expressive tongues in the world.

The musical arts likewise found a new and congenial home in Lucknow. Music, although proscribed by the orthodox *ulema* (doctors) of Islam, had nonetheless always played a prominent part in Muslim life. The sufis (mystics) of Persia and Iraq had sought ecstatic inspiration by means of it, and in India, where there was a strong indigenous musical tradition, most Muslim rulers succumbed to its charms. The Delhi Sultans and their successors the early Mughals, together with provincial rulers such as those of Gujurat and Jaunpur, all patronised the musical arts, and the invention of the sitar has been attributed to Khasrau, a Muslim musician of the Khalji court in Delhi. The Lucknow dynasty inherited and sustained this tradition of patronage. During the reign of Shuja-ud-daula (1756-75) thousands of minstrels and singing and dancing women made their way to Faizabad from Delhi while other performers, including the male dancers called Kathaks, came from the old centres of Hindu music at Benares and Ajodhya. Lucknow society became particularly fond of the dance. Dancing boys dressed as women were an especially admired feature of the performances of the Kashmiri Bhands, and there were few wealthy households that did not have a private establishment of Domnis, or Hindu women of the Dom or dancing caste.

Lucknow owed much to Delhi, but it would be a mistake to imagine that its culture was merely an extension or imitation of that of the Imperial capital. Conditions obtained here which were absent from Delhi, and these gave Lucknow literature and architecture a highly distinctive character. In the first place the court and most of the influential Muslims of Lucknow were of the Shia, and not the Sunni sect; in the second, the province of Oudh enjoyed the protection of the British, a circumstance which made not only for stability and security of a type that Delhi had not known for generations, but also for the introduction of Western influences.

All Muslims accept the 'five pillars of Islam', namely, belief in the one God and in Muhammad of Mecca as His Apostle; five prayers a day; almsgiving; fasting during Ramadan, the month during which the holy book or Koran was revealed to Muhammad; and pilgrimage to the holy places of Arabia. All, furthermore, abominate idolatry and abjure the flesh of swine, naturally deceased animals and beasts of prey. But on issues of doctrine beyond these fundamentals they differ, and two great schools or sects have developed within the Muslim world – the Sunni, or orthodox, and the Shia, or schismatic. Shiism began as a political protest in Iraq in the seventh century A.D., soon after the death of Muhammad, when there was a struggle for the Caliphate, or headship, of the new Muslim empire. The Shias, mostly non-Arabs with grievances against the Arab ruling class, supported Ali, son-in-law of the Prophet, and ever afterwards maintained that he had been the only authentic Caliph. The movement soon developed a doctrine and a hagiology of its own. Shia doctrine is based on the view that the Koran is not, as the Sunnis hold, uncreate and eternal, but created by God and therefore full of occult meanings which only an enlightened leader can interpret.

These gnostic guides are the *imams*, whom all Shias accept as sinless and possessed of the power of intercession with God – a power which makes them equal in status to the Prophet. The largest group among the Shias are 'the Twelvers' (*ithna ashariya*), who maintain that there have been twelve Imams, the first of whom was Ali and the last of whom was the Mahdi, or expected one, who disappeared in about 873 A.D. but who is still alive. During his absence supreme authority in spiritual and legal matters is exercised by theologians called *mujtahidin* (singular *mujtahid*). His reappearance will be preceded by the rise of a usurper corresponding to the occidental Antichrist and will inaugurate a reign of righteousness corresponding to the Christian Millenium. Shia hagiology centres on the 'Five Pure Ones' (*panjtan-e-pak*) – Muhammad, his daughter Fatima, her husband Ali, and their sons Hasan and Husain. Ali and Husain, and possibly Hasan too, were killed by their political enemies and thus attained to the status of martyrs. The death of Husain in battle at Karbala in 680 has acquired in Shia estimation an importance almost equal to that which Christians attribute to the crucifixion, for, notwithstanding that the doctrine of atonement is foreign to Islam, the Shias attribute to their martyr a redemptive mission similar to that of Christ.

Shiism was very strong in Persia, and after the foundation of the Safavid dynasty in the early sixteenth century became the state religion there. From Persia it spread to India. The Mughals were all Sunnis; but Shia troops and associates from Persia and central Asia had come to India in their train, so until the firm reassertion of Sunni orthodoxy under the Emperors Shah Jahan and Aurangzeb there was always a powerful Shia party at the Delhi court. The founder of the Oudh dynasty, Saadat Khan, brought Shiism with him from his Persian homeland; and as a result of the eradication of Shia influences from Delhi and Aurangzeb's extinction of the Shia kingdoms of southern India (Bijapur and Golconda), his court became the most important centre in India of this brand of Islam. Eminent Shia *ulema* settled in Lucknow and thus made available to the Shias of the city the sort of education that was provided for the Sunnis by the Farhangi Mahal. Shia congregational prayer, rare in India, was introduced into Lucknow during the reign of Asaf-ud-daula, and continues to this day. A substantial proportion of the Muslim population of Lucknow was Shia, largely as a result of the conversion of Sunnis anxious for court favour or personal advancement.

The zealous Shiism of its rulers gave Lucknow a distinctive religious atmosphere. The festival of Moharram, in commemoration of the martydom at Karbala of the Imam Husain with his son (Ali Akbar), brother (Abbas) and nephew (Qasim), was – and is – observed with remarkable piety. [15] During this time all luxuries were eschewed. Women discarded jewelry and cosmetics and all classes forwent *pan*, the scarlet-juiced digestive, consisting of betel leaf smeared with lime-and-catechu paste and ground areca nut, rolled into a cone. Coloured turbans and sashes were exchanged for black ones, save in the case of the Sayyids (descendants of Fatima and Ali), whose mourning colour was green. The ceremonies centred on the *imambaras,* or halls of the Imams. Here models of the tombs of the martyrs (*taziyas*) were deposited, after being borne about in procession and before ritual burial in the graveyards known as *karbalas.* Twice a day mourning services were held which generated intense emotion. The oratory of the *maulvis* who recited the exploits of the martyrs often provoked passionate outbursts of grief among the congregation, who would interject with sobs and cries of *Hasan! Husain! Hasan! Husain!* while beating their breasts, tearing their hair and bleeding from self-inflicted injuries. There was little love lost between the Shias and the Sunnis in Lucknow, and the ceremonies of Moharram were especially calculated to provoke clashes, since the Shias then indulged in virulent execration of the first three Caliphs, whom Sunnis revered as companions of the Prophet. In 1828 there was a particularly serious conflict between members of the rival sects. Six people were killed and nine wounded, and as a result the King ordered the houses of the offending Sunnis to be plundered and destroyed. [16]

Shia martyrolatry found literary expression in the *marsiya* (pronounced 'marthiya' in Arabic), or threnody, which had its Indian home in Lucknow. During Moharram traditional threnodies were intoned or sung by professional elegy singers (*soz-khwanan*) like the renowned Haidari Khan, a musician whose performances used to attract thousands of listeners. Wives and womenfolk among the Shias supplemented their private devotions with musical laments for their revered martyrs, and often, at night in the month of mourning, the plaintive and haunting cadences of their voices would break the silence of the *karbalas:*

> The band defeated on Karbala plain
> Came to Damascus in fetter and chain;
> A spear bore aloft the head of Husain
> Before the unveilèd wives of the slain!

The *marsiya* (plural *marasi*) was an old form that had been known in Arabia and Persia; but until the poets of Lucknow adopted it and introduced it into Urdu its prestige had been low. They rehabilitated the form and expanded it into true epic literature, thus adding a new genre to the repertoire of Urdu writers. Mir Zamir, an eighteenth-century Lucknow poet, wrote the first *marasi* in Urdu, and, by introducing exordia with descriptions of battles and landscapes, transformed them from short epicediums into heroic verse. Anis and Dabir, who lived and worked in Lucknow during the first half of the nineteenth century, were the supreme exponents of the form, and critical consensus has awarded their *marasi* a place in the forefront of Urdu literature. Anis was especially renowned for his battle scenes, of which the following is a sample:

> Then tabors were struck, and did amplify
> The vibrant drumnote, till it shook the sky;
> Death's trumpet sounded at the prince's cry
> And the farthest wilderness made reply.
>   The martial clamour from above the ground
>   Startled the dead in their slumber profound;
> With noise of stallions the cohorts rushed;
> The air like an hourglass was filled with dust.
> The sun's shining face was awestruck and flushed
> As it sank to earth in the gathering dusk;
>   Then the combat waxing with doubled roar,
>   The sky grew thicker, and it showed no more.

The *marsiya* was Lucknow's major contribution to Urdu letters; and it was a contribution of historical, as well as aesthetic significance. By introducing Urdu writers to a genre that demanded fresh responses to nature and everyday experience, it weaned them from their preoccupation with the abstract and the symbolic and prepared them for the Western influences that were to transform their work in the second half of the nineteenth century. It was a point of growth in a largely dead and decadent environment.

In Delhi Urdu poetry had been profoundly influenced by a sense of insecurity and tribulation. It was a twilight bloom, which burgeoned in the Imperial sunset, and tears clung about it like vespertine dew. Its themes were elegaic – the agony of unrequited love, the transience of worldly joys and the absurdity of human vanity – and its mood was one of resignation to the tyranny of fate. All these qualities are prominent in the work of the three most important poets of late-eighteenth-century Delhi: in the aching love-poetry of Mir; in the mordant satire of Sauda; and in the mystical resignation of Mir Dard. In Lucknow, on the other hand, poetry developed in an atmosphere of gaiety and ease. Relieved by the British guarantee of all worries concerning the defence of their dynasty and realm, the Nawabs ceased being soldier-statesmen like Saadat Khan, Safdar Jung and Shuja-ud-daula and became philanderers, sybarites and poetasters like Asaf-ud-daula, Nasir-ud-din and Wajid Ali Shah, who lavished their money on every form of personal gratification. The morals of rich society came to reflect those of the court. Cultivated courtesans were patronised by the powerful and exchanged favours for wealth and influence. The Lucknow brothels were notorious, and catered for every taste. Every evening in the old Chowk Bazaar prostitutes would appear provocatively on the balconies of the shops and houses and seek to attract the attention of passers-by.

They were all bare-headed [wrote the German traveller von Orlich, who visited Lucknow in 1843] and their beautiful black hair fell down in braids or was interwoven with jewels. Most of them wore large nose-rings, which hung over the corners of the mouth, and their large earrings touched their shoulders. Very few of them could be called pretty; but they have piercing eyes which look the more brilliant because their eyelids are blackened with antimony. A coloured scarf was thrown lightly and gracefully over the neck and shoulders, and displayed rather than concealed the fine contour of the upper part of their persons. They did not fail to make many remarks upon us, and sought to draw our attention by laughing, joking and tittering; but it is by no means advisable to pay any attention to them, as these bayadères are extremely importunate. [17]

The existence of male brothels is confirmed by the Lucknow hospital report for 1848-9, which notices cases of venereal disease 'proceeding', as Dr Leckie delicately put it, 'from other than the irregularities of female prostitution'. [18] These practices had been made fashionable by the Nawab Asaf-ud-daula, a notorious catamite.

Lucknow literature reflects this security, wealth and preoccupation with pleasure. It is witty, clever, indecent or sentimental; but seldom, save in the case of the *marsiya,* profound. Its aim was to amuse and to avoid probing and disturbing the turbid depths of the soul. The musical drama *The Court of Indra* (*indar sabha*), which the Lucknow poet Amanat modelled on the sort of *rahas,* or pantomime, popular at court, in which Hindu folklore was married to Perso-Urdu forms of versification and Muslim outlook, [19] is in many ways the epitome of Lucknow culture. It is a work in which the prevailing ethos and sense of values have found expression. The city and the court might well be portrayed in it. The setting is the aerial city of Indra, who in old Sanskrit literature figures as the god of rain and thunder but who in this drama is a music-loving monarch much like those of Oudh. His celestial paradise, where the flowers are in perpetual bloom and where the inmates are beguiled with a never-ending feast of song and dance from *gandharvas,* or bards, and *apsarases,* or lotus-eyed nymphs, is irresistibly suggestive of Lucknow itself, with its fairytale appearance, its music and poetry, and its isolation from the mainstream of reality. The plot, which is based on the stock theme of a fairy's love for a mortal and the consequent amorous intrigue, is developed with songs, ballet and magical stage effects. This work, which dates from 1853, was the first written drama in Urdu, and it became the prototype of many imitations. Nor, perhaps, was it inappropriate that Lucknow, in many ways the most theatrical of Indian cities, should become the home of Urdu theatre.

Lucknow poetry plumbs no great depths of feeling, empties love of its spiritual content and parades eloquence and verbal brilliance as substitutes for sincerity. The Delhi poets, like their romantic contemporaries in Europe, distilled their verse from the anguish of personal experience. Mir's dictum to the effect that 'poetry is a task for men whose hearts have been seared by the fire of love and pierced by the wounds of grief' recalls Hugo's preface to *Les Contemplations*: *'L'auteur a laissé, pour ainsi dire, ce livre se faire en lui. La vie, en filtrant goutte à goutte à travers les évènements et les souffrances, l'a deposé dans son coeur.'* Lucknow poets, on the other hand, knew no such debt to experience and, with little to communicate, became obsessed with the manner of communication. Their verse is highly contrived. It is full of difficult metres, intractable rhymes and extravagant imagery; and when it does not aim to dazzle it is content to titillate. The most notable among the earlier generation of poets was Insha (d. 1817), and his verse is in many ways typical. He was a man of formidable erudition, who wrote in several languages. He liked to impose artificial restrictions on himself in order to demonstrate his virtuosity, and thus produced such exercises as poems without diacritical marks and tales without any words of Persian or Arabic origin. Among the younger generation, Nasikh (d. 1848) was a talented poet whose work was of a high order when based on observation and experience. But often he was content to take the stock themes and imagery of the Perso-Urdu repertoire and re-work them into fantastic conceits. In these cases his starting point is not experience, but fancy. Instead of translating reality into imagery he accepts imagery as reality. The old metaphors are treated as statements of literal truth and subjected to the process of logical inference. Traditionally, poets had compared the face of the beloved with fire and called it hot on account of its glow. Nasikh used this as a scientific statement and proceeded by deductive reasoning to a patent absurdity:

> The warm reflection of thy glowing face
> Melts from the mirror every silver trace.

The poetry of Jurat and, later, of Rangin, reflects the prevailing promiscuity of the Lucknow court and aristocracy. Jurat (d. 1810) wrote *masnavis* (narratives) and *ghazals* (lyrics) in which erotic themes predominate, often developed with obscene imagery and at extreme length. The Delhi poet Mir remarked of him that he could not write poetry, but that he could well versify kisses and cuddles. Jurat's work is however redeemed from complete frivolity by an undercurrent of melancholy, a result of penury and blindness:

> These eyes were swift to fade, like jonquil bloom;
> I have no companion save solitude.
> What should I know of pleasure, O my friend!
> Ask me rather of chagrin and of pain.
> I have been encaged while spring after spring
> Came trembling into the flower garden;
> I am a dead tree in the world's orchard:
> Let spring do what it will, I'll bear no fruit.
> But what is the matter with me today?
> Yesterday my heart was not so heavy.

Total abandonment to puerility came with the invention of *rekhti* (the feminine form of *rekhta,* the traditional name for Urdu), which is verse written in the language peculiar to the female apartments of Indian Muslim households. The contriver of the form, Rangin (1756-1834), used it to versify his dalliances with courtesans and dancing girls; and the best-known exponent of the subsequent generation, Jan Sahib (1818?-97), not only wrote verse in the style of women but also performed in public as a female impersonator.

Security, ease and promiscuity were the conditions of this decline into effeteness and artificiality; but they were not its causes. The tendency to degeneracy was already strong in Urdu poetry, for it had been born congenitally weak, offspring of a Persian literature already in decay. Persian poets had been attracted to Delhi in large numbers by the generous patronage of the Mughals, and Indian Muslim poets never escaped the trammels of their influence. They adopted, and later bequeathed to the Urdu poets, not only the traditional forms of Persian verse – principally the *ghazal* (lyric), the *masnavi* (narrative), *qasida* (ode, panegyric) and *rubai* (quatrain) – but its imagery, symbolism and folklore as well. In what has been aptly called its Indian summer, Persian poetry was therefore an academic art, fettered by rigid rules and cut off from the sources of its inspiration. Its practitioners ignored the Indian folklore and the Indian landscape, and continued instead to describe the loves of Laila and Majnun, Shirin and Farhad, Yusuf and Zulaiqa; the mountains and rivers of Persia, the flowers and trees of Transoxiana and the deserts of Arabia – all of which had acquired a tyrannous fascination as characteristic elements in the Muslim cultural heritage. Poetry thus became an intellectual exercise, in which the only modes of innovation were esoteric refinement and excessive stylisation. As a broad generalisation it could be claimed that Delhi poets chose the former and Lucknow poets the latter; but it was difference of outlook rather than of technique which deeply divided the two schools and prevented any cross-fertilisation between them. It was this that caused most of the émigré poets from Delhi to be unhappy in Lucknow and view with distaste the work of the rising generation of local writers. Sauda, Mus-hafi, Mir and Mir Hasan were all attracted to Lucknow by the patronage of Asaf-ud-daula; but none developed any fondness for the place. Mir Hasan wrote a bitter satire on the city in which he called it 'misfortune seeking to impose itself on the world' and claimed that its streets stank 'like an Abyssinian's armpits'. Mir cut a pathetic figure there; an old man alone with his memories and pining for the city he had left:

> One ruined Delhi is worth ten Lucknows.
> I should have died there, not come here to weep.

The wealth and security which Lucknow enjoyed under the British aegis also attracted, as might have been expected, large numbers of European and Eurasian adventurers. Some among this exotic community came as traders and shopkeepers; but the ambition of most was to obtain service at court. Many, like those encountered by Bishop Heber, were disappointed.

I had applications made to me for charity by a Spaniard from Lima in Peru [he wrote] who had come in search of service, and a Silesian Jew, who pretended that he had been an officer in the Russian army and had been encouraged to bend his course in this direction by the golden dreams which men in Europe build of the opening for talent and adventurous spirit in India ... He was exceedingly ignorant, spoke wretched French and German with a strong Jewish accent and, instead of having served in the army, had every appearance of having sold oranges all his days in Leipzic. [20]

Others, however, were successful, for British influences had begun to work a change in taste and manners, and there was in the court a prevailing fondness for all things European. The Nawab Asaf-ud-daula accumulated a vast and whimsical collection of European pictures, clocks, mirrors, crockery and candelabra, and his successors developed a fascination for mechanical devices such as steam engines, telescopes, watches, hot-air balloons and self-performing cabinet organs. Court entertainments were modelled on English forms and became a weird simulacrum of English upper-class life.

The dinner was French [wrote Lord Valentia, who enjoyed the Nawab's hospitality in 1803] with plenty of wine, which, although the Muslims drank none, yet they had all the appearance of it, as the forbidden liquor was served in abundance at the table and they had two glasses of different sizes standing before them. The room was very well lighted up and a band of music ... played English tunes during the whole time. The scene was so singular, and so contrary to all my ideas of Asiatic manners, that I could hardly persuade myself that the whole was not a masquerade. An English apartment; a band in English regimentals, playing English tunes; a room lighted by magnificent English girandoles; English tables, chairs and looking-glasses; an English service of plate; English knives, forks, spoons, wine glasses, decanters and cut-glass vases — how could these convey any idea that we were seated in the court of an Asiatic prince? [21]

The Nawab Nasir-ud-din professed himself anxious to 'imitate the English in everything', and to this end made a habit, as the British Resident reported, of 'drinking wine or spirits to excess; giving public toasts at his table in a noisy manner; dressing at all times in the English costume, which he [did] completely, excepting that he [wore] a crown instead of a hat; eating his meals after the European manner; and having English furniture and English books (which he [could] not read) in his rooms,' [22] All the Nawabs liked to surround themselves with European courtiers or, failing Europeans, with fair-skinned Eurasians. [23]

By the terms of their treaty of 1775 with the East India Company, the Nawabs were precluded from employing Europeans without British permission. Where military employment was concerned, this permission was generally refused. In 1820 the Court of Directors of the Company wrote from London that 'it would be highly inexpedient to introduce into [the King's] corps ... Europeans not in our service or British subjects born in India, the sons of European fathers by native mothers'; [24] and in 1825 the ban was extended to all British officers in India. [25] The Company authorities in Calcutta consequently refused to allow the rulers of Oudh to employ European officers in military capacities. 'European' in this context included sons of European fathers by Eurasian mothers; but sons of Europeans by native women they did not deem to be Europeans, [26] and they therefore felt unable to apply the prohibition desired by the Directors. The service of the Nawabs was doubly attractive to these men, because it offered opportunities which were denied them in British India. In an effort to stem the alarming tendency of its servants to contract marriages with native women, the Company had decreed in 1791 that the children of such liaisons were not to be employed as officers in its military, marine or civil services, and this ban held good until the Charter Act of 1833. Eurasian males therefore, unless they were prepared to go into indigo planting or silk manufacturing, had no prospects of employment save as petty clerks or bandsmen in the army. Such held little attraction for men who were generally the sons of military officers, and large numbers of them came to Lucknow to enlist in the army of the King of Oudh. In 1837 the British Resident reported that two battalions of the Oudh army were entirely officered by Eurasians and commanded by Mr

W. Roberts, the natural son by a native woman of Lieutenant-Colonel Abraham Roberts of the Company's service.[27] In 1836 the two sons of Major Hyder Jung Hearsey, himself a prominent Eurasian, had likewise entered the King of Oudh's service.

Granting permission for the employment of Europeans in civil capacities appears to have been a mere formality, for only one case of refusal seems to be on record. It involved Colonel William Gardner, an Englishman who had never been in the Company's service, but who had been granted a pension and the brevet rank of lieutenant-colonel in return for his contribution as a commander of irregular troops in the Nepal War. Gardner lived with his Muslim wife on an estate at Khasganj, near Delhi, and he often came to Lucknow, where he had mercantile and banking interests. He became an intimate at court (his son, James, married a sister of one of the queens) and in 1831 the King wanted him to superintend the revenue settlement of one of the districts. The Calcutta authorities refused to sanction this appointment because of 'the embarrassment that would result in cases of misconduct, real or pretended, on the part of British subjects so employed, it being impossible that the British Government should leave them to be dealt with according to the usual practice of the Oudh Government towards defaulters'.[28] Usually, however, no objection was raised when permission to employ a European was sought, and each of the rulers of Oudh counted Europeans among his courtiers and servants. The highest number of Europeans and Eurasians at court was recorded in 1849, when the total was thirty-four.[29] The normal number was about half of this. The Eurasians monopolised the military posts, for the reasons outlined above, while the Europeans filled a variety of positions, including those of physician, engineer, horticulturist, hairdresser, artist and saddle and harness maker. When the Governor-General, Lord Hastings, visited Lucknow in 1818 he was entertained by an Irish bagpiper whom the Nawab had taken into his service; and George Mundy, a traveller who visited the court in 1827, mentions the performance of a Piedmontese conjurer. In 1831 Nasir-ud-din appointed Captain Herbert of the Company's military service his Astronomer

Royal and had an observatory built 'as well for the advancement of that noble science by new discoveries as for the diffusion of its principles amongst the inhabitants of India'. [30]

Several of these individuals acquired great influence and made handsome fortunes. Most remarkable in this respect was Claude Martin, a French soldier who began his career under Lally at Pondicherry, continued it in the Bengal army of the East India Company, and ended it as one of the most powerful men in Oudh. His nominal function in Lucknow was that of superintendent of the Nawab's artillery park, to which he had been appointed, with British permission, by Shuja-ud-daula; but his influence penetrated to the innermost recesses of the court and as the Nawab's confidante he accumulated plenty of money in the form of emoluments, presents and bribes. This he increased by banking and pawnbroking activities and by acting as purveyor of European goods to the court. He left over £300,000 when he died in 1800, besides extensive property. [31]

Another of these characters, more notorious than remarkable, was George Derusett, an English barber who came to Lucknow in 1831 in search of custom and fortune. This happened to be the time when the King, Nasir-ud-din, was on the lookout for a European hairdresser. He heard of Derusett from the Resident, and forthwith employed him as valet-de-chambre on a salary of 300 rupees a month. Derusett soon ingratiated himself by pandering to the King's taste for debauchery and heavy drinking. 'Not only the King's private servants', reported the disgusted Resident in 1837, 'but eighteen or twenty Indo-Britons, composing the King's English band, have several times seen His Majesty dancing country dances as the partner of Mr. Derusett – the latter after some grotesque masquerade fashion, and His Majesty attired in the dress of an European lady.' Nor was this all, the Resident hinted darkly. There were reports of other, 'most shocking indecencies'. Derusett, who was joined in Lucknow by his brother William and then, after William's death, by another brother called Charles, both of whom were employed by the King as valets, became rich as he became favoured. He received many presents and made a large profit on the various commissions that he executed for the King in Calcutta and elsewhere. In 1837, sensing that his star was waning, he discreetly withdrew from Lucknow, carrying with him a substantial fortune and leaving his unfortunate brother Charles to account to the fickle King for the family's financial swindles. [32]

British influences on morals and manners should not, however, be too heavily stressed. Such influences as existed were superficial. They affected outward behaviour but produced no fundamental change in ideas or outlook. Mechanical devices were enjoyed as toys, but not appreciated as applications of scientific principles. Nasir-ud-din's observatory was inspired more by the traditional preoccupation with astrology than by an interest in astronomy. The celebrated incident at one of Saadat Ali Khan's banquets, when Staffordshire chamber pots were set out as milk jugs, stands perhaps as the most eloquent example of foreign culture mimicked but not understood. Influences were, moreover, largely confined to the court. They were resented and resisted by the artisans, small shopkeepers, teachers and physicians who made up middle-class Muslim society and who, as a minority jealous of their political privileges and proud of their cultural superiority, reacted strongly against any innovation tending to erode their special identity. As the Muslims had shut themselves off from Hindu influences, so now they did likewise from European ones and jealously preserved their customary values and practices. Traditional scholarship and education; traditional seclusion of women; the traditional forms of Muslim dress; the traditional equation of politics with religion – all survived intact the advent of the science and the sartorial styles, the secularism and the social licence of the British.

Western influences on Lucknow architecture were more important. Elements from the European Renaissance, romantic and neo-classical traditions, such as turrets, battlements, pediments, columns, pilasters, cornices, friezes and semicircular arches, predominate in the secular buildings of the Nawabs and Kings; and even their mosques and tombs, while faithful to stereotyped Islamic patterns, include European details. The entrance to the Jama Masjid, for example, is flanked by Corinthian pilasters and has Corinthian shafts on its piers. The tomb of Saadat Ali Khan is Italianate in much of its decoration. Their knowledge of these motifs derived partly from report and (in the case of Saadat Ali Khan) observation of Calcutta architecture, but mainly from buildings erected in Lucknow by resident Europeans. One such was the Kurshid Manzil, a mock-medieval castle built by Captain McLeod during the reign of Saadat Ali Khan; but the most influential was undoubtedly Constantia, a bizarre palace erected by Claude Martin, which, after his death, became first a hostel for visiting Europeans and then La Martinière Christian Boys' College. Martin's main concern in designing this place seems to have been to incorporate as many different architectural motifs as he could remember, and the result is a weird jumble of classical columns, arches, pediments and balustrades, with Gothic battlements, turrets and statues, and heraldic lions rampant. This was one of the first large buildings of a European type to be erected in upper India, and its impact was great. The Nawab Asaf-ud-daula signified his desire to acquire it, and it was in order to obviate its seizure after his death that Martin had himself buried in the basement. Elements in its exterior design, as well as its rococo interior, were adopted extensively by the Nawabs. Sometimes they tried to blend them with Saracenic arcades, kiosks, crenellations and domes – as in the Chattar Manzil, the Begam Kothi and the various structures of the Qaisarbagh; at others they attempted to use them to produce buildings of a less hybrid, European character, such as the strange cross between French château and Palladian villa that was Dilkusha, the hunting lodge of Saadat Ali Khan. Neither type of experiment can be called successful, since the Palladian laws governing the proportions of the classical orders were unknown and the ornamentation and colouring were travesties of their baroque models; but the architecture undoubtedly has an historic significance. It demonstrates a receptiveness to foreign ideas unmatched since Akbar's attempted synthesis of Hindu and Islamic styles, and therefore signalises Lucknow not so much as the graveyard of an exhausted convention as the meeting point of two cultural currents; a place of aesthetic turmoil, whence a new and vigorous style could well have emerged.

II

By Lucknow standards the British Residency was a modest building. It had three storeys; and with its colonnaded west front, classical portico, semicircular fanlights, striped canvas awnings and Italianate roof balustrade gave the impression rather of a spacious summer villa than of an embassy or palace. Only the somewhat incongruous decagonal tower, with its ribbed dome and finial, hinted at greater pretensions. Yet the overall impression was not unworthy of the symbol of British ascendency. The building was situated on a low mound on the south bank of the river Gomti, to the west of the Farhatbakhsh palace – one of the most elevated and desirable sites in the city. Extensive gardens surrounded it on every side, full of mango, cypress, roses, oleander and scarlet hibiscus; and its yellow-washed walls were restful to the eyes even in the fiercest sunlight.

The main building was begun by Asaf-ud-daula in 1780, but the whole complex of Residency, church and outbuildings for Residency staff was not finished until some twenty years later. The Residency remained the property of the Nawabs, who on several occasions regretted its loss. Ghazi-ud-din signified his wish to retrieve possession of the buildings and grounds in 1822, but allowed the matter to drop when the Resident objected to both the sites proposed for a new Residency.[1] In 1832 Nasir-ud-din opened discussions with the Resident, Colonel Low, with the object of acquiring the site, which he wanted to use for 'a very large and splendid palace and . . . an avenue of trees from it to the new iron bridge'. The King's minister selected a spot for a new Residency in Dilkusha park and the Governor-General, Bentinck, was happy about the proposed change. He considered that the present house, with its elevated position, 'bore an appearance of over-bearing command and control that was almost offensive'; and he furthermore reckoned that if the Resident was removed to a position outside the city he would be less prone to become involved in 'the intrigues of the city and ... those details of the administration which properly belong[ed] only to the sovereign and his ministers'. The King, however, found the idea of having the Resident in Dilkusha park intolerable. The project consequently lapsed, the Resident stayed where he was, and the iron bridge lay in its packing cases for ten years more. [2]

In addition to his official city residence, the Resident had a country retreat. This was a large bungalow beyond the northern suburbs of the town, across the river near the military cantonment of Muriaon. It was set in gardens, with an English-style farm and dairy attached. The place appears to have been built by the Resident Mordaunt Ricketts, in the 1820s, and to have been bought from him by the King, who put it at the disposal of his successors. [3]

Until 1829 a retinue of 146 servants, gardeners, blacksmiths and camel and elephant keepers was attached to the Residency for the repair of the buildings, the upkeep of the gardens and the personal comfort of the Resident. All were paid for by the King, who provided in addition a 'state establishment' of camels and elephants for use by the Resident on ceremonial occasions. Captain Lockett, officiating as Resident in 1829, felt that this system, as well as inviting extravagance and peculation on the part of the *daroga* in charge, impeded the Resident's freedom of action by making him beholden to the King; and on his recommendation the policy was adopted whereby the servants were reduced to sixty-five and made chargeable to the Calcutta government. The King was, however, still allowed to bear the cost of repairs to the Residency fabric. Lockett suggested reducing the number of camels and elephants to four each – 'the lowest establishment for state purposes the Resident can keep here' – but he was informed that 'under the revised rules recently laid down for regulating the office and allowances of Residents, Government [did] not intend to provide them with any establishments for state purposes and [left] them, like other high public functionaries, to consult their own taste and convenience in such matters'. [4]

But it does not appear that, in practice, these retrenchments impaired the Resident's regal way of life. In all forms of etiquette he was treated as the equal of the King. He was allowed the shade of an umbrella, the traditional symbol of royalty, in the presence of the King; and he smoked his hookah as of right before him. He and the monarch sat in each other's presence, and they travelled together on the same state elephant on the occasion of a new Resident's entry into the city. He was still authorised to borrow elephants and conveyances from the King if he required them for special occasions, and it seems that few Residents scrupled to avail themselves of the permission. Prince Soltykoff, who visited Lucknow in 1841, reported that the Resident then had twelve elephants at his disposal. When the Resident went out it was usually in a barouche and four, with postilions and attendant horsemen from the Residency escort. When General Sleeman made his tour through the kingdom in the winter of 1849-50, he and his European guests and colleagues travelled on elephants and were accompanied by some 200 sepoys and a cavalcade of servants and camp followers which extended for twelve or fourteen miles. The Resident entertained frequently and in style.

Besides a daily table for the members of his own family [the Calcutta government explained in 1816] the Resident must be prepared to entertain in frequent rotation the officers belonging to the portion of the Subsidiary Force stationed at the capital, as well as all officers joining or departing from that corps; officers visiting the Residency or the cantonment on their route to or from the headquarters of the Subsidiary Force, or the neighbouring military posts; and all strangers visiting the station for business or pleasure. All these various guests must be entertained by the Resident in a manner superior or at least equal to that of the generality of gentlemen filling public situations. [5]

He was in addition expected to entertain the King and court 'on periodical occasions, such as the anniversaries of Christmas, the New Year, His Majesty's birthday, etc.'. [6] Until 1821, the Resident had to meet these expenses from a consolidated allowance of 84,000 rupees a year (£8,400) and provide his own furniture and plate. In that year, however, it was decided to furnish the Residency at the Company's expense to the limit of 30,000 rupees, and to divide the Resident's pay into an entertainment allowance of 4,000 and a personal salary of 3,000 rupees a month. [7] The salary was later raised to 5,500 rupees, but even then demands on a Resident's personal resources could be something of a strain. On his appointment he was still expected to provide certain furnishings at his own expense – generally by purchasing the property left by his predecessor. Sir William Nott hesitated before accepting the appointment in 1842 because Colonel Low intended to leave property worth between £2,000 and £3,000, which he would be expected to buy. [8] The cost of entertaining also tended to exceed the allowance. Ricketts's table expenses for the month of October 1824, during which time he was entertaining Bishop Heber, amounted to nearly 9,000 rupees. [9] Thus although the appointment was, in terms of prestige and importance, what Governor-General Dalhousie called 'the first . . . under the Government of India', it was not one in which an honest man could grow rich. In 1833 the Governor-General, Lord William Bentinck, made soundings to discover how Low viewed the prospect of a transfer from Lucknow to the Residency in Rajputana. Low begged not to be moved –not because the salary in Lucknow was higher (it was but marginally so) but because the expenses incurred in establishing himself in Lucknow had exhausted his private means. 'The expenses which I incurred first in marching to this place without civil salary and afterwards in furnishing the two houses here were so heavy', he wrote in November 1833, 'that it was only in December last . . . that I again reached the same point towards independence which I had attained a month before I left Gwalior.' His father had died insolvent, with debts amounting to £5,500, and Low reckoned that it would not be until January 1836 – four years after his arrival in Lucknow – that he would have saved enough to pay the creditors. Initial outlay and marriage expenses absorbed two years' savings, so the indications are that Low's savings amounted to some £2,750 a year after the first year. This means that even if a Resident stayed in Lucknow for ten years, which was Low's term of office and which was exceptionally long, he could not hope to amass more than about £25,000, which, although a handsome sum, was by no means princely even then. [10] It certainly cannot bear comparison with the fortunes amassed by the Company's servants in the heyday of extortion and corruption, after the devolution of power in Bengal.

The Resident's duties were generally monotonous and jejune. He had, officially, nothing to do with the interior management of the country, beyond the offering of the advice stipulated by the treaty of 1801, and whenever he offered this he did so as the instrument of the Calcutta government. Everyday duties consisted of what Low called 'a variety of petty matters connected with guaranteed families, complaints of sepoys, training matters and alarms connected with the apprehension and trial of thugs and dacoits [bandits]'. [11]

The 'guaranteed families' were pensioners whose stipends were paid by the Resident from the interest on sums invested in Company loans, and whose persons and property were protected by the Calcutta government. Making loans with such conditions attached was a favourite expedient of the monarchs of Oudh, since it was both a way of making provision for relatives and protégés that would be unaffected by subsequent political vicissitudes, and a means of circumventing the Islamic prohibition of usury. The idea was first adopted by the Bahu Begam ('Princess of Wales'), the wife of Shuja-ud-duala, who had herself, together with her extensive property at Faizabad, been under British protection during her long widowhood – a protection which had been bought by considerable financial concessions in 1775. [12] In 1808 she made a will in which she bequeathed the bulk of her fortune to the British government, with the stipulation that a given amount be invested in Company bonds and the interest therefrom paid partly as stipends to listed beneficiaries and partly for the upkeep of her mausoleum at Faizabad. When she died, in 1815, the Calcutta government renounced the benefits of the bequest and made over the Begam's estate to the Nawab, her son; but at the same time it insisted that a sum of some half a million sterling be donated to the Company as a loan, the interest upon which, at six percent, would provide for the numerous bequests made by the deceased.[13] Already the previous year a loan of a million sterling had been received from the Nawab, the interest on which was assigned, together with a guarantee of British protection, to some 120 stipendaries; and the same thing was done on a smaller scale in 1825, 1829 and 1838.[14] When beneficiaries died without heirs, the interest was diverted to paying off the principal; but when, as was generally the case, there was more than one heir, division of the stipend was usual, and this caused the number of pensioners benefitting by the scheme to mount steadily. By 1857 nearly a million rupees annually were being distributed among 965 stipendaries.[15]

As the Resident was the medium by which most of these people were paid, the agent to whom the majority of them looked for protection and the judge to whom they were accountable, they came to regard him alone as the object worthy of their propitiation and loyalty. The guarantee system thus turned him into a sort of minor monarch in his own right, and for years the Residents at Lucknow lorded it over their dependents with all the appurtenances of royalty. Until 1831, the Resident held a durbar of his own each Saturday, to which the various pensioned princes, princesses, nobles and favourites sent their *vakils* (agents) to present grievances and pay respects with all the elaborate punctilios of oriental etiquette.[16]

This system led, understandably, to friction between Resident and monarch. The King saw his own wishes and courts of justice set at naught by a privileged group, who invoked the Resident's authority in cases relating to internal administration and even in private domestic matters. With a naturally officious Resident, like Colonel John Baillie (1808-15), the interference could go to humiliating extremes. Saadat Ali Khan's relations with his mother, the Bahu Begam, were strained; and as the Begam was a protégée of the Company, she made a habit of referring all her complaints to the Resident. A spectacular row blew up over the Nawab's dismissal of Tahsin Ali Khan, the eunuch who had for many years managed the *khurd mahal* (gynaeceum) of his late father's establishment at Faizabad. Prompted by the Begam, Baillie invoked all the weight of his authority and bullied the Nawab into reinstating Tahsin Ali. This caused a revolt of the ladies of the *khurd mahal*, who despised the old Begam as a virago and complained that Tahsin Ali cheated and insulted them. An unruly crowd of them actually quitted Faizabad in August 1812 and came to Lucknow, where they lodged themselves in the Imambara and implored the Nawab to redress their wrongs. Baillie insisted that the revolt had been fomented by the Nawab in order to confute the Begam; and the Nawab, embarrassed and embittered, was compelled to stand by helplessly for four months, until the ladies finally gave up their sit-in and made their way back to Faizabad, hungry and cowed.[17]

But it was the treaty of 1825 that gave rise to the most notorious case of interposition by the Resident between the monarch and one of his subjects. By that treaty the King, Ghazi-ud-din, had lent a crore (ten million) of rupees to the Company in return for a guarantee that a stipulated portion of the interest would be paid as a pension to his minister, Aga Mir, and his family, and that the Company would protect the 'life, honour and property' of those individuals. A new King, Nasir-ud-din, succeeded in 1827, and within a year Aga Mir had fallen from power and from favour. He was accused of gross malversation and embezzlement during his fifteen years in office and required to surrender accounts of all his transactions. This put the British authorities in an awkward position. They were pledged to protect the ex-minister; and since the late King had, on his deathbed, absolved him from all responsibility for financial irregularities, they seemed liable to protect him from the consequences of all such crimes committed in the previous reign. The Resident was therefore required to put the ex-minister under house arrest as a means of protecting his person and property against the King's officers, and to inform the King that accounts relating to the previous reign could not be admitted as evidence. Specific charges of peculation during the present reign would be received and investigated by the Resident. Thus, to quote the Assistant-Resident, Lieutenant Paton, 'the residence of the British representative became a civil court in which the sovereign himself was a suitor, and in which he preferred his enormous claims, amounting to one crore 76 lakhs of rupees [£1,760,000]'. Nearly three years elapsed before the Resident submitted his report; and as there seemed to be no claims that invalidated Aga Mir's right to British protection, the Resident was instructed to release him forthwith and provide Company troops to escort him and his personal chattels across the Ganges into Company territory. His houses and gardens in Lucknow, plus a sum of two million rupees, were left in the Resident's custody as provision for any claims subsequently allowed. So was an ex-minister, accused of major crimes, together with a vast portion of the wealth he was charged with having embezzeled (it occupied 800 carts and was valued at between one and twenty-five millions sterling), transported out of the kingdom against the King's wishes by foreign troops at the behest of a foreign representative. [18]

The Aga Mir affair made the Calcutta authorities fully alive to the invidious nature of the role the Resident was compelled to play under the operation of the guarantees, and thereafter efforts were made to modify the system. Ghazi-ud-din had made a temporary loan of five million rupees in 1826, and by the terms of his will this was converted into a permanent loan on condition that the Company's protection be extended to the stipendaries in receipt of the interest. These terms Calcutta declined, as bound to 'impair the legitimate rights of the native government of Oudh and involve the British authorities in endless disputes and vexatious interference regarding the domestic concerns and private interests of individuals who, so long as they reside in the Oudh territory, should look to their native sovereign alone for justice and protection'. The money was finally accepted as a permanent loan from the new King only when he agreed to restrict the stipends to his female relatives and abandon the demand for a formal pledge of protection. [19] When Low became Resident he discontinued the durbars and ceased receiving appeals from the protégés, save in cases where they had applied in vain to the tribunals of the country.

In the judgement of Lieutenant Paton, this mitigated the worst tendencies of the system and improved relations with the court; but, he added, 'many troublesome and undefined duties still fall to the lot of the Resident'. He mentioned especially the 'exercise of an undefined and uncertain jurisdiction over Europeans and Indo-Britons residing in Lucknow'. As the Anglo-Oudh treaty of 1775 forbad the settlement of such individuals in Oudh without the consent of the Calcutta government, they remained there only during the pleasure of the Resident, and cases of peremptory expulsion were not unknown. The Resident also exercised over them what amounted to civil and criminal jurisdiction, for it was tacitly accepted that they were not amenable to the King's courts, and individuals with complaints against them invariably addressed themselves to him. [20]

The 'complaints of sepoys' mentioned by Low constituted the most onerous of the Resident's duties. The East India Company maintained three native armies (under British officers), one at each of the Presidencies of Bengal, Madras and Bombay. The Madras force consisted of local recruits; but the other two contained large numbers of men from Oudh. They made up about two thirds of the Bengal army, for until the Mutiny of 1857 the principality was one of the main recruiting grounds of India. One in ten of its Rajput and Brahmin population served as mercenaries all over the subcontinent. Most of these troops came from the class of petty landholders who held village estates as coparcenary communities. As a special privilege, Oudh men in the Company's service and, after the 1840s, those who had been drafted from the Company's regular corps into the service of protected princes – some fifty or sixty thousand in all – were allowed to submit petitions relating to their domestic concerns to the Resident at Lucknow. Every month about a hundred such petitions, duly signed by sepoys' commanding officers and countersigned by their colonels, were received by the Assistant-Resident, in charge of the Sepoys' Petitions Department. The Assistant's job was to pass them on to a special officer deputed by the Oudh government, who investigated the complaints, reported back to the King, and obtained his orders where necessary. In theory, therefore, the Resident was only the channel through which the petitions were passed to a royal official; but the process of consultation between him and the King's official and the constant pleas for redress from sepoys and their officers often involved him in the investigation and settlement of the suits. In practice therefore he found that much of his time was consumed by grievances concerning 'rights of *qanungo* and *chaudhri* [petty local offices]; *zemindari* [tenurial] disputes; rights of *sir* [demesne lands, subject to lower assessment] and *nankar* [perquisite in the form of part of the state's share]; plunder of property; destruction of houses; cutting down trees; wounding, maiming or imprisonment; demands in excess of revenues; deprivation of contract before the expiration of the term agreed on; requisition that *ilaqas* [estates] be made *huzur tahsil* [paying revenues directly into the royal treasury]'.

The system, besides involving the Resident in invidious and time-consuming mediation between the King and his subjects, spawned abuses. Sepoys used the threat of an appeal to the Resident to tyrannise their opponents, and sometimes sold the use of their name and their right of petitioning to neighbours or relatives. Lieutenant Paton wrote: 'Oudh zemindars [landholders] who cannot get justice from their own government again and again manage thus to get the British Resident to fight their battles with the durbar'; and ten years later the Assistant in charge of the Petitions Department complained in much the same vein: 'There are many cases which have been worked up by the sepoys as of much cruelty and severity whereas their origin has been either very paltry or without foundation ... [and] very many complaints have no reference to sepoys but are brought forward in their names for the purpose of being referred to the durbar and advocated by the Resident.'

Low made efforts to check the worst abuses of the system. He refused to receive any petition which related to grievances antedating a sepoy's enlistment or to complaints older than six years when first brought to court. Relatives on behalf of whom a sepoy was allowed to petition he limited to parents, wife and children. In 1846 the King agreed that all sepoys with coparcenary shares in village estates might pay their dues directly into the royal treasury, and it was hoped that by thus obviating contact between them and the royal *amils* the causes of complaint would be reduced. But the restrictions on eligibility merely increased the incidence of fraud. In 1852 the Resident, Sleeman, condemned the whole scheme, which created a feared and privileged class in Oudh society and involved the British representative, and even the Calcutta and London authorities on occasion, in the pursuit of spurious and iniquitous claims. [21]

The value of the Resident's moral support was so great that not only pensioners and sepoys, but powerful courtiers and ministers, and even the King himself, used every art of flattery, cajolery and bribery in order to obtain it.

He is ever experiencing [reported Lieutenant Paton in 1835] the greatest civility and marks of personal courtesy from the King and minister. No attempt is left untried to heap favours upon him; and lakhs of rupees, if he would take them, are ever ready to be lavished upon him, and lucrative appointments in the King's service are offered to his friends and relations ... The indication of a wish on his part is often enough to obtain a situation for almost any person. [22]

Captain Lockett, Acting Resident in 1829, wrote that the King had personally offered to send him two of the most beautiful women in the city in return for a favour concerning the employment of a favourite at the Residency. [23]

The British now frowned on approaches such as these, for things had changed since the old days, when Company servants were unscrupulous adventurers and speculators, intent on making quick fortunes by private trading and venal abuses. The orgy of corruption and extortion that had followed the British acquisition of power in Bengal had been so ruinous to both the Company and the economy of the Indian possessions that public opinion had swung sharply against the 'nabobs', as the *nouveaux riches* from India were called, and enabled Parliament to impose controls over the administration of the Indian empire. The Regulating Act of 1773 had reorganised the structure of government in British India and forbidden the acceptance of private gifts from natives; and Pitt's India Act of 1784 had subjected the affairs of the Company to the supervision of a ministerial Board of

Control. The Company itself had also undergone changes. Increased territorial responsibilities and the gradual removal of its trading monopoly (finally extinguished in 1813) had ensured the decline of its commercial operations and the impairment of its mercantile ethos. It had acquired a more distinctly bureaucratic identity, requiring standards of purity, efficiency and regularity, and offering fixed salaries and allowances in place of the old commissions and irregular perquisites.

Since the impeachment of the Governor-General Warren Hastings for, among other crimes, the receipt of illicit presents from the native princes of Benares and Oudh, the prohibition in the Act of 1773 had been scrupulously enforced. In conformity to oriental etiquette, gifts were still exchanged between native princes and Company representatives acting in an official capacity, but all were treated as public property. The Calcutta government both provided the presents offered and appropriated those received, and if a recipient wished to keep his gift he was expected to pay its value to the public exchequer. Lord Comberemere, Commander-in-Chief in India, had to pay over 5,000 rupees for a portrait of the King, set in diamonds, which was presented to him during his visit to Lucknow in 1827.[24] In the same year the Governor-General, Lord William Bentinck, having decided that the system of exchanging presents was 'empty, vexatious and unmeaning', ordered all the Residents at native courts to discontinue it.[25] Thereafter it ceased as a regular practice, though high-ranking British visitors were still required to go through the elaborate charade of give and take.

For one Resident, Mordaunt Ricketts, the temptations proved too great, and he became the centre of what promised to develop into the biggest scandal since the time of Warren Hastings. After an undistinguished career, Ricketts was appointed Resident in 1823, probably as a result of the influence of his relative, Lord Liverpool, who was Prime Minister.[26] He failed to give satisfaction. He seemed to be too closely involved in court intrigue, and there was a disturbing strain of evasiveness and petty mendacity in many of his reports. The Calcutta government, with the approval of the home authorities, therefore removed him in 1829. [27]

It was the King's efforts to get Aga Mir to disgorge his ill-gotten gains that gave rise to the suspicion that Ricketts was guilty of something more serious than incompetence. Shortly before Ricketts left Lucknow, the King had suddenly reduced his claims against Aga Mir by twelve lakhs (1,200,000) of rupees, and Captain Lockett, temporarily in charge of the Residency, reported that it was generally believed that this had been done as a result of pressure from the Residency, where the money in question had been received as a coronation gift from the King. Certain phrases in the correspondence of Aga Mir implied that Ricketts had some special knowledge of or connection with this sum; and when Lockett's investigations revealed that he had recently been exchanging large amounts of gold for native bankers' bills on mercantile houses in Calcutta, Bentinck felt bound to ask him for an explanation. Ricketts denied that he had done anything wrong, but then set sail for England with suspicious haste. He did not offer for examination his accounts with the Calcutta houses in question, and this determined Bentinck to institute a formal inquiry.

The investigations, conducted by the new Resident, Thomas Maddock, disclosed no incriminating evidence on the charge relating to the twelve lakhs of rupees. Aga Mir prevaricated when questioned, and the Governor-General decided that it would be indelicate to interview the King. Other specific charges of corruption preferred against Ricketts by Lockett were either refuted or declared insubstantiated for lack of evidence. But Maddock established beyond doubt that Ricketts had remitted to Calcutta over 700,000 rupees by means of native bankers' bills of exchange, as well as nearly 100,000 rupees in government bills. Maddock took no official cognisance of Ricketts's personal circumstances, so there was no evidence to suggest that the money was not legitimately his; but this was unlikely. The sum was, in the first place, suspiciously large. Secondly, most of it had been remitted by means of native bankers' bills, whereas the normal mode of remittance for Europeans was buying bills on government treasuries. Finally, most of these bills (half a million rupees' worth) had been bought with gold. Where, Maddock wondered, had the Resident obtained so much gold? The currency used in all ordinary transactions was the silver rupee. The only man who could answer this question was the quondam Residency treasurer, Inder Narayan. Inder Narayan had acted as Ricketts's personal agent in his financial transactions and had, strange to tell, left Lucknow at the same time as Ricketts, taking with him all his current ledgers and native staff. Maddock wrote to him at Benares, where he was now settled; but he denied all knowledge of the private transactions of Ricketts and claimed that he was unable to explain the sale of gold.

That was as far as the investigation went, and no criminal charges were ever brought against either Ricketts or Inder Narayan. It is likely that Ricketts was saved from prosecution by his high connections. The Court of Directors had certainly learnt enough to prevent his return to India. With the approval of the President of the Board of Control, he was superannuated and the inquiry quietly abandoned. [28]

This affair marks a turning point of some significance. Hitherto the Residents and their European staff had been a part of Lucknow high society. Informal contacts with members of the court had been frequent, and the Resident himself had often formed ties of companionship with the monarch. Baillie used to attend Saadat Ali on his hunting excursions, and Ricketts and his wife had been among the ornaments of the court. [29] But after the Ricketts scandal all this changed. Purely social intercourse between members of the court and the Residency staff was discouraged, and any sign of private understanding between the King and the Resident was liable to land the latter in very hot water. Maddock discovered this in 1831, when he asked the Governor-General's permission to go to England as the King's representative at the court of William IV. Bentinck's reaction was not only to forbid the project absolutely, but to remove Maddock forthwith to the Residency at Kathmandu. 'That Mr. Maddock', he wrote, '. . . should even for an instant have brought himself to listen to this proposition did appear to me so objectionable, that my first impression was to consider even his conditional assent to betray such an erroneous judgement of the obligations of a confidential agent of the Governor-General's as to disqualify him from further political employment.'[30] The demeanour of the Residents changed; and from being accessible, sociable and complaisant, like Ricketts and Maddock, they became remote, censorious and sternly uncorruptible, like Low and Sleeman.[31]

Perhaps we can see in Ricketts a last reflection of the way of life and the morals of the old 'nabobs'. Like them, he was ready to mix with native society, adopt native ways and share in the perquisites of native official life. That such readiness was incompatible with equitable government must be conceded, and the notion of pure administration, introduced by Cornwallis and rigorously applied by Bentinck, can be considered as one of Britain's most valuable legacies to India. But purifying crusades have a tendency to breed their own vices, and it is open to question whether the old abuses were worse than the racial arrogance, insulting *hauteur* and sense of moral superiority that were the price of their removal.

III

When Wellesley made his treaty with Oudh in 1801, he was principally influenced, as his predecessors had been in their dealings with that state, by strategic considerations. The position of the East India Company in India was as yet far from secure. The Mahrattas, still predominant in western and central India, had by no means relinquished their claim to the reversion of the Mughal authority – indeed, Delhi itself, and with it the person of the Mughal Emperor, was in their hands; and the Afghans, under their restless monarch, Zaman Shah, still seemed disposed to re-enter the struggle for supremacy. The British made Oudh an object of special vigilance in these years of interregnum, for it was important by virtue both of its wealth and of its position as a buffer state between their own territories in Bengal and those of the Mahrattas and Afghans in the northwest. The Oudh government was almost bankrupt when Saadat Ali Khan became Nawab in 1798, and he himself admitted that he would have great difficulty in meeting the cost of the Subsidiary Force, which Wellesley had insisted on bringing up to a strength of twelve battalions of infantry and four regiments of cavalry, plus supporting artillery. Wellesley reckoned that the ideal solution to the problem was outright annexation of the province to the territories of the Company. His hectoring and menacing drove the Nawab to drink and the edge of a nervous breakdown, but failed to induce him to sign away his kingdom. The Governor-General had to settle for half the Oudh territories. By the terms of the 1801 treaty, a crescent of territory, comprising Rohilkhand, the Doab and Gorakhpur, was pared away from the central districts of the province and its revenues applied to the upkeep of the protective force in lieu of the cash subsidy. This territory, combined with lands conquered from the Mahrattas in 1805, became known as the Ceded and Conquered Provinces. The Company undertook to guarantee the remaining part of the

Oudh dominion to the Nawab and his successors, and to preserve them 'against all foreign and domestic enemies'. [1]

The advantages of the treaty as part of a defence policy were considerable. It surrounded Oudh with an insulating fence of British territory and it put the financing of the Subsidiary Force upon a secure basis. But these advantages soon became redundant. The rapid extension of British hegemony over the subcontinent, culminating in the final overthrow of the Mahrattas in 1817, removed all external threat to the stability of Oudh, and the treaty survived in practice as a mandate compelling the British to protect the Nawabs from their domestic enemies. As such it proved an embarrassing liability. It forced the British to act as the reluctant accomplices of the Nawabs in their efforts to tax and subdue an unruly and sometimes desperate population. It compelled them to underwrite an administration based on all the devices they professedly detested – venality, peculation, oppression – and to support a dynasty whose weakness they contemned and whose proclivities they despised.

But this thraldom was not the result solely of Wellesley's treaty. If that treaty had left the remedy undefined, it had nevertheless specified the wrong, and the Nawabs' refusal to conform to the administrative standards demanded constituted a breach of the treaty on their part. [2] Legally, therefore, the British were free to go the way that conscience pointed and emancipate themselves from a painful partnership. But the legal condition was not sufficient. The British were shackled by other bonds, which long resisted the pull of ideological inclination and moral obligation.

The government of Oudh, like that of all Indian states, lived by its land revenue. All land, save uncultivated waste, owed dues either to the crown (such were *khalsa* lands) or to its assignee (*muafi* or *jagir* lands). The land revenue subsumed all other forms of income, since customs duties, town and market cesses and road tolls were all credited to the taxable assets of the landholders, who were left to realise them and pay their value as part of the government share. Bureaucracy was therefore designed essentially a means of realising land revenue. The sixteen administrative subdivisions of the country (*chaklas*) were determined on a fiscal basis, and the crown's provincial governors (*chakladars*) were generally called 'collectors' (*amils*), even though they acted as civil and criminal judges and chief constables as well as tax-gatherers. [3]

Under normal circumstances the net income of the Oudh government, which reached an average of about one and a quarter millions sterling a year, [4] was more than adequate to cover public expenditure, which one Resident, Colonel Low, estimated in 1836 at 8,600,000 rupees, or £860,000. [5] What had been the biggest single drain – the British subsidy – had no longer to be set off against the exchequer income, and the defence of the kingdom was looked after by the Company. Hence in times of reasonable restraint on the part of the court outlay was more than comfortably covered by income. But this never entailed a relaxation of the revenue demand, because the court's appetite for funds remained voracious. All the monarchs of Oudh had a predilection either for squandering or for hoarding money. The reckless extravagance of Asaf-ud-daula had become proverbial and had brought the state to the verge of bankruptcy. His successor, Sadat Ali Khan, had just as great an appetite for money, but his propensity was to hoard, rather than spend, what he got. The British Resident of his time, Colonel Baillie, attributed this to an avaricious disposition. It is true that the Nawab was disliked as tight-fisted in certain quarters; but the accusation ill accords with what we know of Saadat's way of life. His dress was always splendid, his hospitality lavish, and his passion for building uncurbed by reluctance to loosen his purse-strings. The impression of niggardliness was perhaps no more than an effect of the contrast that was bound to exist between Asaf-ud-daula and whoever followed him, and the new Nawab's unpopularity probably did not extend beyond those who suffered by the retrenchments he was compelled to make. An Indian historian has suggested that he was given to amassing wealth because he had ideas of buying back from the Company, at some stage, the territories he had so reluctantly given up in 1801, [6] and it may well be that such thoughts were in the back of his mind. But whatever the cause, the effect was indisputable. He grabbed all he could get, and at his death left a fortune of some £13 millions. It did not long survive him. His son and grandson, Ghazi-ud-din and Nasir-ud-din, both spent large sums on buildings, and the latter squandered the remaining vestiges of his legacy in a way that drove the Resident, Colonel Low, to despair.

Since His Majesty's accession [he informed the Governor-General in 1836] he has expended the average annual sum of 66 lakhs [£660,000] in excess of his ample revenues ... Even subsequently to the exhaustion of the old treasury, he, amongst other acts of extravagance, squandered in one day the sum of 150,000 rupees upon two head dresses of which he has already more than an abundance and 50,000 more in making up dresses for the celebration of the birth of some imaginary prophet. He has established some absurd ceremonies which he calls *achhutas* (the form of which most Muslims think idolatrous) which originated entirely with himself and which entail a tremendously heavy annual expenditure, as they are held on each of the supposed anniversaries of all the twelve saints, and each procession ... costs not less than a lakh of rupees [£10,000].[7]

The throne reverted to the eldest surviving son of Saadat Ali in 1837 and both he (Muhammad Ali Shah) and his son (Amjad Ali) resumed the ways of Saadat Ali. Retrenchments were made, and in Muhammad Ali Shah at least the Resident recognised the makings of a capable and conscientious ruler. But the obsessive concern of both, again, was to lay by a stack of treasure.[8]

The demand for money was therefore constant and heavy, and the revenue assessments were high, varying between a third and two thirds, or even more, of the gross produce of the cultivated land.[9] Resistance to the demand, on the other hand, was equally persistent. The revenue actually collected seldom, if ever, equalled the amount due, for the rural population of Oudh consisted of martial Hindus, who were traditionally turbulent and more than usually recalcitrant when it came to coughing up their taxes. In order to reduce losses and stabilise income, recourse was had to the system whereby the office of *chakladar* was farmed out to a contractor who, instead of receiving a fixed salary, paid a fixed sum in commutation of the estimated revenues and pocketed any surplus he realised in his collections. This policy was begun in the reign of Asaf-ud-daula and was continued, with variations, for sixty years. It was applied on an extensive scale by Saadat Ali Khan, who grouped *chaklas* together into larger revenue divisions called *nizamats* when an individual wealthy enough to undertake a large-scale contract could be found. Such was called a *nazim,* and exercised the full powers of a *chakladar* over his assigned territories. [10]

The system was attractive to the court because, in theory at least, it stabilised income and minimised bureaucratic business. Its appeal was especially strong to an indolent monarch like Nasir-ud-din, whose aversion to public affairs was such that he wanted to consign the farm of the entire kingdom to his minister.[11] But the disadvantages of the system were equally obvious. It secured vast powers to men whose chief qualification was not administrative competence or experience, but ability to pay or, rather, to promise to pay. It put gubernatorial appointments at the disposal of unworthy courtiers, rash speculators and, occasionally, rich bankers, who were assigned territories in liquidation of claims against the state or in mortgage as security for the payment of such claims.[12] 'It has frequently happened', wrote the Assistant-Resident in 1836, 'that low individuals as uneducated as unprincipled have been thus elevated as the governors of districts, to which they proceed in state, dignified by a title from the government, seated upon a royal elephant with the *noubat* or state drum of authority sounding before them and backed by an army of some thousands of mercenary troops henceforth devoted to their bidding.' [13]

These men, without experience or knowledge of local conditions, were left to wring from an intractable population, in a short space of time, the revenues that were their only means of profit. Incapacity and urgency combined to create methods of collection which, while they produced the funds, caused widespread disruption and distress in rural society. One of these methods was *qabz* ('sequestration'), by which a collector assigned a portion of his district to his military escort, in commutation of their pay. The troops were left to squeeze what they could from the cultivators, while he received credit for amounts supposed to have been paid on their account. This form of billeting was tantamount to a dragonnade for the cultivators. 'This practice', wrote the Resident, Sleeman, in 1849, 'is the source of much evil . . . The commandant of troops commonly takes possession of the lands . . . assigned . . . and appropriates the whole produce to himself and his soldiers without regard to the rights of landholders, farmers, cultivators, capitalists. The troops too are rendered unfit for service by such arrangements, since all their time is taken up in the more congenial duty looking after the estate until they have desolated it.' [14]

Sleeman remarks that this method tended to be reserved for emergencies. Much more usual was the practice of subcontracting, for this was a means of harnessing the knowledge and influence of the local chieftains. As lords of the soil whose ancestors, or putative ancestors, had been in occupation before the Muslim conquest, these claimed prescriptive rights of a seigneurial nature. [15] Unable, or disinclined, to make their revenue assessments and collections in the prescribed way, directly with the cultivators, and constantly harassed by the chieftains, jealous of their traditional rights, the crown collectors often decided to make a virtue of necessity and subcontract for the revenues with these local lords.

The sufferers by this system of contracting and subcontracting were the small landholders. These were men who, through the effects of generations of partible inheritance, had come to hold single villages as coparcenary brotherhoods. The chieftains who became subcontractors often used the powers of their new position to depress these brotherhoods; while powerful capitalists stepped in to buy up the villages of brotherhoods reduced to bankruptcy by the excessive demands of the revenue farmers. Small landholders were thus depressed and in their place a new breed of magnates, or *taluqdars*, sprang up. [16] This process was obnoxious to the British, who fancied that they saw in the coparcenary communities landholders of a type corresponding to the sturdy and admired yeomen of England. The only class of landholders – and it was a very small one – exempt from this degradation comprised those who held their villages by a tenure called *huzur tahsil* ('royal collection'), which prescribed their paying their dues directly into the royal treasury in Lucknow, through a special official. They had no contact at all with the collectors.

The oppressive tendency of the Oudh farming system was increased by the fact that it allowed no elasticity in the crown's requirement; and when a contractor defaulted, through incompetence, cupidity or misfortune, it was the taluqdar or small landholder that had to atone. Saadat Ali devoted much of his great energy to squeezing from his *nazims* and *chakladars* the balances due under their contracts. He made tours of inspection, summoning insolvent *amils* to account for themselves; and when they failed to cough up, or absconded, he would pounce on the smaller fry.[17]

The later monarchs, whose energies were pre-empted either by paramours or by priests, dispensed with these personal visitations and simply made over the district of a delinquent collector to someone more amenable; but the result was much the same. In 1831 the Resident, Maddock, wrote to the Calcutta government deprecating 'the present system under which the country is parcelled out amongst a set of great farmers whose only object is to enrich themselves'.

> The misery and ruin which they occasion to thousands of his subjects [he reported] are unknown to the King, who is satisfied if they make good the rent they have stipulated to pay; and these petty governors being allowed almost absolute power in their own districts, there exists no sympathy between the people and the government, while the latter, unwilling to believe the defalcations in the revenue arise from over-assessment under exactions, takes its revenge on the farmer for balances unpaid and sends another to succeed him who, finding his farm deteriorated and its resources diminished, must have recourse to still more grievous exactions to make good his bargain . . . and thus a succession of *amils* takes place, each more oppressive than his predecessor . . . till at length no-one will accept the farm but on terms which involve a vast sacrifice of the revenue, that comes too late to save the district from temporary ruin.[18]

All these were evils to which the revenue system could and

did lead; but they did not invariably follow its application. Potentially the system was bad; but there is nothing to suggest that in practice it produced the devastation which so many British observers prognosticated. Landholders and cultivators did, apparently, occasionally flee the country and take refuge in neighbouring British territories; [19] but these migrations were temporary. There is no evidence of a sustained drain on the population of Oudh, and travellers who ventured beyond the naturally unfertile land that bordered the well-trodden road between Kanpur and Lucknow generally found that the country was like a garden and the inhabitants prosperous and robust. [20] Even after a decade of misrule by that *roi faineant*, Nasir-ud-din, the Resident was forced to admit that 'the people generally speaking in the interior have not suffered more of late years than the subjects of Indian governments do in general'; [21] and Colonel Low took pains, a few years later, to dispel the notion that 'the mass of the people throughout the kingdom of Oudh were in a state of wretchedness and discontent'. [22]

The fact is, that antidotes were not wanting to neutralise the worst effects of the system. Excessive exaction produces its own antidote, for there is nothing to be gained by continuing to squeeze a sponge when it is dry; and the rhythm of excessive harassment interspersed with periods of relaxation is psychologically less demoralising than harassment that is bearable but inexorable. In Oudh, even in the days of darkness, there was always the hope – the certainty, even – of better times to come; and this gave the population a remarkable tenacity and resilience.

> The agricultural population [wrote the Resident in 1831] may be considered as a machine of wonderful elasticity, for however they may be wronged and oppressed, and even when deprived of their all and forced to desert their villages . . . their natural love of home will recall them to cultivate again their hereditary fields on the slightest prospect that gleams upon them of better treatment; . . . and when a district has been ruined and depopulated and little or no revenue can any longer be extracted from it, it has been customary to farm it on moderate terms for a number of years to some man of property and good management, whose interest it has immediately become to

lure back the fugitive zemindars and ryots [peasants] till, by keeping faith with them for a time ... he has succeeded in restoring the district to order and raising the revenues to their former standard. [23]

Sleeman made the same point twenty years later; and he added the interesting observation that the land itself benefited from temporary depopulation, since this normally resulted in a switch from agrarian to pastoral exploitation. He attributed the great fertility of the soil of Oudh to these periods of fallow. [24]

Then again, contractors were not all flagitious monsters. Many among them, if not exactly benevolent, were canny enough to appreciate that a due regard for the welfare of the cultivators was in their own long-term interest. It was not unknown for wealthy and well established contractors to make advances to their landholders in periods of drought, to enable them to irrigate and dig wells. There was striking evidence of this disposition during the famine of 1837-8, when the Governor-General's camp was passing up country. No forage was procurable in the British territories, but it was available from the estates of the Oudh revenue farmers along the Ganges between Kanpur and Fatehgarh. [25] One of the most notorious and powerful of the Oudh revenue contractors was Darshan Singh, a court favourite of Saadat Ali Khan and Ghazi-ud-din, who acquired the contract of Partabgarh and Sultanpur. He was tyrannical and jealous and, disdaining to collect through intermediaries, pursued a policy of dispossessing landholders large and small alike by fixing revenue demands so high that they resulted in confiscation for arrears. He thus got a large number of villages under his own management and realised the ideal of collection direct from the cultivators. He was always concerned to protect the cultivators from the oppressions of the royal troops, and the districts under his control were remarkably settled and peaceful. Low, the Resident who advised his removal in 1834, in response to complaints against his alleged excesses, was glad, eighteen months later, to have him re-appointed, so manifestly more suited was he to managing the turbulent chieftains and taluqdars than the salaried officials who had replaced him. [26] He was subsequently given the contract of the *chakla* Gonda-Bahraich, and thus became *nazim* of nearly a third of the kingdom. He was long remembered in his districts – if not with affection, then at least with respect. [27]

If the collectors do not merit unqualified denigration, neither do the taluqdars. No doubt they were eager to aggrandise themselves at the expense of the village brotherhoods; and no doubt they were sometimes the medium by which oppression was transferred, for it is hardly open to question that many, when an extra twist was given to the revenue screw operating on them, compensated by giving two twists to that operating on the cultivators. But it is also true that many treated their cultivators well, and acted as a cushion between them and the collector, for good husbandmen and retainers were in short supply and taluqdars competed for their services.[28] It was not unknown for village communities to place themselves voluntarily under some powerful taluqdar, and pay seigneurial dues to him in return for his protection against the crown *chakladar*. The most prominent feature in Oudh rural history during the first half of the nineteenth century is the constant tussle between the crown collectors and royal troops on the one hand, and the taluqdars and their henchmen, armed with cross-bow and sword, on the other. The taluqdars' mud forts, enclosed by impenetrable bamboo jungle and mounted with old ships' guns brought up by merchants from Calcutta, were a characteristic feature of the Oudh countryside. Reducing them formed a customary routine in the bi-annual harvest-time collections; and their regrowth with the quickening of the new season was as regular as the nesting of the blue jays or the ripening of the mustard crop.

It was, ironically enough, the resistance to the evils of the system, rather than the evils themselves, that was the source of British embarrassment. The treaty of 1801 committed the Company to protecting the King against his domestic enemies, and their resistance to his officers automatically qualified the taluqdars as such. The King's collectors were consequently entitled to the aid of the British Subsidiary Force in their efforts to coerce the taluqdars and, as the royal army itself was ill trained, ill armed and mutinous, this was a right that they often desired to make use of. Requests for the services of the Subsidiary troops became so alarmingly frequent that the British authorities began to envisage themselves as the handmaids of oppression.

> It is to be feared [wrote the Political Secretary to the Resident in 1808] that the employment of the British troops for the suppression of disorders within the territories of the Vizier has too frequently been occasioned by the misconduct of His Excellency's *amils* in exciting these disorders by their injustice and rapacity; at the same time Government is aware that requisitions for the employment of our troops on such occasions could not be rejected consistently with the obligations of the engagements subsisting between the British Government and the state of Oudh.[29]

The dilemma was as persistent as it was embarrassing.

> Neither is the aid thus afforded at all effectual [wrote the Governor-General in 1824] . . . as is clear from the annual repetition of the same scenes of resistance. As fast as disorders are suppressed in one quarter they spring up in another. Forts which are this year dismantled are restored again in the next . . . The same process has been again and again gone through, whilst contempt and odium attaching to a system of collecting the revenues by the habitual intervention of the troops of another state infallibly tends to aggravate the evil, by destroying all remains of confidence in His Majesty, or respect for his authority.[30]

This obligation to support the Nawab's authority was anathema to the British, since it compelled them to forswear a principle that they held dear. It was a cardinal article of their political faith that, by virtue of civil rights, an oppressed society is justified in rebelling against its ruler. This was the major inference to be drawn from the fiduciary political theory of John Locke, which in effect places sovereignty not in monarchs but in their subjects, who assign it on trust to their rulers and retain the right to withdraw their obedience in cases of breach of trust. This doctrine had been invoked to justify the Glorious Revolution of 1688, of which the British were inordinately proud and which they regarded as the foundation of their liberties. It is not surprising, therefore, that they felt acutely uncomfortable when they found themselves acting as the instrument by which that same right of rebellion was being denied to others. They came to envisage their own presence in Oudh as the means whereby an artificial and undesirable situation was perpetuated, in which the forces of resistance were checked in their natural tendency to cancel out the forces of oppression. In 1810 the Calcutta government admitted itself open to the 'imputation of being the instrument of abuses which, unsupported by the military power of the Company, would speedily produce their natural consequence – successful resistance to the authority of the Vizier and general anarchy and confusion throughout His Excellency's dominions'.[31] Such a disturbing construction brought forth an uncharacteristic note of self-admonition from the Court of Directors in 1828:

> We should deceive ourselves were we to suppose that, for the state of [misrule and oppression] thus depicted, the British Government is in no degree responsible ... Had it not been for our connection with Oudh, oppression and disorder, although [they] might have attained as great a height, could not have been of equal duration. The subversion of the government by which it was produced or tolerated and the substitution of more moderate rule would have been the speedy result. It is the British Government which, by a systematic suppression of all attempts at resistance, has prolonged to the present time a state of disorganization which can nowhere attain permanence except where the short-sightedness and rapacity of such a barbarous government is armed with the military strength of a civilized one.[32]

The subsidiary system was discussed at great length both in contemporary writing on India and during the Parliamentary investigation of the affairs of the Company prior to the renewal of its charter in 1833. Most commentators agreed that it vitiated the administration and oppressed the population of native states; but they were sharply divided on the issue of what to do about it. One school was in favour of modifying the system; the other of abandoning it altogether.

Those who wanted to modify the system explained that this could be done in one of two ways. The first was taking the right of offering advice to the limit of active interference and exercising political pressure through the Resident; the other was the shock treatment of withdrawing from all but the legal minimum of association with the native government concerned. The first possibility was opted for by the historian Henry Prinsep, who wrote in 1825: 'The obligation of interposing in such cases [of bad government] seems to be a necessary consequence of our holding the military power; for we wield it with so strong an arm as utterly to deprive the population of their natural tendency to rebellion, and the aristocracy of theirs in faction and conspiracy. Unless, therefore, the corrective come from the British Government, there can be no limit to vice and tyranny, howsoever intolerable.'[33] This view was echoed by Lord Macaulay, who wrote in his influential essay on Warren Hastings: 'Is anything more plain than this, that whoever voluntarily gives another irresistible power over human beings, is bound to take order that such power shall not be barbarously abused?'

Another historian, Horace Wilson, writing twenty years after Prinsep, put forward the other view. He questioned Prinsep's assumptions. 'There is no record in Indian history', he wrote, 'of the despotism of its princes being curbed by popular insurrection. Deposal and [unnatural] death have not infrequently been the fate of Indian monarchs, but they have been the work of treacherous ministers or competitors for the throne, in whose selfish policy the people felt little concern.' In his opinion, subsidiary forces should be excluded from revenue collecting, and interference should be resorted to only 'when universal disorder is to be apprehended, or when the conditions and objects of the alliance are imperilled'.[34]

Such was the alternative that could be contained within the system, and both methods were tried in Oudh, as they were also in Hyderabad.

In Oudh, the experiment with interference lasted until 1815. Resident John Baillie (1808-16) turned himself into something of a prime minister. The premise which underlay this policy was that 'the origin of the evil [was] the vicious system of His Excellency's administration',[35] and its object was to persuade the Nawab to make reforms – especially in the revenue department. The plan which the British were intent on realising in Oudh was the abolition of revenue farming and the introduction of management by salaried officials (*amins*). This was first urged on Asaf-ud-daula by Lord Cornwallis, and was thereafter cherished by the Calcutta government almost as a panacea for the ills of Oudh.

In 1810 Baillie had certain districts placed under *amins* with instructions drawn up by himself, and the following year, after the way had been prepared by a stern wigging of the Nawab by the Governor-General, he submitted a comprehensive plan for the reform of the administration. This prescribed the division of the territory into four or five large *zillas*, to be subdivided into districts. Each district was to be under the charge of 'an upright and intelligent *amin*', who was to receive a fixed salary and conduct a revenue survey upon which a triennial settlement could be based.[36] This attempt to impose the British will upon the Nawab failed, and its failure proved that the interference policy could not work. The Nawabs deeply resented the degree of British control which such a policy postulated. Having been stripped of so much authority, they clung jealously to what they retained. In the case of a strong personality like Saadat Ali Khan such a reaction was only to be expected. He let Baillie have his way over the appointment of *amins* in 1810, but jibbed at the proposals, as formulated in the 1811 plan, that the new *amins* be appointed in consultation with the Resident and that the proclamation inaugurating the new system announce that it was adopted 'with the advice and consent of the British Government'. He insisted that such proposals were contrary to the spirit of the 1801 treaty, since they were detrimental to his dignity and authority. The point was conceded and the proposals were withdrawn; but even then he continued to drive Baillie to exasperation with his evasions and objections. He told the Resident: 'I continue to apprehend the subversion of my authority, the retirement and disaffection of my subjects and general disorder in the country, and other injurious effects, from the ignorance of the *amins* and the want of a measurement of the lands.'[37] Even Ghazi-ud-din, who was a much weaker character than his father, exhibited the same sensitivity when the subject of introducing British officials to conduct reforms was raised. He complained that it amounted to placing himself and his subjects in the relation of defendant and plaintiff.[38] Muhammad Ali Shah's reaction to a similar proposal in 1837 was one of nervous prostration. 'The idea... so hurt the old man's feelings', reported the Resident, Low, 'that it had an immediate effect on his disease by producing an instant attack of spasms in the toes of both his feet, which put him to much pain at the time and from which he did not entirely recover for twenty-four hours.'[39]

While Lord Minto was Governor-General (1807-12), pressure was maintained on Saadat Ali, and relations between him and Baillie grew very strained. Baillie's tone became insistent, even imperious; and the Nawab, old, ill and sick to death of this overbearing man, responded with tearful taciturnity, 'retiring for a time from his palace, withdrawing his attention from business, suspending the progress of the reform, expressing a distaste for the exercise of sovereign authority, and a wish to depart on a pilgrimage'.[40] Minto showed himself harsh and inflexible in his response to the Nawab's pathetic complaints, and one of his last acts before leaving India was to send him a scolding and minatory missive, in which he promised him a lifetime of torment: 'However desirous Your Excellency may be to evade the performance of your engagements, the British Government will not cease to require you to fulfil them, and... no lapse of time and no change of circumstances will induce the British Government to relinquish a measure which it considers to be so essential to the welfare and happiness of Your Excellency's subjects... and to the reputation and interest of both governments.'[41]

There seems to be a law which decrees that the probability of an eventuality increases in direct proportion to a politician's insistence on its impossibility. Within a year of this unequivocal declaration of Minto's, the policy of interference had been abandoned. The co-operation of the Nawab must be obtained if the policy was to be reconciled with the 1801 treaty, since that treaty restricted British action to advising and precluded the use of British officers in Oudh; and as such co-operation was obviously not forthcoming, to continue with the policy could produce only sterile argument and bad relations. Such was the reasoning of the new Governor-General, Lord Moira (later the Marquis of Hastings), who dropped the plan of reform and with it the whole policy of the Minto era. A crisis was mounting in central India, and Hastings was anxious to avoid driving the Nawab to the point of 'throwing himself with all his treasures into the hands of any power that would take the field against us'. [42]

It is evident from the whole tenour of the treaty [he wrote to the Court of Directors] that an uninterrupted exercise of his own authority within the reserved dominions was assured to him in order to qualify the very strong step which we took in appropriating to ourselves ... so large a portion of his territories. The Nawab is consequently to be treated in all public observances as an independent prince ... The Resident should consider himself as the ambassador from the British Government to an acknowledged sovereign; a respectful urbanity and a strict fulfilment of established ceremonials should thence be preserved by the Resident towards His Excellency. [43]

Hastings doubted from the start that this new policy could be implemented by Baillie, in whom he noticed 'a captious disposition and a domineering tone, of themselves highly calculated to excite irritation in a prince whose situation would naturally render him acutely jealous of his independence'. [44] His impressions were confirmed when Captain McLeod arrived in Calcutta from Lucknow late in 1813. Saadat Ali had unburdened himself to McLeod, an officer in his service, concerning Baillie's harassment and bullying, and McLeod, who had access to Government House by virtue of his family's associations with the Governor-General's wife, made all this known to Hastings.[45] Baillie's removal was discussed, but was postponed in view of the Governor-General's own pending visit to Lucknow and of the death of Saadat Ali Khan in July 1814. What Hastings saw in Lucknow convinced him that the new Nawab, Ghazi-ud-din, was as unhappy with Baillie as his father had been; but, inhibited by fear of the Resident or by fear of the Governor-General's displeasure, the new ruler had made accusations only to withdraw them, and positive grounds for replacing Baillie were wanting.[46] But Baillie soon fell a victim to his own arrogance. He had got wind of the Governor-General's conferences with McLeod and these so incensed him that he publicly accused Hastings of plotting his removal and sabotaging the plan of reform. The vain and status-conscious Governor-General would have been the last person in the world to tolerate such language in a subordinate. Baillie was removed forthwith, and Richard Strachey summoned from Gwalior to take his place. [47]

This change was the result of something more than a mere clash of personalities. The sacrifice of Baillie was probably inevitable in any case. He was too closely associated with the policy of interference and too emotionally committed to the plan of reform to be able to pursue a policy of disinterested aloofness. As defined by Hastings, that policy was 'to observe strictly the true and obvious spirit of our engagements with the sovereign of Oudh, by leaving him a free agent in the internal government of his own dominions, interfering with that advice which to him must be injunction only in cases where the real importance of our mutual interests required it'.[48] Hopes of persuading the Nawab to introduce some reforms were not abandoned, but the Resident was no longer to intrude with spontaneous and overbearing counsel. He was to 'stand aloof, and keep himself entirely unconnected with any party. He must be ready to offer disinterested advice whenever His Excellency may solicit it, and his conduct should be so shaped as to encourage His Excellency's frequent recurrence to his counsel; but his suggestions should not be obtrusive . . .'[49]

Hastings's concern to dissociate the Calcutta government from the internal affairs of Oudh led him to ignore the issue of administrative reform and concentrate on inducing the Nawab to refurbish his own army – possibly with the help of British officers. If the Nawab's troops were made efficient, the British forces would be relieved of the odious job of coercing the rebellious rural classes. But the policy was thwarted by the inhibiting pressure of vested interests in Oudh and the refusal of the London authorities to allow Company officers to be employed in the Nawab's forces. The appalling state of the Oudh army remained the subject of sterile remonstrance with successive Governors-General. [50]

The policy of non-interference was adopted with regard to all the states in the subsidiary system; and in the case of Oudh, as in that of Hyderabad, it was carried to the furthest extreme compatible with the maintenance of the treaty. One of the many sins of the unfortunate Ricketts was his hostility towards Aga Mir, whom Nasir-ud-din chose as his minister on his accession in 1827, and his apparent involvement in the court intrigues which led to that individual's removal the following year. Aga Mir was *persona non grata* to the British, for he was reckoned to have exercised a baneful influence over the mind of Ghazi-ud-din and to have made him hostile towards projects of reform; but Ricketts was told that his appointment should have been acknowledged nevertheless, in conformity to 'the policy of leaving to the sovereign of Oudh the free and unshackled selection of his own minister'. [51] The British military presence in Oudh was made as inconspicuous as possible by reducing the Subsidiary Force and by attaching inhibiting conditions to the use of the remaining troops. The Resident had been told to investigate and arbitrate all demands for military assistance as early as 1812, and in 1826 it was decreed that in future no assistance was to be given without sanction from Calcutta. [52] Non-interference was carried to the point of non-cooperation in the matter of extradition, on which subject the British policy was that neither state should surrender revenue defaulters to the other 'except in special cases where there might be circumstances of fraud or other misconduct'. [53]

Great faith was had in the therapeutic value of aloofness coupled with a respectful but constant urging from the Resident of the necessity of equitable government. 'The principles of native government', the Calcutta authorities explained in 1830, '[are] so simple, that if the will exist[s] where the powers of administration [are] placed, relief to the people and comparative prosperity to the country [are] sure to follow. To excite this will it must be the Resident's difficult and laborious, but honorable task ... It [is] hoped that by pursuing this course steadily, amelioration [may] be produced and become progressive.' [54]

The Resident's task under this new system was in fact more than difficult and laborious. It was hopeless. The monarchs of Oudh who followed Saadat Ali Khan were, with one exception, supine characters. Reform, with all that it implied in the way of personal exertion and personal sacrifice, was as odious to them as it was to the powerful vested interests about the court. Given this situation, the system was unworkable. A reforming minister could hope to survive only if he had the active support and protection of the Resident, and such support and protection the system precluded *a priori*.

Two ministers dominated the political history of Oudh during the period 1814-32. They were the great rivals Aga Mir and Mehdi Ali Khan. Both tried to implement reforms, and both failed to do so because of the absence of support from the Resident.

Aga Mir, a megalomaniac whom Bishop Heber described as 'a dark, harsh, hawk-nosed man, with an expression of mouth which seemed to imply habitual self-command struggling with a naturally rough temper', had risen from menial status in the royal household. A favourite of Ghazi-ud-din, he was made minister, with the title Moatamud-ud-daula ('Pillar of the State') soon after that King's accession in 1814, and he remained in power, save during one short period of disfavour, until his master's death in 1827. At first he responded to Baillie's demands for reform. He divided the country into six districts (*zillas*), each under a salaried *nazim*, and made preparation for a new revenue settlement. [55] But with the removal of Baillie and the appointment of a new Resident on whose support he could not rely, Aga Mir knew that it would be political suicide to continue with these plans. Ghazi-ud-din was like some easy-going medieval abbot. Jovial, ingenuous and of falstaffian girth, he was religious in his own peculiar way; but he lacked a strong sense of duty and moral propriety and, without such fibre to strengthen his character, was always yielding to the attractions of sensuous pleasure and somnolent ease. Aga Mir was astute enough to realise that if he failed to lead the King along the primrose path of dalliance, others would, and he abandoned reform as the only way of consolidating his hold over his affections. [56] He admitted that he was forced to this by the removal of British support. He told a later Resident, Maddock, that 'the removal of the controlling influence of the Resident over the affairs of this government in the time of Lord Hastings was the greatest misfortune that it could ever have sustained'. [57]

The experience of his great rival, the *hakim* (physician) Mehdi Ali Khan, was similar. He made his fortune and reputation as a revenue farmer, in which capacity he had earned the approval of the British authorities. [58] He made his first bid for political power in 1815 and it was his machinations which, in the opinion of Baillie, caused the temporary disgrace and removal of Aga Mir; but not till Ghazi-ud-din died did he fully succeed in supplanting his rival. He was made minister in 1830, when he was already infirm, bald, and sinking beneath the weight of years, and set about reforming the administration with a will. He planned the division of the kingdom into four great revenue districts with the substitution of *amani* or trust management for revenue farming, and began to make extensive retrenchments in court and public expenditure. [59] Within a year he had achieved results which induced the Resident, Low, to write enthusiastically to the Governor-General:

> I beg to mention some ... facts for your Lordship's satisfaction. *First*, that no open rebellion or public warfare of any kind at present exists in any part of Oudh; *second*, that since the end of January no less than thirteen zemindars of importance have come in and made up their quarrels with the durbar – all of whom had long been refractory and most of them openly disobedient to their government for many years back; *thirdly*, that upwards of 14,000 troops have been disbanded; and *fourthly*, that several districts have been taken from the farming system and placed in amani, while the police, especially in those districts bordering on our provinces, is decidedly much better than it was in former times. [60]

But however much they approved of what he was doing, the British refused to associate themselves with the *hakim* in his drive for improvement. The Resident's participation did not go beyond general expressions of encouragement, and when the *hakim* asked whether British officials would be available to implement the reforms, he was told that the British government would be better pleased if these changes were effected by the King's own agents. [61] Calcutta was especially anxious not to be associated with the minister's unpopular measures. 'You must be cautious', Low was instructed on his appointment as Resident in 1831, 'not to make such a display of unanimity as shall enable the minister to represent every ungracious, violent or unpopular act as the result of your urgency.' [62]

Such a policy could lead to only one result, for nowhere about the court could the minister find support to compensate for British diffidence. Never was a king less disposed to fulfil the duties and observe the standards of his office than Nasir-ud-din. His intellect was weak; he was bibulous and lecherous; and his distaste for affairs of state was complete. His wealth he squandered on paramours, panderers and sycophants, whose task was to devise ever new and more perverted forms of titillation to occupy his never-ending leisure. Any intrusion into this life of dissipation and self-gratification was resented. 'When he goes out', wrote Low, '... sowars [cavaliers] scour the streets to prevent any person delivering petitions, and instances have occurred of complainants for justice being severely flogged by his order.' Reared in the zenana by a doting mother and female relations, he exhibited all the symptoms of arrested psychological development. He pursued the gratification of every whim with childish monomania, and lost interest with childish capriciousness. He was full of childish vanity and childish tantrums. He was childish in his attachment to those who had won his favour, and childish in his cruelty to those who had lost it. He was too squeamish and sentimental to be a bloody tyrant, and shrank from inflicting capital punishment; but his vengeance could be sadistic when he felt his religious susceptibilities to be offended. [63]

Powerful parties about the court bitterly resented the *hakim's* economies, which had eaten deeply into many pensions and privileges and, led by the queen mother, they induced the unstable King to get rid of the offender. Precluded by his instructions from offering anything more than remonstrance, the Resident stood by with his feelings working strongly within him while 'an old and highly meritorious man humble[d] himself to the dust before a young one who ha[d] neither capacity to appreciate his merits nor feeling enough to sympathize with his distress of mind'. [64]

Mehdi Ali Khan was dismissed in November 1832, and succeeded by Raushan-ud-daula, whom the Assistant-Resident described as 'a most amiable and good-tempered man, of high family and pleasing manner, but ... more suited to be[ing] a king than a laborious minister'. He made attempts to take up and complete the *hakim's* work, but he was pusillanimous and feared offending the King, whose riot of extravagance had by this time brought the state close to ruin. Increasingly unhappy, Raushan-ud-daula often signified his wish to resign, and, failing to derive any political support from the Resident, felt compelled to cultivate this in other quarters by the bestowal of large bribes and *douceurs*. These he partly paid from his own resources and partly embezzled from the treasury. [65] Reform, needless to say, stalled.

The *hakim* Mehdi was recalled from his exile at Fatehgarh by Muhammad Ali Shah on his accession (1837), and the combination of his talent with the sincere determination of the new King to put things in order bade fair for a real change without recourse to British interference. The *amani* system was introduced on a wide scale, and the pruning knife applied unsparingly to the army and all durbar establishments. [66] The *hakim* died six months after taking office and a period of instability followed, under the ministry of the heir-apparent; but after the accession to the deputy ministry of Sharf-ud-daula the King's wishes were again effectively translated into actions. [67] Sharf-ud-daula was young, high-born and prone to make enemies by a haughty demeanour; but he was amenable to those hints and suggestions which, after nearly ten years' experience as Resident, Low knew exactly when and how to offer. This period was probably the most promising in the long trial of the non-interference policy. It demonstrated that the policy could work, given only an able and well disposed monarch.

But to demand so much was to demand too much of the dynasty which ruled in Lucknow. Muhammad Ali Shah, whom Low judged to be 'the most respectable native sovereign ... that [he] [had] ever been associated with on official duties in any part of India', [68] was unique among the later monarchs of Oudh. Already sixty-three and suffering from an acute nervous disorder when he succeeded, he lived for only another five years; and in his son, Amjad Ali Shah, all the characteristic vices of the family reappeared. When he succeeded in 1842, he was already middle-aged, and fat and scant of breath. His behaviour was the result of a narrow, religious education on a voluptuous and passionate nature. He carried to the point of real hatred the aversion which, as a Shia Muslim, he traditionally owed the Sunnis, and in all cases where choice was admitted allowed the satisfaction of bigotry to take precedence over the interests of efficiency. In public he made a parade of piety which was belied in private by the rebel impulses of a gargantuan sexual appetite. Like most men who are tortured by the powerful and conflicting sensations of desire and guilt, he found it extremely difficult to make decisions, and most of the time that he devoted to public affairs was wasted in procrastination. [69] To make matters worse, his accession coincided with the retirement from Lucknow of the sober, sagacious and experienced Low. Thereafter the Residency was managed in swift succession by two veteran generals of the Afghan War, Sir William Nott and Sir George Pollock. Neither was well qualified for the job. Nott was cantankerous and prosaic; Pollock unassertive and inarticulate. Nott, who was given the high-sounding title of Envoy to the King of Oudh by Governor-General Lord Ellenborough as a reward for services in Afghanistan, arrived in Lucknow early in 1843, but was forced by bad health to retire after a few months; and Pollock, who arrived in December 1843, as Acting Resident, stayed only a year, before being recalled to Calcutta to take up a seat on the Council. This unsettled state of the Residency combined with the weakness and vacillation of the King to produce the most chronic ministerial paralysis that Oudh had yet experienced.

As he could not tolerate the idea of having a Sunni as his minister, Amjad Ali Shah dismissed Sharf-ud-daula and nominated as his successor Amin-ud-daula, the son of Aga Mir. The supersession was resented by Nott and Pollock, and they treated the new minister with studied insult. A rift developed between court and Residency, and co-operation became impossible until Pollock left Lucknow and was succeeded by the more urbane and experienced T. R. Davidson, a Bengal civil servant. In his report on the state of the kingdom, dated May 1846, Davidson confirmed that the revenue system was still radically as bad as ever: 'So long as the plan of farming the revenues of districts to *amils* prevails, Oudh can never become a prosperous state. The King and the minister are not insensible or ignorant of the grievous evils attendant on the present faulty system; yet so many interests are involved in its continuance that to them its extinction seems to be impossible.' [70]

Remittances received by the treasury in Lucknow had begun to fall off alarmingly. This was due partly to the fact that the minister, in the face of British hostility or reticence, was forced to propitiate the revenue collectors by allowing them to claim false expenses and send in diminished balances; and partly to the increased difficulty of realising the dues of taluqdars and zemindars now that the assistance of British troops was withheld in all but exceptional cases. [71]

The experience of forty years had shown that both forms of the subsidiary system were unworkable. Intervention had proved itself incompatible with royal rights and pretensions; non-interference had precluded ministerial efficiency. The reforms achieved during the period were meagre. In response to the new standards demanded by the British, infanticide and *sati* (or 'suttee' – the ritualistic burning of Hindu widows) had been prohibited in Oudh in 1833; but the decrees were never enforced, and in the crucial area of fiscal administration the situation was still basically the same as that which had obtained under Saadat Ali Khan. Thus after forty years the British still found themselves supporting a dynasty whose practices were anathema and which were, in the words of one

Resident, apparently 'fast leading to the devastation of the fairest province of India'.[72]

Experience therefore added weight to the arguments of those who wanted to abandon the system altogether. There was a legal case to be made out for cancelling the treaty, since the King had failed to honour his obligations to reform his government in conformity with the advice of the Resident and to keep his army within the stipulated limits. The alternative was still basically the same – interference or non-interference; but with the treaty removed interference could be carried to the point of assuming the administration and pensioning off the King, while non-interference could be turned into complete withdrawal and abandonment of the dynasty to the unrestrained play of the forces of rebellion.

The treatment accorded to Mysore and Coorg, where conditions of misrule were similar to those in Oudh, set a precedent for assumption. In 1831, invoking its rights under the treaty of 1799, the Calcutta government divested the Raja of Mysore of all political power and placed the administration of the country under British officers. In 1834 the principality of Coorg, in southern India, was invaded and annexed to the Madras Presidency as a penalty for the Raja's incompetence and oppression. The conviction was growing that the policy must soon be applied to Oudh. 'It must come ultimately to our assumption of the administration', wrote the Governor-General, Bentinck, to Low, in 1832;[73] and in 1837 his successor, Auckland, noted that 'the choice appear[ed] to be only between an assumption of the administration by British officers . . . or a transfer of the sovereignty on improved conditions to a more capable member of the royal family'.[74]

The idea of confiscating the administration was fostered by the powerful lobby of liberal and Evangelical opinion. Both liberals and Evangelicals owed much to the notion of progress and to the belief that Western civilisation was its manifestation and its agent; and both therefore came to accept it as axiomatic that good government meant British government. Indian governments they regarded as incorrigibly corrupt and inefficient, and their continued existence was held to be incompatible with the happiness of the Indian people. Replacing them by British methods of government was therefore considered to be a moral duty. 'In my opinion', said James Mill, when giving evidence before the House of Commons in 1832, 'the best thing for the happiness of the people is that our government should be nominally as well as really extended over those territories; that our own modes of governing should be adopted, and our people put in the charge of the government.' [75] These convictions played their part even in the annexation of Sind (1843), though strategic and commercial motives, as well as the personal ambition of Sir Charles Napier, were in this instance paramount. Lord Ellenborough justified the measure on the grounds that 'nations have claims to consideration as well as Princes', and Napier saw it as the means of bringing the benefits of civilisation to the oppressed and deprived subjects of the Sind Amirs.

Such arguments had strong influence on the 'Reform' Ministry of Whigs and liberals which took office in 1830, and in 1834 the Court of Directors, at the instigation of the minsterial Board of Control, authorised the Governor-General in Council to assume the entire administration of the King of Oudh's dominions. It seemed, therefore, that the days of the dynasty, as a political influence at least, were numbered. In fact, it lasted for another twenty years. The threat of assumption was uttered four times, in 1831, 1835, 1844 and 1845; but it was never followed by action. The reason was that the British were not yet so intoxicated by liberalism that they were oblivious of other vital considerations.

Their sense of moral obligation was as yet weaker than their respect for international law. 'Such a necessity', wrote Hastings in 1815, 'though it might morally exist, could never be made out to the world, and the seizure of the Nawab's possessions would be universally stigmatized as a premeditated usurpation arising from a base cupidity'.[76] The East India Company had a treaty right to confiscate the administration of Mysore in the event of maladministration and the ultimate sanction for the deposition of the Amirs of Sind was the legal right created by their supposed treachery.

But no such legal justification existed for similar measures with regard to Oudh. In the second place, Englishmen were not wanting in India who warned against the tendency, so pronounced in liberal circles, to equate indictment of the native system of government with vindication of the British. Low warned the Calcutta government in 1841 that native preference for the British system should not be taken for granted:

> The experience of the last sixty years has proved that the inhabitants of Oudh greatly prefer their own country to any other and also that, unless on particular occasions when they have been oppressed to a very great extent and, I may say, in a peculiar degree, they have evinced a steady preference for their own irregular government and their own rough usages, over other governments and other systems which, according to our notions, ought greatly to be preferred ... I do not admit the existence of what can be called general discontent in Oudh ... There are many ... parts of this kingdom in which the people, generally speaking, are, to the best of my belief, well contented with their lot in life. [77]

Then again, while the native states were despicable for moral reasons, they were valuable for political ones. 'The preservation of the existing states in India is a duty imposed on us by the obligations of public faith as well as the dictates of interest', wrote the Secret Committee of the Court of Directors in 1838. 'The continued existence of such states will afford the means of employment to respectable natives, which they cannot at present obtain in our service; and until such means could be provided in our own provinces, the downfall of any of the native states under our protection might, by depriving numerous influential natives of their accustomed employment, be attended with consequences most injurious to our interests.' [78]

The fourth consideration was the enormous debts of the Oudh government. It was Captain Paton, the Assistant-Resident, who pointed out in 1835 that if the Company assumed the administration of the principality it would inherit many claims from creditors. 'Though the Oudh Government has hitherto turned a deaf ear to those claims, the British Government might find itself bound in honour to pay many of them to a heavy amount.' The likelihood was increased by the fact that one of the largest claims, that of the Das brothers, bankers of Calcutta and Benares, had recently received powerful support in London. The debt dated from 1794, and had originally amounted to about 200,000 rupees; but it was common practice to issue new bonds each year for amounts combining principal and interest (at thirty-six percent), so within a short time the nominal loan had become some 1,160,000 rupees, or about £116,000. The Das brothers, through their agent, Mr Prendergast (who was accused of having bought the debt), had tried for many years to induce the Company either to persuade the King to pay the debt, with interest, or to settle it itself. Hastings, when Governor-General, had acknowledged that the claim was a special one, deserving the countenance of the British authorities, since the Das brothers were British subjects and their claim had its origins in the Nawab's efforts to discharge arrears due to the Company. The Court of Directors had rejected this pleading, and directed that a policy of strict aloofness be followed in all cases involving a pecuniary claim by a private individual on a native sovereign. It insisted that to acknowledge one such claim would be to invite scores of others, since it was known that other native creditors, who were supposed to have been settled with in 1796, had in fact never been paid. In 1832, however, the Dases' claim had received the support of the President of the Board of Control, Charles Grant, who subscribed to the reasoning advocated by Hastings. A dramatic struggle had ensued when the Court still demurred and Grant, invoking the legal powers vested in the Board, applied to the Court of King's Bench for a writ of mandamus which would compel the Directors, under pain of imprisonment, to send the necessary orders to India. He desisted at the last minute, suddenly aware that to acknowledge such a debt would saddle the British with an enormous liability when they assumed the administration of Oudh; but it was now inevitable that such an assumption would lead to claims, complicated investigations and commitments of the type that had already produced so much embarrassment in the Carnatic following the take-over of its administration in 1801, and in Hyderabad in the days when Resident Charles Metcalfe had attempted to clean the Augean stables of the Nizam's administration. Grant had been very vague on the issue of interest; but he had suggested that the Das brothers were entitled to the terms which the Nawab's European creditors had obtained in 1796. These were principal plus compound interest at thirty-six percent. To settle the claim of the Dases on the same terms after a period of thirty-six years would render their debtor liable for the fantastic sum of some seven thousand millions sterling. Obviously, such an amount could never be paid; but, armed with an acknowledgement of its theoretical validity, it was not to be expected that the creditors would compound for modest compensation. A crore of rupees, or a million sterling, was the sum mentioned by Paton. [79] There were, furthermore, extra debts, contracted since the treaty; and the British authorities had already been directly involved in the efforts to recover that of the Lucknow banker Shah Behari Lal, which amounted to half a million sterling. [80] The Lucknow treasury, on the other hand, was confidently reckoned to be empty. In 1836 the Resident reported, quoting figures, that 'all available assets were insufficient to cover current arrears due to public establishments'. [81] The Calcutta government would obviously have hesitated to involve itself in such an unhealthy situation at the best of times; and these times were far from the best. The Company had been running at a loss for some time, and its finances were in a parlous state after 1833, when it was deprived of its monopoly of the China trade, the profits from which had long subsidised territorial administration in India. Bentinck was compelled to pinch and scrape in order to find the funds needed by the Directors to defray expenses in England; while Auckland, who succeeded him, had to find money for the disastrous First Afghan War. Small wonder, then, that the permission to assume the administration of a bankrupt state was never acted on.

There remained the possibility of complete withdrawal. This had much to recommend it. Such a procedure would salve the British conscience on the moral issue without pricking it on the legal one. The accusation of underwriting the iniquities of the native administration would be removed, while that of indulging in unprovoked aggression would be avoided. It seemed the perfect compromise. But this policy too was eschewed. Indeed, there was never a chance of its being adopted, because the strongest of all pecuniary arguments militated against it. The standing arrangement with Oudh may have been offensive to British principles; but it was nevertheless very convenient for the British pocket.

Extensive territories had been ceded to the British in return for their protection. If they withdrew that protection, it was only logical that they should return the territory. This was not an attractive idea, since the Ceded Provinces now yielded something near two millions sterling a year, of which less than a third was absorbed by administration charges. Captain Paton, in his report of 1836, suggested that withdrawal could be reconciled with retention of the territories, since protection against external enemies could continue to be afforded by a force based outside Oudh; but this was a specious argument. The fact was, that Oudh had no external enemies now that British hegemony was effectively established over the subcontinent. The King's only enemies were his domestic ones, and the treaty prescribed quite specifically protection against these. To retain the Ceded Provinces as the price of defence against foreign aggressors would have been tantamount to receiving two millions a year for meeting a threat that did not exist and ignoring one that did.

But the British would never have abandoned the monarchs of Lucknow even if it had been possible to do so without giving up the ceded territories. Tiresome and embarrassing though they were, the fact remained that they were useful – even essential. They had, as Hastings put it, 'vast command of money'; and they survived for so long because they found the fatal chink in the British moral armour – vast need of money. Even the British, it was discovered, had their price; and the Nawabs bought instalment after instalment of reprieve by pumping vast sums of treasure into Company loans in times of crisis. They literally paid for one of the Company's major wars, and afforded large subventions to two others. They reckoned, and with reason, that the British would never abandon them while their money and their complaisance lasted.

A short-term loan was negotiated from Asaf-ud-daula by Lord Cornwallis, to help finance the Third Mysore War; but it was Lord Hastings who first tapped the wealth of the Nawabs on a large scale. Preparations for the Nepal War were going forward after June 1814, a time when funds were short. The Calcutta treasury was depleted, and there was little hope of raising another public loan at the current rate of interest, because government securities were on the market at a sixteen percent discount and officials in the upper provinces were forced to borrow at twelve percent in order to defray current expenses.[82] Hastings's thoughts therefore turned towards the private hoard of Saadat Ali Khan. In October, when the Governor-General's tour of the upper provinces had brought him to Kanpur, Baillie was summoned to the viceregal camp and privately instructed to negotiate a loan of ten million rupees (£1 million) from the Nawab, conducting the business in such a way that the offer would appear on record as a spontaneous one.[83] Baillie played his part well, and when Hastings met the Nawab at Kanpur he was gratified by his 'volunteering' to lend the Company ten million rupees. The amount was subsequently increased to 10,800,000 rupees, so as to make the interest, at six percent, sufficient for some 120 stipends.[84]

This delicate negotiation had caused Hastings to suspend his ideas of removing Baillie, for he alone had the influence and *savoir-faire* necessary to bring it to a successful conclusion. His removal would have caused the fall of his ally Aga Mir and brought to power the *hakim* Mehdi Ali Khan, who was known to oppose the loan. Hastings therefore turned a blind eye to the distress which Baillie was causing Ghazi-ud-din. 'It is not my business to develop this intrigue', he wrote in his journal. 'If the power which Major Baillie has over the Vizier's mind, aided by the cooperation of Aga Mir, be exerted beneficially for the furtherance of public affairs, I can have no call to make objections.'[85] It soon became obvious that further recourse would be necessary to Baillie's influence. News arrived of unforeseen disasters in the Nepal War and reports from Calcutta stated that the authorities had, without the Governor-General's consent, diverted the funds made available by the loan to the liquidation of the old government debts. Hence there was still no war fund, at a time when the war was demanding immediate extra resources. Another ten million rupees were required, and early in December Baillie was asked to do his utmost to get this from the Nawab.[86]

The business proved difficult, and the Governor-General grew anxious.[87] By mid-February the tone of his Private Secretary's correspondence with Baillie was importunate:

> According to a statement just received by His Lordship from Edmonstone [Vice-President in Council], nearly three crores in addition to our surplus revenue will be required to meet the war extraordinaries up to the 30th April 1816 ... Unless, therefore, you can enable me to rejoice His Lordship by informing him that you have succeeded in getting another crore from the Vizier, fifty lakhs [500,000] from the Begam and fifty lakhs from your monied men, we shall be in a very desperate state.[88]

Baillie, with the help of Aga Mir, finally extracted a second loan of ten million rupees from the Nawab in March 1815, and Hastings's expressions of gratitude were profuse. How long his gratitude would have maintained Baillie in the post of Resident, if Baillie had not been so unwise as to traduce the Governor-General, it is difficult to say. It was certainly not true, as Hastings implied, that Baillie was dismissed as part of a tacit bargain with the Nawab.[89] Not the prospect of Baillie's absence, but the fact of his presence was the essential condition of these loans, and Hastings only pretended otherwise because he was anxious to vindicate before the London authorities the removal of Baillie and the adoption of a non--interference policy. He implied that he had got the money by adopting a non-interference policy. In fact, he had risked wrecking that policy (by retaining Baillie) in order to get the money.

This second loan was more than adequate to cover the whole of the extraordinary expenses of the Nepal War, which proved less than had been anticipated; and as the entire amount was liquidated after the war by the cession of territories partly conquered from the Nepalese and partly owned but never exploited by the British, Hastings was able to claim that the war had not cost the Company a single shilling. The entire charge had been borne by the Nawab of Oudh.

Ten years later, when the Burmese War was dragging on and costing far more than the original estimates, the treasure of Saadat Ali Khan, lying in rotting sacks in some subterranean chamber in Lucknow, began to exercise a fascination over the mind of the new Governor-General, Lord Amherst. The Resident, now Mordaunt Ricketts, was duly applied to, and he induced the Nawab to promise a third loan of ten million rupees. There was, however, a hitch concerning the rate of interest. The Nawab wanted six percent, but Amherst would offer only five and made it plain to Ricketts that if he could not secure the loan on these terms he would be replaced by someone who could: '. . . the successful management of this negotiation will be in no slight degree creditable to you; on the other hand I am bound to say . . . its failure will seem to evince a want of influence with the King and minister greatly to be regretted in one holding an office for which the command of influence in this quarter is one of the most essential qualifications'.

Fortunately for Ricketts, Aga Mir was as anxious as the Governor-General for the deal to be clinched. He saw in it a means of insuring himself against the fall from favour which was sure to follow the death of Ghazi-ud-din. He persuaded the King to offer a five percent loan, with the condition attached that the interest be paid by the Company as pensions to nine specified individuals. Aga Mir, his wife, daughter and son were the stipendaries who figured most prominently in the list. They were guaranteed, under British protection, pensions amounting to 25,000 rupees a year. The following year, Amherst pressed Ricketts to apply for another five million rupees to offset 'heavy and accumulated expenses attendant upon the close of the war', and this was procured by the minister in return for a recognition by the Governor-General of the titles conferred on him by the King.[90] The total contribution of Ghazi-ud-din to the Burmese War was therefore fifteen million rupees, or one and a half millions sterling, which was far in excess of that of any other native prince.

Nasir-ud-din, who succeeded in 1827, made substantial investments in Company loans. He converted the loan of 1826, which had been short-term, into a permanent one, and added a million and a quarter rupees to make the interest sufficient for the pensions of selected begams.[91] Three further loans followed, totalling some four million rupees, most of the interest on which was assigned as a pension to one of the King's wives. The rest was divided between a new hospital with a medical school attached, and a charity for the poor of Lucknow.[92]

The death of Nasir-ud-din, in 1837, came at a critical time. The machinations of Russia in Persia and central Asia were causing grave concern to British statesmen. Lord Auckland, the Governor-General, had written to Sir Charles Metcalfe in September 1836: 'I share with you in the apprehension of our being at no distant date involved in political and possibly military operations upon or beyond our western frontier.'[93] In order to provide against such an eventuality – to materialise three years later with the outbreak of the First Afghan War – Auckland decided to use the occasion of the accession of Muhammad Ali Shah to squeeze more money from Oudh. With this object in view he resorted to methods that recall the worst extortions and venal excesses of Clive and Warren Hastings.

Nasir-ud-din had two putative sons – Kaiwan Jah, the elder, and Munna Jan, the younger. The former was almost certainly spurious, the son of one of the King's wives by a former husband; and the latter, while probably genuine, had been turned into a little monster by his doting grandmother, the Padshah Begam. In 1832 the King had publicly disowned both boys. Kaiwan Jah was rejected because his mother had been replaced in the King's affections by another begam; Munna Jan suffered the same fate at the instance of Mehdi Ali Khan, who was anxious to destroy the influence of his arch-enemy, the Padshah Begam.[94] Given the dubious parentage of the one prince and the psychopathic mentality of the other, the British authorities had not been disposed to quarrel with the King's pronouncement and had recognised his uncle, Muhammad Ali Shah, the only surviving son of

Saadat Ali Khan, as heir to the throne.⁹⁵

In July 1837 Nasir-ud-din died quite suddenly in the middle of the night, aged thirty-six. Alcoholic poisoning seems the most likely explanation, but another sort of poison could have been responsible, administered by some agent of the Padshah Begam. She was a fiercely ambitious woman and was reputed to have blood on her hands. The fact that she was so well prepared for the King's death reinforces the case against her. While Low was preparing to announce the accession of Muhammad Ali Shah she marched with 2,000 henchmen to the throne room (Barahdari) of the Farhatbakhsh palace, took possession, and seated Munna Jan on the principal throne. The next three and a half hours were critical. Low's expostulation with the Begam proved unavailing; the crowd of her supporters became larger and more hostile; and looting and all the first signs of popular insurrection occured in the city. Only with the arrival of British troops from the cantonments north of the river was the situation retrieved. They stormed the throne room and inflicted casualties amounting to thirty or forty according to Low, and to five hundred according to native accounts. The Padshah Begam and Munna Jan were made state prisoners and spirited quickly away to Chunar fort, where they both spent the remainder of their days.

Low's first action on hearing of the death of Nasir-ud-din was to present himself before the acknowledged heir with a paper ready for his signature. This paper read: 'I hereby declare that in the event of my being placed on the throne I will agree to sign any new treaty that the Governor-General may dictate'. After being woken in the middle of the night, shocked by the unexpected news of his nephew's death and dazed by the urgency of the Resident, Muhammad Ali Shah was in no state to question or deliberate, and he signed the paper thrust under his nose hardly knowing whether he was awake or dreaming. It was not long before he discovered that he had signed what was a blank cheque in more than the figurative sense.⁹⁶

The Governor-General disapproved of Low's initiative. He complained that the promise extracted from the King was 'liable to misconstruction'. But this disapproval was for the record only. Auckland's real sentiments can be judged by his speed in making use of the promise. Within a few days the draft of a new treaty was on its way to Lucknow. One of its provisions was for the introduction of British officers into Oudh in the event of persistent maladministration, and Auckland made much of this, implying that the object of the treaty was to give the Oudh people a remedy for oppression. In fact its object was nothing of the sort. Auckland himself admitted that he had no intention of dropping the policy of non--interference in practice. The real significance of the treaty lay in those clauses which stipulated the replacement of the British Subsidiary Force by an Auxiliary Force consisting of the King's own troops and commanded by British officers. This new force was to be paid for by the King but controlled by the Resident. 'I can see in no other arrangement', said Auckland, '... any chance of combining the good and orderly government of that kingdom and the consolidation of our military strength.'[97] The object of the treaty was to release the Subsidiary Force for military operations outside Oudh by compelling the King to provide a replacement, at his own expense. Auckland ignored the fact that the Oudh princes had already ceded half their territory to pay for their protection.

The honest Low was aghast to find how unscrupulously Auckland had used the promise extracted from the King. He confessed himself averse to a treaty so blatantly 'more for our own purposes and interests than for [the King's] or for the direct advantage of his subjects'. The gravamen of his argument, which was that the monarchs of Oudh were being required to pay twice for the same service, was unanswerable, and Auckland could only reply with evasion and threat. In a shameful mess of ungrammatical verbiage, he explained that the sovereigns of Oudh had nullified the 1801 treaty by their failure to observe its provisions; but then, sensing that this line of reasoning could only lead to the inference that the lands transferred under that treaty should be restored, he switched tactics and told Low that there was no question of compulsion. The King was at perfect liberty to revert to the 1801 arrangement if he wished. But he warned that in that event the treaty would have to be fulfilled to the letter, and this was bound to lead to 'endless collision and embarrassments and ... temporary anarchy and misery to the people and an early reduction of the sovereigns of Oudh to the condition only of pensioned princes'.[98] In Auckland's private correspondence there is the same thinly veiled ruthlessness. He let Low know that it was not his job to question the morality or legality of measures deemed necessary for the good of his country, but to get them adopted. 'I am well aware that you share with me in an anxious desire to support the honour and consolidate the power of our country; and if I had not the most perfect confidence in the zeal and ability with which you will pursue those objects, I should look upon your residence at Lucknow with different feelings from those of the satisfaction with which I have been accustomed to view it.'[99]

The draft of the new treaty aroused considerable bitterness in the durbar, but the King's hands were tied and the agreement as finally signed incorporated only trivial modifications.[100] That was not the end of the matter, however. The projected treaty caused considerable embarrassment in London. Iqbal-ud-daula, a cousin of Nasir-ud-din whose claim to the throne had been passed over in favour of that of Muhammad Ali Shah, had gone to London to seek redress. He had there found powerful support among the political opponents of the Melbourne ministry, and Hobhouse, who as President of the Board of Control was ministerial agent for Indian affairs, was aware that a treaty such as this would strengthen their case considerably.

Be good enough [he wrote privately to Auckland in August 1838] to inform me that you have abandoned all intention of carrying your projected Oudh treaty into execution. We could not sanction or defend any such treaty, and the sooner it is dropped the better ... Even while I write this Lords Brougham, Lyndhurst and Ellenborough who, probably, have heard of your preliminary treaty, have denounced the bargain as unjustifiable and I know not what, connecting it with the elevation of the present King of Oudh to the exclusion of more rightful claimants – which, altho' nonsense, it is as well to be able decidedly to contradict.[101]

Hobhouse had sent his official instructions for the abrogation of the treaty through the Secret Committee of the Court of Directors in April, but Auckland ignored them. After further, peremptory instructions from London, the King was informed, in July 1839, that he would not be required, after all, to pay for the new Auxiliary Force; but he was never told that the treaty as a whole had been disallowed. Indeed, it remained legally valid, since the Governor-General in Council never issued an instrument of cancellation. [102] Auckland was later condemned in Parliament for this 'gross and scandalous concealment of the facts from the King'. [103]

Auckland's attempt to mulct the King of Oudh of another £160,000 a year therefore failed; but Muhammad Ali Shah did nevertheless make considerable investments in government securities. He sank £170,000 in the current four percent loan to provide pensions for selected individuals; and his contribution to the new five percent loan, opened in 1841, to provide for the expenses of the Afghan War, totalled some four and a half million rupees (£460,000). [104]

Thus during the period 1814-42 contributions totalling not less than 48 million rupees, or nearly five millions sterling, had been lent by the Kings of Oudh to the Calcutta government. [105] The British were always anxious to demonstrate that these loans were to the advantage of both parties, and they often claimed that they were a means whereby sterile wealth was turned into productive investment. It is difficult to find much justification for such a claim. The capital was largely used to finance wars, and the interest, with the exception of that on two small investments by Nasir-ud-din, did not find its way into philanthropic or economically constructive projects. It was absorbed by court stipendaries and either found its way back into private hoards or circulated within the constricted nexus that linked the aristocracy with the luxury commodity market. Furthermore, while the loans themselves provided a powerful inducement to the British not to abandon the Oudh sovereigns, the mode of paying the interest extended the Company's aegis to a whole sector of the aristocracy and thereby restricted still further its freedom of action in relations with the court.

These pecuniary services were not the only advantages reaped by the British from their connections with Oudh. Valuable assistance in the form of elephants and horses was provided during the Mahratta War of 1802-5 and during the 1814-16 Nepal War. Moreover, the hospitality of the Nawabs, and their willingness to employ Europeans, put valuable patronage at the disposal of the Governors-General. Hastings presumed to offer several of his protégés employment at the court of Lucknow,[106] and Auckland used his influence to get Mr Gattie appointed as successor to the notorious barber, Derusett.[107]

Nineteenth-century English liberalism was a rationalised expression of English optimism and English self-confidence. It had its origins in the astonishing developments in English industry and technology, in the rapid expansion of English trade, and in the remarkable political stability of the British Isles during the period of the Industrial Revolution and Revolutionary and Napoleonic Wars. As a creed, it drew on those elements in Whig political theory, Enlightenment philosophy and modern political economy that the English experience seemed to vindicate: the constitutional doctrine of Locke, Blackstone, and the apologists of the Glorious Revolution; the belief in moral progress and human perfectibility as pronounced by the eighteenth-century *philosophes*; and the principles of free enterprise, free trade and utility formulated by Adam Smith and Bentham. Liberalism was not confined to one party or group. Its influence affected the whole climate of English thought, and in the 1830s and 1840s its anti-dogmatic, anti-mystic and anti-authoritarian message was accepted as axiomatic by all save the extremist elements of the Tory Party and Anglican Church. Several prominent liberals were associated with the government of the Indian empire. James Mill, like his equally famous and equally liberal son, spent most of his working life at India House – first as Examiner and later as Head Examiner of Correspondence. Thomas Macaulay spent part of his career as Law Member of the Calcutta Council. Two of the Governors-General – Bentinck and Auckland – were men of liberal and even radical political persuasion and affiliation. All liberals believed in representative government; but they likewise all accepted that this could not yet be applied to India. Indian society they regarded as enervated by tyrannous custom and benighted by false religion; it was, in a word, 'uncivilised', and they saw 'civilisation' as the prerequisite of the representative system. They differed concerning the best means of regeneration. Whigs like Bentinck and Macaulay believed in the efficacy of English education and the stimulation of economic *laissez-faire*, while James Mill and the Utilitarians put more emphasis on strong paternalistic rule; but all agreed that India was not yet civilised, and that Indian government was therefore still necessarily despotic. Burke's powerful pleading had reinforced the liberal and humanitarian conviction that the characteristic feature of such despotism must be benevolent rule. This conviction inspired important reforms in the Indian territories under British rule in the 1820s and 1830s; but it did not fundamentally influence relations with the most important of the subsidiary native states. Translated into action that conviction must have meant either assumption of the government of those states, or withdrawal of all moral and military support from their princes, since experience had conclusively demonstrated that the operation of the existing treaties could not be made to accord with liberal principles; yet both Hyderabad and Oudh survived this powerful sense of moral obligation. The history of the Company's relations with Oudh affords an instructive insight into the breakdown of the liberal experiment in India. It reveals that the force of conservative opinion had some part in the process; but it shows that the financial difficulties of the Company were more important. These difficulties, caused partly by the loss of the China trade and partly by expensive and engrossing wars, made the Calcutta authorities not only reluctant to assume a government already saddled with debt, but even disposed to maintain the princes who were so ready to afford handsome relief from their private resources. There were no further loans from the Kings of Oudh after 1842; but wars in Sind, the Punjab and Burma followed that in Afghanistan and distracted viceregal attention for another decade. Only with the emancipation of Lord Dalhousie from such preoccupations in 1854 was liberalism, in alliance with the new and powerful force of Victorian Evangelicalism, able to work the final overthrow of the native dynasty in Lucknow.

IV

In 1847 an oriental prince became King of Oudh and a Scottish nobleman was appointed Governor-General of British India. Each quitted his office in 1856, when the King went into exile and the nobleman returned home to die. Neither had seemed destined for a station which would bring him into contact with the other. Wajid Ali Shah was his father's second son, and in the ordinary course of events would have lived the inconsequential life of a wealthy Lucknow aristocrat. The Earl, later Marquis, of Dalhousie was a younger son who might easily have ended his short career, after his brief term of office at the Board of Trade, in the political wilderness with the Peelite Tories. These two men, coinciding in India after beginning their careers so far asunder, call to mind two planets, moving in widely separated orbits yet finally coming into close conjunction within some constellation; and it would require a belief in historical determinism no less dogmatic than that held by an astrologer in the influence of the stars to claim that without this particular configuration of time, place and personalities things would have been much the same.

If he had not been such an unsuccessful king, Wajid Ali Shah might have been remembered as a successful man of letters. Literature and music were the ruling passions of his life, and his talent as a writer was real. Under the *nom de plume* of Akhtar he published some forty works, including six collections of *ghazals,* three volumes of *marasi* and many *masnavis* and *qasidas,* besides a treatise on music called *saut-e-mubarik* ('Joyous Sounds'). The last work is still valued by scholars, though Wajid Ali's personal taste in music has been condemned as debased and he is reproached by some for having encouraged music of a trivial nature and ignored the purer and more serious art. Much of his poetry has the flavour of sexual fantasy or insipid melancholia. These were the after-effects of precocious concupiscence. A childhood and youth in the moral squalor of the royal female apartments had turned him into a bloated, androgynous sybarite, yearning for the gratification which ever eluded his jaded senses:

> This aching defies your physician's art;
> Mine is the sickness of a broken heart.

Some of his verse is in the style of the Islamic mystics, whose worship of human beauty as a reflection of divine beauty demanded the use of language and imagery associated with profane love in invocations to the Deity:

> Love has made me a slave; Oh let me stay
> To live in adoration, night and day.
> Body and soul in abject attendance,
> But utter thy will and I must obey.
> Vain to test the strength of my devotion:
> Rather the sharpness of thy sword assay.
> Thus to die were to attain to glory;
> My blood will stain deep – throw henna away.
> Look not angry on Akhtar, O Lord God!
> For my heart is thine and all else alway.

There is something of philological interest in much of his early work, for Wajid Ali was intrigued by the rural dialects of Oudh and his vocabulary is often unexpectedly Hindi in idiom and bucolic in flavour.

His intelligence, aesthetic sensibility and sociability made him popular in sophisticated Lucknow and when, on his father's disowning of his elder brother, he became heir apparent, high society gravitated gratefully towards him as the natural leader of the reaction against the puritan régime of Amjad Ali Shah. He was only twenty-seven when he succeeded to the throne, and at first he devoted himself enthusiastically to the duties of kingship. The glamour of his new position appealed to him and it had that element of novelty which alone has value for those to whom price is nothing. He especially enjoyed the music and glitter of parades, and for a short time found satisfaction in the role of military supremo. Vernacular histories relate how early every morning he would don his general's uniform, mount a thoroughbred horse and ride out to drill his troops. Regiments were reorganised and given Persian titles. He worked diligently at his desk, and in order to keep himself informed of the grievances of his subjects adopted the system whereby during his evening drives two Turkish sepoys rode ahead with a silver casket. All complainants were invited to place their petitions in this casket, whose contents the King made it a personal duty to examine.

But all this lasted only two or three months. Wajid Ali was timid, and an attempt to assassinate his prime minister, Amin-ud-daula, in April 1847 made him scared to stir beyond the precincts of his palace. Moreover, the attraction of his new position lay in its novelty, and when this faded there was no incentive in the form of shame or fear of failure to replace it, for the King was insulated by flatterers and a fond mother from all the consequences of his own shortcomings. He lapsed again into *ennui,* and sought distraction in more compatible pastimes, such as philandering, music, literature and his own imagined illnesses. State affairs were abandoned to the new minister, Ali Naqi Khan, while the King passed his days secluded with minstrels, poets and paramours, on whom he bestowed lavish presents and sinecure appointments. In 1848 work was begun on the Qaisarbagh, a vast and meretricious agglomeration of apartments, courtyards and parterres which, after its completion in 1850, became the temple of those cults of wit, gaiety and licentiousness that had made Lucknow proverbial throughout India. Every August a great *fête champêtre* was held here, to which the ordinary public was admitted. For these occasions the King devised a dramatic and musical entertainment based on the traditional Hindu erotic ballet (*rahas*) of Krishna and the shepherdesses, in which he himself acted the part of the love-lorn hero. The shepherdesses (*gopis*) were played by court beauties and, we are told, under the intoxicating influence of the dancing and music audience and performers alike would shed all their inhibitions. 'During these festivals', wrote the Lucknow historian Sharar, 'the ordinary folk participating were completely unrestricted, save for the stipulation that they must come decked out in bright clothes. The result was that even doddering grandfathers became gay young sparks, and filled the cup of their senility with the wine of the King's youthful merriment.' [1]

While the King was thus seeking distraction in a life of pleasure and literary pottering, official business began to slide into a morass of corruption and confusion. The minister, Ali Naqi Khan, was rumoured to be a *roué* whom the King had met in a brothel. His urbanity made him agreeable on a social level, but apart from his hold over the King's affections he was without a qualification for his office. All the old symptoms of maladministration began to reappear, and in November 1847 the Governor-General, Lord Hardinge, took advantage of his presence in the upper provinces to visit Lucknow and make his displeasure known personally to the King. A solemn caveat of the usual type was delivered to Wajid Ali, in which he was reminded of his treaty obligations, warned that his case would be reviewed again after two years, and offered the assistance of European experts. [2]

The offer came too late to find acceptance. Ali Naqi was not a reforming minister. His overriding concern was to devise not a system that would satisfy Calcutta, but one that would fill his own pocket. In response to the demands of the Governor-General and Resident, the *amani* system of revenue collection was introduced experimentally in parts of the kingdom; but it was vitiated by a spirit of venality. Collectors were permitted to remit to the treasury sums diminished by false claims for expenses, on the understanding that portions of the gain went as *douceurs* to the minister, his wife and other relatives. This scheme of malversation was even connived at by the King, who shared in the illicit profits and thus as a private individual cheated himself in his official capacity. [3]

Lord Hardinge was succeeded at the beginning of 1848 by James Andrew Ramsay, Earl of Dalhousie. He was only thirty-five, but had the self-assurance of a veteran. Dalhousie and kingship were as compatible as Wajid Ali and kingship were incongruous. This Governor-General was born to rule, and rule he did, in a way that India had not known since the days of the great Mughal Akbar. He was a *roi soleil*; a source of intellectual brilliance and motivating energy, and intensely jealous of any minor luminaries. He was not unamenable to counsel from men older and more experienced than himself; but he insisted that such counsel be subsumed in the expression of his own will. There must be no intrusion of strong personalities between himself and the governed. 'It does not do', he wrote, 'for [the Governor-General] even to *appear* to play second fiddle.'

A crushing weight of responsibility and solitude is the price of an autocracy such as this, and Dalhousie was sustained under the load by powerful Presbyterian convictions. A measure once decided on, he would pursue it with undeviating determination, secure in his knowledge of a higher mandate and almost relishing the idea of martyrdom for its sake. His dogma was duty and he was severe with himself in its cause. He was never in good health, yet as Governor-General he worked a day of crippling length, personally drafting most of his public dispatches and writing his minutes with his own hand. He spent long periods of his term of office dragging himself about on exhausting tours, which covered the length and breadth of the now vast British Indian empire – from the Punjab to Pegu; from Simla to Mysore. After the devastating experience of the death of his wife, in 1853, he carried self-discipline to the point of self-mortification, and finally went home in 1856 incurably ravaged by disease and the effects of overwork. He died in 1860, at the early age of forty-eight.

Despite the distractions of two wars – one in the Punjab and the other in Burma – his achievement was remarkable. He found British India encumbered by the accumulated effects of a generation of drifting and haphazard rule. Administration was confused; the native army was dangerously inefficient; public works, traditionally regarded in India as the token of good government, had been lamentably neglected; and relations with the protected native states were ill defined and embarrassing. During his nine years as Governor-General, Dalhousie grappled with all these problems. His administrative reforms included the foundation of a legislative council in Calcutta, of a separate provincial government in Bengal and of the basis of the future Indian Civil Service. He laboured to expel from the army such sacred cows as seniority promotion, clothing off-reckonings and the Military Board. His introduction of the railway into India was historic. He devised a policy which would both reduce the number of protected native states and make those that remained strictly accountable for any failure to observe treaty obligations. The first object was achieved by invoking the 'doctrine of lapse', by the operation of which, in accordance with Hindu law, dependant Hindu principalities escheated to the paramount power in the absence of natural heirs. The second involved a strict observance of rights as defined by treaty and international law. This could lead to annexation – as it did in the case of the Punjab, where the Sikh rulers were technically guilty of rebellion; but it could also result in the continuation of British protection of even a defaulting native prince – as in the case of Hyderabad, where the Nizam's debts were liquidated by the cession of territories. The treaty was Dalhousie's only inspiration and mandate in this business. 'If the policy declared', he told the President of the Board of Control, 'had been to put the treaty in the fire and walk over [the Nizam] – a policy which has abundance of advocates both in this country and at home – I am afraid I must have asked you to find some other hand to guide it.' [4]

It is important to stress this concept of legality, because it dominated Dalhousie's attitude towards the protected native states and precluded his acceptance of the notion of a British moral responsibility to redeem them from oppression. It is true that Dalhousie said some rude things about the native princes. His own self-discipline and his lofty conception of public office as a sacred trust made him hard on the malefactions of inept and effete rulers. It is also true that he believed in the superiority of Western methods of administration and in the benefits of Western trusteeship. But he expressly rejected the idea of an overriding moral duty to diffuse those methods and those benefits in defiance of the rights of princes and of popular will. 'As for the moral obligation', he wrote to Colonel Low in 1849, 'which some assert that we are under, by reason of our paramountcy, to rescue the subjects of native powers from what we call oppression, whether they ask for rescue or not, I regard it as nothing else than an ambitious and hypocritical humbug.' [5]

The problem of Oudh was a rankling one. The policy of drift hitherto pursed with regard to that state was an irritant to Dalhousie's methodical mind, and public opinion was mounting in favour of a decisive line of conduct. In an editorial of 1850, the *Delhi Gazette* confronted the government with a stark alternative: 'What we contend for is, that our countrymen should either govern Oudh or abandon its rulers to their fate. As it is, we are powerless for good and unwilling accomplices in evil. We do infinite and perpetual wrong, because some of our nation in times past made treaties which it is immoral to observe.' [6]

There was little doubt as to which of these possibilities better suited Dalhousie's temperament and predilections. The Lucknow court represented everything that he most abhorred – disorder, self-indulgence, sensuality, stagnation. Right from the time of his arrival in India he had itched to take Wajid Ali Shah ('the wretch at Lucknow') by the scruff of the neck and remove him and his ministers from the positions of power they had abused. After the death of his wife his antipathy deepened. The laughter and revelry of Lucknow seemed like a living affront to his own inner anguish; a mockery of his own self-mortification in the cause of duty. He hated the court and all it stood for, and emotional compulsion added urgency to his desire to 'swallow' it before he left India.

He did not want to annex Oudh. What he planned was a reversion to the system of decisive interference, to be implemented this time by British officers. The King he proposed to reduce to the status of a titular sovereign with a pension. [7] The great stumbling block was the treaty of 1801 (he assumed that of 1837 to be invalid), since this made no provision for the introduction of Company officials to carry out reforms. What he needed, therefore, was a justification for setting this aside and replacing it with another treaty, which would provide legal authority for British assumption of the administration. Had the King been a rebel, the operation could have been accomplished in one stage, and Dalhousie frankly lamented that Wajid Ali would not give him legal justification for outright confiscation. 'The King won't offend or quarrel with us', he grumbled in 1855, 'and will take any amount of kicking without being rebellious.' [8] Given the King's refusal to be a rebel, and Dalhousie's concern to act legally, a two-stage operation became necessary.

The first stage – cancelling the 1801 treaty – was straightforward, for there was plenty of evidence on record concerning the maladministration of Oudh, and that treaty had stipulated good government. The second stage – negotiating a new treaty – might have presented more difficulty; but as it happened Dalhousie was spared the embarrassments that his own scruples might have caused him. If he was concerned not to transgress the canons of international law, others were more concerned with notions of moral duty, and they accepted his reason for cancelling the treaty as a vindication for outright confiscation. This was not because his evidence was overwhelmingly persuasive. It was rather because it was produced at the optimum moment, at a time when prevailing opinion was that good government meant British government and that the paramount duty of the British in India was the moral one of diffusing the benefits and civilising influences of their own way of life.

Dalhousie's indictment of the native government was far from conclusive. The greater part of his evidence was supplied by Major-General Sleeman, who was Resident at Lucknow from 1849 until 1854; and Sleeman was a man whose judgement was clouded by psychological disorder.

At the time of his appointment to Lucknow William Sleeman had spent forty of his sixty-one years in India. Although he was a Bengal army officer, his military duties had ceased after the Nepal War and it was in a civil capacity that he had made his name, notably as the supressor of 'thuggee' (*thdgi*), the cult involving ritual strangulation. He had acquired an unrivalled knowledge of the rural life and dialects of central and northern India and with it a great affection for the Indian agricultural classes. He especially admired the Indian village communities, in which he found all the best civic virtues. But he had no sympathy for native government at the executive and legislative levels. Indian princes he detested as parasites battening on the sturdy rural classes that he loved so well. 'I could not help thinking', he wrote of the native government of Gwalior, 'that it would be an immense blessing upon a large portion of our species if an earthquake were to swallow up this court.' [9] Of the superiority of British government at the executive and legislative levels he had no doubt. 'We give to India', he wrote, 'what India never had before our rule and could never have without it – the assurance that there will always be at the head of the government a sensible ruler trained up to office in the best school in the world; and that the security of the rights and the enforcement of the duties presented and defined by law will not depend upon the will or caprice of individuals in power.' [10] The natives under British rule, he asserted, were convinced 'that they never had a government so good as ours and that they could never hope for another so good, were ours removed'. [11]

Sleeman detested the court of Lucknow even more than Dalhousie did. 'Such a scene of intrigue, corruption, depravity and neglect of duty and abuse of authority I have never before been placed in and I hope never again to undergo.' [12] His bitterness was the result partly of puritan revulsion against profligacy and frivolity, and partly of frustration, caused by his own political impotence. Sleeman was a man of action and open air, never happier than when stomping around the Indian countryside in his shirt sleeves, supervising the construction of a bridge here, a reservoir there, and chatting with the village landholders in their own patois about the state of the crop or the fluctuations in the market. In Lucknow he felt like a giant in fetters. He longed to set to work and turn the country into a garden; but he was compelled to stand by instead and observe its spoliation, offering advice that was never heeded. 'Had I come here when the treasury was full', he lamented, 'and Nasir-ud-din Haider was anxious to spend his money in the manner best calculated to do good and please our Government, I might have covered Oudh with useful public works; and much do I regret that I came here to throw away the best years of my life among such a set of knaves and fools as I have had to deal with.' [13]

But the style of Sleeman's dispatches and his quirks of

behaviour suggest something in addition to puritan bias and personal frustration. He was not without a sense of justice, and it is unlikely that he would have allowed himself to be governed by prejudice. All the signs are, in fact, that he was the victim of not prejudice but delusion, which made it impossible for him to view the court with anything but the deepest aversion. He was obsessed with the notion that the royal palace was a nest of personal enemies, perpetually conspiring to thwart, remove or even assassinate him.

It is only in the terms of such an obsession that his attitude towards his colleagues and subordinates can be understood. He regarded any association by them with courtiers as a form of treachery. His Assistant, Captain Robert Bird, was on familiar terms with men in the royal circle, and Sleeman deduced from this that he was plotting to get rid of him. Early in 1849 he tried to have Bird transferred to another post, at Ludhiana; and when this stratagem failed he became overtly hostile and began to exercise an inquisitorial interference in the Assistant's private life. Bird was fond of the turf, and ran horses at the Lucknow races. Sleeman insisted that this must stop, for it brought Bird into contact with the minister and court eunuchs, the only natives who patronised the sport. In October 1849 he wrote to the King and requested that the races be discontinued, since they were 'prejudicial to the character of young men by bringing them into intimate companionship with disreputable people, and to their circumstances by inducing them to gamble and incur expenses beyond their means'. The King, understandably, ignored this impertinent letter; so Sleeman, in March and May 1851, brought the case before the Governor-General, complaining of Bird's racing activities and his want of proper deference towards himself. He hinted strongly that Bird was intent on using his high connections to undermine the Resident's authority. 'I have always considered Captain Bird, since he returned from Simla', he wrote, 'as suffering from a notion which has ruined many a young man of average ability – that the influence of relations, connections and family and personal friends in high places would relieve him from the necessity of attending at all to the views and wishes of his immediate official superiors.'

Dalhousie was far too upright to allow such considerations to influence him, and he signified his support of the Resident. Barred from racing at Lucknow, Bird transferred his operations to Kanpur, where he continued to associate with Lucknow hidalgos and to run horses under the aptly chosen name of Mr Hope. This incensed Sleeman, who stooped to the dangerous device of accusing the Assistant of corruption. He complained that Bird had used his official powers to halt and get transferred to Kanpur legal proceedings in which a native horse dealer was defendant. His implication was that Bird and the defendant were in collusion. In a revealing sentence he again betrayed his fear that Bird was using his connections to sabotage his position: 'I have ... too much reason to apprehend that [Captain Bird] has long been diligently and, unhappily for the people of Oudh, successfully employed in persuading the minister that he has more influential relatives and friends at the seat of government than the Resident has.'

The irascible and vindictive tenor of Sleeman's dispatches caused some perturbation in Calcutta. One member of Council, Currie, was startled by 'the apparent animus which pervad[ed] Colonel Sleeman's report'. Dalhousie heard Bird's explanations and came to the conclusion that while Bird's behaviour had been ill-advised, Sleeman's accusations were quite unwarranted. More for the sake of keeping the peace than for the purpose of stigmatising Bird he decided to remove the latter to the post of Assistant to the Superintendent at Ajmir, with no loss of salary. [14]

Another *bête noire* in Sleeman's deluded mind was Dr Bell, the Residency Surgeon. Bell, like Bird, kept company with people about the court of whom Sleeman disapproved – especially with Mr Brandon, an Englishman whom the Resident described as 'an inveterate and unscrupulous intriguer'. Brandon was, it is true, an unsavoury character. He had first come to Lucknow as an associate of the notorious barber, Derusett, and had been employed as a horticulturist by Nasir-ud-din. He shared in Derusett's fall from favour in 1837 and was expelled from Lucknow; but he returned ten years later under the patronage of one of the court minstrels, as a shopkeeper and purveyor of amusements. He began to associate with the minister's secretary, Wasi Ali Khan, whom Sleeman detested and whom he had tried, unsuccessfully, to get removed. 'It was the game of Wasi Ali and his party', he complained in characteristic fashion, 'to persuade His Majesty that all my advice and suggestions might be disregarded . . .; that our Government had never carried out its threats, though it had been threatening for half a century.' At the instigation of Brandon and Wasi Ali 'great efforts were made, by every possible sacrifice of truth and money, to get me out of the way'. It was apparent even to the King that the activities of these people had assumed an exaggerated importance in Sleeman's mind.

His Majesty [wrote Sleeman] expressed some surprise that I should consider a person so contemptible [as Brandon] as capable of influencing anyone, since he looked upon him as a buffoon upon whom his servants were in the habit of playing-off low practical jokes. Mr Brandon had often told me that he was obliged to submit to such humiliations in order to sell his goods and exhibit his amusements. I explained to His Majesty that this person's influence consisted in the ascendency he had obtained over Dr. Bell.

The Resident was convinced that there existed an 'organized system of hostility' in which Bell's part was to boast of 'the influence which he had at the court of Oudh and about the Governor-General'. So firm a hold had this persecution complex taken on his mind that he considered resigning in December 1851; but on second thoughts he deemed this 'pusillanimous and dishonourable' and requested instead that Bell be forbidden to attend Brandon professionally, and that the conduct of the Residency post office, traditionally a function of the Surgeon, be removed to other hands, since it brought Bell into contact with Brandon, who held the contract for the mail carriages and cattle between Lucknow and Kanpur. Bell solemnly denied that he had ever associated with Brandon for any but professional reasons, and the Governor-General explained that he could not act on the basis of unsubstantiated imputations. As Sleeman had no proof to offer, no action was taken against Bell; but Brandon and his wife and family were unceremoniously ejected from Lucknow on orders from the Resident.[15] Sleeman's behaviour in this affair caused the erstwhile Resident, Colonel Low, now Military Member of the Council, to observe: 'He writes rather as the head of a party or clique than with the firmness, forbearance and dignity which becomes His Lordship's representative at a foreign court; and . . . he has shown a proneness not only to listen to, but to believe, the wretched tittle-tattle of the place.'[16]

That this proneness was pathological became apparent late in 1853. In October that year there was a dramatic incident at the Residency, caused by a sepoy who dozed off while on guard duty. His relaxed arm set off his musket, and in order to save himself from the charge of sleeping at his post he invented a story about intruders, at whom he had fired. The truth of the matter was obvious, for no sign of intruders was found, the sepoy's hand and wrist had been injured by the musket shot, and the ball itself was found lodged in the ceiling. Sleeman himself acknowledged, in a letter to Dalhousie, that the sepoy's story was demonstrably false;[17] yet in a letter to Low written shortly after he wrote: 'that the minister and Wasi Ali got up the attempt at the Residency either to make away with me or to alarm me into going away, I am persuaded'.[18] This sort of illogicality is an acknowledged symptom of paranoid delusion.

Secure in his conviction that the present administration was incorrigibly evil, Sleeman began to urge on Dalhousie a plan which would make himself effective ruler of Oudh. He wanted a council of regency set up, composed of the first members of the Lucknow aristocracy but headed by the Resident. The King was to retain only the title of sovereign and control of his houschold.[19]

The Resident [he warned] is helpless for purposes of good. His advice is disregarded, or his efforts to secure redress for wrongs or remedies for widespread evils are thwarted, or the sovereign's orders founded upon them are perverted for their own vile and selfish purposes, by those who have his ear and confidence, and persuade the minister that he may continue to disregard the advice and remonstrances of the Resident, since he has done so with impunity for so long.[20]

He met Dalhousie at Fatehgarh at the end of 1851 and pressed him to adopt the plan; but the Governor-General's attention was soon after diverted by the outbreak of the Burmese War, and the problem of Oudh was shelved. Nothing daunted, Sleeman submitted his scheme again in April 1852. It was now embedded in his report of a tour of inspection of the kingdom, made at Dalhousie's request during the winter of 1849-50. In his eagerness to sell his idea, Sleeman turned this report, which began as a simple journal embodying his observations of rural life, into a vast tendentious tract – discursive, disorganised, and obsessively repetitive. Paragraph after paragraph, page after page, the stories of oppression and corruption, extravagance and bankruptcy, depravity and frivolity are reiterated *ad nauseam*. Samuel Lucas, author of the tract *Dacoitee in Excelsis,* described Sleeman's methods very aptly when he wrote: 'The managers of this impeachment deal with their allegations as the managers of a theatre, of which the resources are scanty, deal with their little army of supernumeraries. The same individual personages are passed over the stage again and again, and the result is to swell to an imaginary total and to heighten to the general eye the effect of the performance.' A promiscuous piling-up of observation, gossip, history, anecdote and scandal was made to masquerade as evidence for the prosecution of the dynasty. Nowhere is there an attempt to sift fact from fiction, for Sleeman was predisposed to accept the truth of any piece of information that denigrated the court and native administration. He retails in detail, for example, the story of the murder of the contractor of Bahraich by the *hakim* Mehdi Ali Khan, without offering any doubts concerning its authenticity. Mrs Parks, on the other hand, in her book *Wanderings of a Pilgrim in Search of the Picturesque,* treats the same story as unfounded bazaar gossip. If the facts admitted more than one interpretation, Sleeman mentioned only the least favourable. In June 1849 he reported that 'it [was] not at all uncommon for the landholders to have the land ploughed and the seed drilled in at night, by stealth, when beleaguered by the King's troops'; [21] and the same piece of information was reproduced in the report: 'The land is ploughed, and the seed sown, often by stealth at night, in the immediate vicinity of a sanguinary contest between government officers and the landholders.' [22] It is instructive to note that another witness offered an entirely different explanation for this nocturnal activity. 'It is the custom in Oudh', wrote William Russell 'to plough by torchlight, as the earth is soft and yields to the plough when moistened by the dew.' Sleeman's chief target was of course the King, whom he tried to make out to be insane – a form of imputation that is common among paranoid personalities.

The general picture of Oudh that is contained in Sleeman's report is a reflection of his own predilections and delusions. It is one of a sterling Hindu peasantry oppressed and ruined by a weak, profligate and maleficent central Muslim administration. The attempt to extend the *amani* system of revenue collection the Resident represents as a total failure, and he recounts in gory detail the cruelties of the great revenue farmers. He describes the 'wild license' of the taluqdars, and their usurpation of the rights of the village communities. There was no system of justice; public works were totally lacking; rich land was lying waste through want of confidence in the government; and rural Oudh was a picture of crime and anarchy.

> There is no indication of the beneficial interference of the government for the protection of life, property or character, and for the encouragement of industry and the display of its fruits ... It is painful to me to walk out of my tent of an evening, for I have every day large crowds seeking redress for grievous wrongs for which I can see no hope of redress ... I feel like one moving among a people afflicted with incurable diseases, who crowd around him in hope, and are sent away in despair. [23]

Such was the chief accuser, and such his arraignment, of the native administration of Oudh. Enough has been said to show that his arraignment was not the product of a calm, balanced and detached mind. As it happened, Sleeman was not the man who put the impeachment into its final shape. By the end of 1854, when the Burmese War had ended and Dalhousie was at last free to devote himself to the question of Oudh, bad health had forced Sleeman to leave Lucknow on furlough. The task of drawing up the case which Dalhousie intended to present to the London authorities fell to Colonel James Outram, who acted as Resident pending Sleeman's return. He was instructed to institute an inquiry into the condition of the country and ascertain whether its affairs still continued in the state described by Sleeman. What in fact he did was something quite different. He merely rummaged in the vast ragbag of his predecessor's reports and dispatches and pieced together, in the space of a few months, a report based almost entirely on the material he found there. Outram, with characteristic ingenuousness, admitted this. 'In the absence of any personal experience in [this] country, I am of course entirely dependent for my information on what I find in the Residency records and can ascertain through the channels which supplied my predecessor.' What he provided, therefore, was in essence a picture of Oudh as Sleeman had seen it. Not surprisingly, that picture was very dark.

Dalhousie called the report 'a tremendous bill of indictment'. In fact, as an indictment it was very weak. As a vindication for British annexation, it was worse than useless.

The report was in seven parts. Part One, called 'The Sovereign and his Minister', purported to show that the King was addicted to frivolous amusements and completely dominated by eunuchs, fiddlers and songsters. The evidence adduced consisted mostly of extracts from Sleeman's reports.

Part Two, called 'Revenue and Finance', consisted of a description of the Oudh revenue system and its abuses. It was based on the reports of Sleeman and of four British military officers stationed in Oudh, of whom only three had been in the province for any length of time and all of whom relied heavily on hearsay and rumour. Such phrases as 'I am credibly informed that', 'it is reported that', 'I have every reason to believe that', 'I hear that', 'I am told that', 'I have heard of', preface most of their statements. Outram told a story of vast public arrears and pending bankruptcy, but admitted that he had had no access to official records. He relied on Sleeman's figures, together with an estimate of exchequer receipts 'obtained by [the Assistant-Resident] ... from a person who had access to the durbar accounts and on which he [thought] reliance [might] be placed'. Outram admitted that he was puzzled by the non-occurrence of the financial crisis so confidently predicted by Sleeman, but he avoided the inference that Sleeman's figures were wrong.

Part Three, called 'Judicial Courts and Police', consisted almost entirely of extracts from the reports of previous Residents, and retailed the same accounts of corruption and venality.

Part Four, 'The Army of Oudh', was based entirely on Sleeman and presented Sleeman's view of the army as oversized, ill equipped and utterly inefficient.

Part Five, 'Roads and Public Works', complained that these were virtually non-existent, whereas vast sums had been squandered on palaces and tombs in Lucknow.

Part Six, entitled 'Statistics of Crime and Outrage', was really the gravamen of the impeachment. With the aid of the reports of the official native newswriters, as transcribed in Sleeman's Residency diaries, Outram demonstrated that during the period 1848-54 the number of people murdered and assaulted in Oudh averaged 1,573 a year, of whom 628 were killed. He claimed to give significance to the statistics by quoting in comparison those of the British Province of the Punjab, whose population was double that of Oudh. Here the crimes of violence were only 886 for the year 1855. But the comparison was false. Even assuming that the casualty figures in Oudh were as high as this – or higher, as Sleeman had insisted – it was unwarrantable to attribute them to what in the British provinces would be classified as crime. If, as Outram admitted, 'a large portion of the casulaties in Oudh [were] to be attributed to faction fights and collisions between the officers employed in the collection of revenue and the landholders who pay it', they related to what would be classified as civil disobedience in the Punjab. There is, in fact, little to support the claim that criminal activity in Oudh was more widespread than elsewhere. Among the reports in the

Residency archives which Outram did not use were those of T. R. Davidson, the Bengal civil servant who officiated as Resident before Sleeman's arrival. In 1846 Davidson had written to the government:

> On comparing the past with the present I cannot say that robberies, dacoities and plunderings have sensibly decreased; still, from having been employed in our own provinces as a magistrate, superintendent of police, and criminal judge, the mass of mischief here has not perhaps struck me to be so enormous as it has officers whose experience of crime has been confined to Oudh alone. Indeed, if due consideration is given to the fact that throughout the country there is nothing which deserves the name of police and that the perpetration of offences is rarely if ever punished, the wonder is not that crime prevails, but that it does not prevail to a greater extent. [24]

The final section, called 'Oppression and Cruelties', was in one sense the most significant part of the report, for implicit in this, the only part based on independent inquiry, was a clear refutation of the very policy the report was made to vindicate. The section was in essence an account of the oppression and exactions of the Oudh revenue farmers; but in three out of five reports from frontier magistrates adduced as evidence it was expressly denied that there had been any appreciable emigration of Oudh subjects into British territories. The clear implication of this, the only unimpeachable evidence in the whole report, was that all the British had done was convince themselves that the Oudh administration was bad. The essential thing that they had failed to do, was convince the population of Oudh that British administration was better. [25]

Hence the evidence collected by Outram, even if it were reliable, amounted only to an indictment of the native system of administration. It did not include a shred of vindication of the British system. Even Sleeman was lucid enough to appreciate this, and he never equated denigration of the one with vindication of the other. His plan for Oudh had involved the placing of native institutions under British executive supervision. He was against wholesale confiscation or annexation, since his own inquiries had made it clear that no one in Oudh wanted the British system of government – mainly because the

British courts of justice had such a bad reputation. Dalhousie, though he seems to have persuaded himself that in this instance there was a native population anxious to be rescued, remained concerned to act legally and intended to use the report only as justification for cancelling the 1801 treaty and withdrawing British protection. 'My duty', he wrote, 'was to propose the best course which was open for our adoption in accordance with international law, and which would be least assailable by critics and opponents.'[26] The plan he submitted to London for approval was therefore that of informing the King that the treaty was dissolved. In its place, the King was to be offered a new agreement, by which he was to be reduced to the status of a mediatised prince, with a fixed stipend from the Oudh revenues, but no civil or military power, the whole of which was to be assigned to the East India Company. It was hoped and expected that the threat of withdrawing the protective force would induce the King to agree to the new arrangement, which would thus be realised in a strictly legal fashion.[27]

But official reaction to the report went beyond what Dalhousie and Sleeman had anticipated or intended. This was the high noon of liberalism, and its imperialist message – that Western trusteeship and Western methods of administration were conducive to the greatest happiness of the greatest number of any black population – had so intoxicated the Victorian mind that even the East India Company's inveterate critics assumed that the people of Oudh must prefer British rule. Seizure of the kingdom was therefore widely preached as a moral duty, the performance of which would earn the British nation the eternal gratitude of the native population. 'Everyday that the annexation of this misgoverned country is delayed', wrote the Lucknow correspondent of *The Englishman*, 'another day of suffering is added to the lot of hundreds, nay thousands, of one of the finest races of Hindustan'.[28] In England press commentators drew the same inference from the same assumptions. In the spring of 1855 a book called *The Private Life of an Eastern King* appeared, whose purported author was one of the Europeans who had been attached to the household of Nasir-ud-din. It is in essence an account of the scandals and excesses of the Lucknow court in the 1830s, interlarded with descriptions of Muslim life and festivals. The book is almost certainly spurious. There are inconsistencies in the text,[29] the style has too much of the glib and stilted flavour peculiar to Victorian journalism to ring true, and there are extensive borrowings from other sources. [30] It is obviously a journalistic concatenation by the so-called editor, William Knighton. Even superficial inquiry would have revealed that *The Private Life of an Eastern King* was not what it claimed to be; yet its reliability was never questioned, because it afforded an irresistible opportunity for the strident assertion of moral duty. 'Are we', demanded the *Edinburgh Review*, 'to be deterred from doing our duty to those millions by a morbid fear that we shall be charged with cloaking ambition and greed under a pretence of humanity?' [31]

Given this prevailing consensus of public opinion the Outram report could have only one effect. It told people what they were expecting and wanting to hear, so they overlooked its weaknesses and welcomed it as a complete vindication of what they felt to be necessary. After studying it, two members of the Calcutta Council, Dorin and Grant, insisted that the outright annexation of Oudh was a moral duty.[32] Dalhousie did not solicit powers to take the country by force. 'It was not for me to suggest it', he wrote, 'since such a course would not be warranted by international law.'[33] Vernon Smith, the new President of the Board of Control, was apprehensive about the political and public opposition which even legal annexation might arouse. 'The public feeling', he wrote in August 1855, 'in which, I own, I agree, is much against any addition of territory to our Indian dominions.' But as the tone of the press hardened, so the Cabinet and the Court of Directors grew bolder; and at the end of November the Court, with the sanction of the Cabinet, authorised Dalhousie to take Oudh by force if the King refused to surrender the administration. 'In that event . . . we are fully prepared to take the responsibility of authorising and enjoining the only other course by which our duties to the people of Oudh can be fulfilled – that of assuming authoritatively the powers necessary for the permanent establishment of good government throughout the country.'[34]

Dalhousie received this dispatch on 2 January 1856; and he was not sorry to have it, even though it authorised a course that was unequivocally illegal. Time was short, for he was due to leave India on 1 March, and since he was now emotionally committed to settling the Oudh business before he did so, he decided at once to make the most of the Court's permission and cut all the legal corners. Hastily, a new plan was devised. The King was to be offered a new treaty, and with it an ultimatum. The treaty assigned the whole of the Oudh administration to the Company and a liberal pension of one and a half million rupees (£150,000), plus his titles and control of his household, to the King. The ultimatum specified that if the treaty was not signed within three days, the kingdom would be taken by force and the King deprived of all rights and privileges. Outram, who had come to Calcutta to await the reply from London, left again for Lucknow on 24 January, armed with these new instructions. At the same time a strong brigade of troops was ordered, by the recently completed electric telegraph, to rendez-vous at Kanpur and march thence on Lucknow.

Outram, travelling post-haste, arrived back in Lucknow on 30 January. He presented the draft treaty and the ultimatum to the minister, who was stunned. On the 31st Brigadier Wheeler crossed the Ganges from Kanpur and began his advance to the capital, in heavy winter rain.

The queen mother requested an interview with the Resident, which was granted. In visible distress, she implored Outram to intercede with the Governor-General and avert this degradation of her son. She begged for a further delay, that the King might implement the reforms required and show the world that he was at last in earnest. Moved, but powerless to depart from his instructions, Outram advised her to use her influence with her son to induce him to sign the treaty and thus secure a liberal pension.

He did not see the King until Monday, 4 February, when Wheeler's advance guard was only eight miles from Lucknow. Foreseeably enough, Wajid Ali's histrionic and poetic sensibilities responded far more readily to the pathos of fallen majesty than they had ever done to the responsibilities of effective sovereignty. Like Shakespeare's Richard II, he turned his deposition into an exhibition not of remorse or resistance, but of self-pity and self-abasement. To emphasise his helplessness, he had the guns before his palace dismounted and his guard of honour disarmed. During the interview with Outram he shed floods of tears and made an impassioned speech, descanting on his own subservience and protesting his inability to sign a treaty, since this would have no meaning from one so humble as himself. With a theatrical gesture, he took off his turban, the symbol of his sovereignty and dignity, and placed it in the hands of Outram, who, like Bolingbroke, was standing by stolid, embarrassed, but obdurate. This performance was only a dress-rehearsal for those he was planning for Calcutta and London. He knew that the Resident had no discretionary power in the affair, and his hopes of reprieve were centred on a personal appeal to the Governor-General and even to Queen Victoria herself. According to Outram, he was fortified in these hopes by the encouragement of Mr Brandon, who, since his expulsion from Lucknow, had resided at Kanpur and edited a newspaper called *The Central Star*. To make his intentions clear, Wajid Ali issued a proclamation to all his subjects, in which he commanded them to pay obedience to the officers of the British government pending the outcome of his own journey to Calcutta and to England.

To the last he resisted Outram's exhortations to sign the treaty; so when, at noon on 7 February 1856, on the expiration of the term of the ultimatum, Outram convened the minister and chief officers of state and formally announced the assumption of the government by the East India Company, he committed what was *de jure,* as well as *de facto* an act of aggression. The Oudh problem was thus resolved by what Dalhousie had all along sought to avoid but which he had in the urgency of his emotional commitment condoned – an illegal act, a contravention of international law, a warlike invasion of one state by another. But this did not detract from the Governor-General's satisfaction. News of the annexation came by telegraph on 8 February, ten days after news that his successor, Lord Canning, had landed at Bombay. Dalhousie's sense of fulfilment was redoubled by the knowledge that he had got what he wanted with so little time to spare. 'So our gracious Queen', he wrote, 'has five million more subjects and £1,300,000 more revenue than she had yesterday. As a present object it would have been better that a treaty had been signed, for an amicable agreement would have looked best. But as regards the future, it is much better as it is. We shall have to bear a much less heavy charge, and we are entirely free prospectively.'[35]

Dalhousie was merely an instrument in the annexation of Oudh – not a reluctant instrument, it is true; but an instrument nonetheless. He had personal reasons for wishing to interfere decisively in the principality; but he did not share in that sense of moral duty that was ultimately responsible for the illegal annexation of the state and the deposition of its dynasty. The solution adopted was not the solution he proposed, because the indictment he presented acted like a catalyst on the powerful elements of Victorian Evangelicalism and Victorian liberalism, combining them into an agent whose effect was death on the native dynasty of Lucknow.

A horror of opulence and sensuality, as the associates of evil and vice, is an essential ingredient in the Protestant ethic. Deriving from the Old Testament depiction of Babylon, the whore city, as an object of divine displeasure, it has exerted a constant influence over the Protestant outlook and Protestant behaviour. It inspired the denunciations of Renaissance Rome by the Lutherans and their millenarian predecessors; it inspired the iconoclasm of Cromwell's Ironsides; and it inspired Milton to describe the halls of Satan as the epitome of magnificence and to portray 'courts and palaces ... and ... luxurious cities' as the abode of Belial. The Reform Act of 1832, by subjecting Parliament to the influence of middle-class Dissenters who were the spiritual heirs of the English Puritans; and the Evangelical movement, by stimulating religious revivalism among Anglican conformists, ensured that the Victorian response to public issues was heavily influenced by the severer Protestant values. The Victorians' detestation of Lucknow was the detestation of a people who had committed themselves to the ideals of earnestness, discipline and sobriety; and the annexation of Oudh – and, even more, the sack of Lucknow and of Delhi by British troops in 1858 – was a consequence of the same sort of compulsion that led to the devastation of Rome in 1527 by the Protestant knights of Charles V and the bombardment of Paris in 1871 by the Protestant armies of Prussia.

If Evangelicalism provided the emotional impulse, liberalism provided the dogma and the moral justification for annexation, for it preached that British institutions were those best calculated to promote the happiness of the Indian people. It also provided an illusion of popular mandate, and this was an essential condition of action in an age morbidly sensitive to the political dangers of offending Indian opinion. The liberals' confidence in the worthiness of their own motives and in the merit of the principles which underlay the British system of government led them to underrate the inadequacies of that system in practice. They accepted its comparative excellence as axiomatic and consequently took for granted Indian acquiescence in its extension. They sincerely believed not only that annexation was good for the people of Oudh, but also that it was what they wanted.

The truth is that Indian opinion was quite different from what the British imagined it to be. The excellence of British government was far from axiomatic in the Indian view. The inhabitants of Oudh may have been – no doubt were – aware that the native administration was bad; but they were certainly not convinced that what the British could offer was any better. There is plenty of evidence which suggests that British revenue administration was popularly regarded as oppressive, and that British courts of law were hated and feared. Furthermore, the notion of a moral duty deriving from the quality of administration was incomprehensible to the Hindu mind, which did not reckon – as the Western mind did and does – the promotion of happiness or virtue to depend on forms of government; while the Muslims found it impossible to attribute morality to any government whose ethos was heathen or even secular. To them a bad Muslim was always better than a good Christian. Political consciousness was still absent among the Hindus, for the state, with its connotations of nationality, patriotism and civil law, was to them still an alien concept. It was the Greek city state, after all, that had given birth to political thought in the West. To Hindus government meant no more than kingship (*raj*) in the traditional Indian sense – that is, a function in which the people had no part and whose impingement on their lives was minimal. Government was often oppressive, occasionally protective, and largely superfluous. Happiness depended on more spiritual things and everyday life was regulated by ties of kinship, familial etiquette, caste rules and, most especially, religious precept. Moral claims could derive only from personal merit, and personal merit derived from conformity to those standards of ethical duty and right conduct which, according to the concept of *dharma*, pertain to one's social station and ensure one's self-fulfilment. The British, far from qualifying for authority, stood shamefully condemned when judged by such criteria. In popular conception their attributes were brutality, coarseness, addiction to drink and forbidden flesh, greed for gold, lechery and (on the part of their women) shocking immodesty. The British saw themselves as the agents of moral regeneration. Indians, Muslim and Hindu alike, saw them as the chief source of the very 'corruption' that they professed to loathe. It had not gone unnoticed that European vices and European courtiers had played a prominent part in the vitiation of the Lucknow court; and it was popularly believed that exposure of the dynasty to such contaminating influences formed part of a deliberate policy, whose object was to demoralise and weaken the native government. 'I fear', wrote Maddock in 1831, 'the impression is not uncommon that we have connived at excesses and allowed the vices and mismanagement of the native government to go unchecked till the general disorder of the country would furnish us with a plea for assuming the government into our hands.'[36] Of religious piety they had little, for their way of life was profane even when judged by their own standards. It was not only among the Muslims, bound to regard them as infidels, that they engendered a sense of repulsion; many Hindus felt it too, and for them it stemmed less from the fact that the Europeans had a different religion than from the fact that they had banished even their own religion from the greater area of their conduct. Christianity and Islam alone among the major religions of the world have a tradition of bigotry and intolerance. The Hindu has a degree of respect for all religions, for he believes that they are all so many different approaches to the same essential truth. But to him religion involves the totality of experience and action. What he can hardly conceive and cannot but shun is a way of life that postulates a distinction between sacred and secular. It is arguable that conversion to Christianity was so rare (much rarer than conversion to Islam) and so generally abominated not because it meant apostasising but because, in popular conception, it meant relinquishing religion altogether and plunging into either a dark abyss of secularism or a bewildering maze of double standards. It is a fact that, during the troubles of 1857-8, many Hindu sepoys equated mere loss of caste with conversion to Christianity.

Thus the plea of moral duty which was invoked to justify the annexation of Oudh was one which had no meaning to the native population of India. Wherever the annexation was discussed – in the bazaars, in the villages, and in the sepoy lines of the native army – it was, as Lord Hastings had foretold, discussed from the legal standpoint that the British had abandoned. In the popular mind, it had significance only as an act of unprovoked aggression. The Kings of Oudh had been the oldest and most faithful allies of the British government; and thus perfidiously to violate their prescribed sovereignty and rights was to shock Indian opinion profoundly. Such an act seemed to harbinger a time when treaties and contracts would mean nothing and the whims and caprices of an alien power would take the place of law.

I remember [wrote H. C. Irwin in *The Garden of India*] on one occasion discussing the subject of the annexation of Oudh with a well-to-do zemindar, a man perfectly well affected to English rule, whose father, moreover, had been put to flight and his estate harried and laid waste by Raghbar Dyal, the infamous Nazim of Gonda-Bahraich, as recently as 1847. 'Why,' he asked, 'had the *sarkar* [British government] deposed Nawab Wajid Ali? He was a poor meek creature, a humble servant and *tabidar* or follower of the British. What had he done to be so summarily wiped out?' And it appeared to be quite a new light to him to be told that the misrule and disorder of Oudh had become more than the British Government could tolerate.' [37]

The Delhi poet, Ghalib, was well disposed towards the English and counted many friends among them; yet even he was sensible only of injustice in the annexation. 'Although I am a stranger to Oudh and its affairs', he wrote to a friend in February 1857, 'the destruction of the state depressed me all the more, and I maintain that no Indian who was not devoid of all sense of justice could have felt otherwise.' [38]

In one sense the annexation was a response to the anomaly of responsibility without power, which the British had themselves created. By reserving control of the only effective troops in the country to the Resident, and making him besides a protective and judicial agent independent of the King, the subsidiary system impaired the authority of the native administration and thus encouraged anarchy and rebellion. Without the British presence the Oudh government probably would not have been any better, but it would have been stronger – either under the present dynasty or under a usurper – and this would have obviated annexation, for what the British reacted to was not so much the badness of the Oudh government, as its weakness. It is doubtful that an efficiently oppressive administration, under which all opposition was stifled, would have evoked the same concern. So, it could be argued, the East India Company penalised the Oudh Kings for a weakness for which it was itself responsible.

But for all this, the annexation did not flow inevitably from the British connection. Other states, similarly circumstanced, survived. The will and determination of Dalhousie were essential ingredients in the process which led to this result. For generations British statesmen had managed to live with the embarrassments and problems arising from the Oudh treaty, and there is no reason to suppose that, but for Dalhousie, they would not have gone on doing so until such time as fashions of thought had changed and prevailing opinion was less hostile to the native princes. As Vernon Smith wrote to Dalhousie in October 1855: 'The policy of inaction which Your Lordship thinks it difficult to defend in Parliament has yet received the sanction of such a number of years, and so many successive governors-general, that it is not easy to say why this moment is chosen for interference.' [39]

This moment was in fact chosen because Dalhousie had promised himself that he would resolve the problem of Oudh before he left India; and annexation came about, even though such was not what Dalhousie advocated, because this was the very moment when annexation was the only solution that public opinion would admit.

PART TWO : THE PLAIN

In India, the husbandmen with their wives and children live in the country, and entirely avoid going into town.

Megasthenes

2 Oudh, *post* 1801 (The District boundaries are those of 1871)

V

Oudh covered an area of 24,000 square miles; yet the first census, taken after annexation, disclosed only eighteen towns with a population of five or more figures, and of these only Tanda, the site of a cloth factory set up by a Scottish immigrant late in the eighteenth century, owed its origins to industry. The rest were either Muslim or Hindu military colonies or, in the cases of Lucknow and Faizabad, court centres. The greater part of the country's teeming population – it must have amounted to about ten millions by the middle of the nineteenth century – lived from the land and on the land in hovels of mud and thatch. The Province was crammed with some 70,000 hamlets, an average of three or four per square mile, each surrounded by its fields and sheltered by its old banyan or peepul tree, and each fostering a way of life starkly different from that of the highly literate and polished society in the two major cities.

This latest addition to the British Empire was part of the great alluvial plain of the Ganges: flat and fertile, with little to suggest the orient save silver pampas grass and wild lotuses on stagnant pools. It was a realm of narrow fields and long perspectives; of winding rivers and deciduous groves. Over this unobtrusive landscape the Indian seasons played with dramatic effect. From July to January the rivers were full. The savannahs were tessellated in green and gold and dappled with the shadows of shifting clouds. The avenues and arbors of mango, mahua, jamum and tamarind were as lush as oak, elm or sycamore in an English summer. From April to June there was no colour save dun and straw; no sound save the rustle and rattle of dessication; no movement save the long, slow passage of the sun, slicing through the sky like a white-hot point through sheet metal. Sometimes a dust storm would turn day into night, and leave everything looking like an ash-and-cinder copy of its former self. The Province was rich in fauna. Wild tigers were plentiful in the central part, and the lucky huntsman could still find the odd leopard. There were wild elephant and buffalo in the sparsely inhabited northern regions, and peacocks and game birds everywhere.

The rural population of Oudh was divided into four main groups: the religious classes, the non-cultivating landholders, the cultivating peasants and the landless labourers. The élite among the religious classes were the Brahmins, or hereditary Hindu priests, of whom there were about one and a half millions according to the post-annexation census. Most were economically unproductive, for considerations of ritual purity precluded Brahmins from doing menial work or driving the plough. Some were landholders, and of the remainder those that could not live by charity and fees for religious ministration took up arms and became soldiers. The Brahmins of the trans-Gogra region, handsome and athletic, were especially renowned for their turbulence and martial bent. They enlisted in large numbers in the private gangs of the powerful landlords and in the armies of the East India Company, and the Brahmin cognomen Pande became a generic name for the sepoys serving under the British flag. At the lower end of the social scale were the *ryots* or cultivating peasants, each with a plot of three or four acres, capital equipment of a few brass pots, a rough plough and well ropes, and livestock of a few skinny bullocks with a milch cow or buffalo. The landless labourers – ploughmen, reapers, cowherds and swineherds – were the lowest of the low among the agricultural classes. Abject and impoverished, they fought a losing battle with hunger and destitution, and many sold themselves and their posterity into slavery in order to avert starvation or seizure for debt. The most powerful group was that comprising the landholders, often a law unto themselves. Most of them were Rajputs, who, although they numbered only six percent of the population, controlled over half the land of the Province.

The term 'Rajput' has no ethnic significance; nor is it the name of a caste (*jati*). The division of society into castes, or groups which are endogamous, commensal, hereditary and, generally, craft-exclusive, was a comparatively late development in the history of India whose significance was never as profound in the north or the country as it was in the south. 'Rajput', meaning, literally, 'royal progeny', denotes rather a social class of the type which antedates caste. It is a survival from the remote time (possibly as early as the second millenium B.C.) when the Sanskrit-speaking, Indo-European immigrants into India, still comparatively fresh from their Mediterranean homeland and anxious to preserve their racial identity in the face of the indigenous Dravidian and Mongolian tribes, divided the society of northern India into four occupational categories, or *varna: brahmin* (priestly), *ksatriya* (warrior) *vaisya* (trading, peasant) and *sudra* (serf), all aboriginals being confined to the last and lowliest. The modern vernacular corruption of the Sanskrit *ksatriya* is 'Chattri' ('Chetri' in Nepal), and since the Rajputs are regarded everywhere in northern India as the modern *ksatriyas* (though they have no ethnic link with the ancient ones), the terms 'Rajput' and 'Chattri' have become synonyms in popular parlance.

The most important unit in Rajput society was the landed lineage. The members of each lineage, which was usually divided into main and subordinate branches, traced their descent by authentic kinship links to the founder of the main branch. The chiefs of these lineages, who were generally addressed as Rao, Raja or Thakur, made up the aristocracy of Rajput society. But a larger unit, comprising a number of lineages, was also recognised. This was the clan (*got*), whose genealogical significance was dubious but whose importance as a determinant of status and precedence was great. Each clan had its peculiar customs and folklore. The Raikwar clan, for example, alone of all Rajputs, were forbidden to use the twigs of the nim tree as toothbrushes. Members of the Bais clan were reputed to be proof against snake bites, owing to their ancestral connection with the son of the World Serpent. Finally, there was the 'race' or 'tribe' – a concept which transcended provincial borders and grouped all the Rajputs into about three dozen classifications, each exogamous and all arranged for marriage purposes in a single hierarchy. These 'royal races' had no genealogical significance. They merely provided a set of illustrious and fabulous pedigrees with which the powerful could disguise churlish or uncertain origin. By virtue of his membership of a tribe or race, every Rajput claimed to trace his descent from the heroes of the Sanskrit epics and thence from either the sun or the moon.

The real origin of the Rajputs is more prosaic. Their entry into India was comparatively late, since most appear to be descended from the White Huns and Gujars, central Asian tribes related to the Huns of Attila, who invaded India and mastered the Punjab in the second half of the fifth century A.D. The first consequences of this immigration were destructive. The political and cultural fabric of the Gupta empire, which had given India what has been called its Periclean age, was wrecked, and an era of darkness and uncertainty ensued. Once settled, however, the Huns and Gujars became Hindus (just as their cousins in Europe became Christians) and were accepted into the social hierarchy as *rajputra ksatriya,* or royal warriors, in deference to their political and military significance. In medieval times, from the seventh to the twelfth centuries, various Rajput ruling houses dominated the country now known as Rajputana or Rajesthan and probably most of the Punjab, Bundelkhand and Oudh as well, with political centres in Delhi, Kanauj, Kalinjar, Ajmir and Lahore.

Much ink has been spilled in discussion about the nature of the Rajput states since James Tod, an East India Company officer, made a minute investigation of them as they had survived in the early nineteenth century and came to the conclusion that they were 'feudal' structures based on ties of vassalage very similar to those which had characterised political life in medieval Europe.[1] Tod's critics have claimed that the analogy is false, despite superficial similarities, because Rajput chiefs or nobles held land not in return for service rendered to their sovereign but by virtue of their kinship with him.[2] What these critics have failed to appreciate is that all claims based on kinship, especially when it is of the 'tribal' kind, need to be treated with great circumspection. Such kinship was a consequence rather than a cause of the political relationship between Rajput chiefs and their sovereigns. Tod was right to ignore the tribal nature of the

Rajput polities; but he cannot be completely vindicated in his insistence on their feudal structure. The word 'federal' would probably have suited them better. Tod himself admitted that the Rajput's first loyalty was not to his sovereign but to his lord (thakur),[3] and if we accept (what Tod, in his eagerness to refute all ties of kinship, denies) that these lords were lineage heads, it follows that the 'states' were really military federations, cemented by tokens of allegiance from the component chiefs to the supremo or war lord, who generally added the prefix *maha* ('great') to his own lineage title. This interpretation is supported by the very restricted legislative and judicial powers of the Rajput 'sovereigns', and by the fact that they nowhere had the admitted right to confiscate estates. 'When Deogarh was established', complained the chiefs of the Maharaja of Deogarh to Tod, 'at the same time were our allotments; as is his patrimony, so is our patrimony.'[4]

The political and social moulds of upper India were again destroyed when the Muslims of central Asia, first under the Kings of Ghazni and later under those of Ghor, poured through the northwest frontier passes and extended their sway over the Punjab and across northern India to Bengal. At the end of the twelfth century the Ghoris expelled the Rajput dynasties from Delhi, Kanauj and Kalinjar, and set up their own viceroys in Delhi. Shock waves of migration and dispersal were set up among the Rajput and Brahmin populations and groups of them found their way north into Nepal, south across the Vindhyas and east into Oudh. Intermarriage with indigenous peoples was the inevitable consequence of this unsettling of old colonies and patterns of behaviour, as was the rise to Rajput status of groups hitherto depressed by the Rajput hegemony.[5] The Rajput class thus became increasingly widespread and hybrid, but there was no impairment of the Rajput ethos. Old and new had the same pride of race, the same military ardour, the same acute, even morbid, sense of honour. These traits made them poor cultivators and unruly subjects. They considered it beneath their dignity to touch the plough, and they left their *sir* or reserved fields to be tilled by paid labour. An outlet for the martial energies of some of the Oudh Rajputs was provided by the Bengal and Bombay armies of the East India Company, and by the contingent forces maintained at the Company's behest by the native princes of Nagpur, Hyderabad and Gwalior. They found universal favour as recruits since they had a strong military bent and were physically impressive. 'The tallest and finest men I have ever seen here, or indeed in Europe', wrote Bishop Heber of them. They, together with the Brahmins of Oudh, formed the mainstay of the Bengal army. The energies of those left at home were absorbed by private vendettas. 'The shield is his cradle', wrote Tod of the infant Rajput, 'and daggers his playthings; and [his] first commandment is "Avenge thy father's feud".' 'Boundary disputes were always causing trouble. Sometimes these were settled by the crude and uncertain method of trial by ordeal, which required the contesting parties to lift a red-hot iron ball.[7] More often they would be resolved by arms. 'I have never seen enmity more strong and deadly', wrote Sleeman, 'than that exhibited by contending co-sharers and landholders of all kinds in Oudh ... In Oudh they always settle such questions by force of arms, and the loss of life is no doubt fearful.'[8] The Rajput code demanded a life of passionate commitments and quixotic stances. It prescribed lifelong devotion for a trivial favour and bitter enmity for a trivial affront. The Rajput must exaggerate his chivalry towards a virtuous woman as much as he must exaggerate his vengeance on an unfaithful wife. It was related of the Raja of Khajuri, in Rae Bareli District, that he made the obscene gesture of raising his thumb when informed by the royal Nazim that his rent assessment was to be raised. Incensed, the Nazim ordered that the thumb be cut off. The Raja thereupon took his betel scissors, cut off the thumb himself, and threw it contemptuously in the official's face. The story may or may not be true; but it is a good illustration of the sort of extravagant reaction popularly associated with the Rajput.

But the Rajput code did not enjoin a pompous and ostentatious style of life. Save on state occasions and at marriages, Rajputs were content with simple comforts and homespun costume. Their diet was modest and unvaried – *chapatis* or cake of unleavened bread, pulses, vegetables and curds – and their dress plain, consisting of quilted cotton in winter and undyed calico in summer, with a turban for holidays. Costume was no badge of prosperity and prestige, and the wealthiest landholders were hardly distinguishable from the poorest. 'It is scarcely possible to imagine the meagre appearance of some of these rich chiefs', wrote Russell, the correspondent of *The Times,* in 1858. 'On ordinary occasions they are conspicuous merely by a silver ring on the finger, or a rich cummerbund, or a fine piece of cloth, and the universal use of the tulwar, which they carry simply thrust through the waist belt.' [9]

Acute sensibility where prestige and honour were concerned was responsible for the practice of female infanticide, which even Sleeman, a confessed admirer of the Rajputs, was compelled to admit was prevalent among those in Oudh. To give a daughter in marriage to a tribe of lower status than his own was intolerably degrading to a Rajput, and as the expense of contracting a suitable alliance was often ruinous, he frequently obviated the alternative by disposing of his daughters soon after they were born. The babies were normally smothered or buried alive, without compunction or social stigma. 'It is strange', observed Sleeman, 'that men who have to undergo such heavy penance for killing a cow, even by accident, should have to undergo none for the murder of their own children, nor to incur any odium among the circle of society in which they live.' [10] Nor did the Rajputs, generally speaking, redeem this craven brutality by beneficent rule. As landholders they were not cruel to their peasantry; but they lacked a sense of civic responsibility. One of the largest Rajput estates in Oudh in the eighteenth century was that of Muhamdi, in Kheri District, which consisted of some 900 villages covering an area the size of Yorkshire. Its rulers were Sombansi Rajputs who had been converted to Islam. Of them a later British officer wrote: 'Only one small mosque throughout their immense dominions was erected by any one of the family ... Several rivers intersect their broad lands, but not a bridge was ever built by them ... No tank or well was ever constructed ... They built nothing but brick forts, girt with deep ditches and towering turrets, to protect themselves and their servants against an oppressed people.'[11] The same was true of the estate of the Ahban Rajputs, based on Mithauli. 'The peasant points to no bridge or temple as proof that any single man in their many generations ever cared for the people or the country where he ruled.' [12]

It is unlikely that the Rajputs came into Oudh in waves of mass migration. A few prominent eastern Rajput clans – the Sombansi, the Bisen, the Raghubansi and the Kanhpuria – preserve no tradition of migration at all, and they are probably descended from Chattri groups that had been here throughout the middle ages or even from aboriginal stocks that had lost the stigma of their churlish origin through miscegenation or political success. Other clans do tell a story of migration, but trace their arrival rather to the wanderings of disinherited or dispossessed individuals than to great waves of conquest and occupation. But the disruptions caused by the Muslim inroads were not the only stimulus to the Rajput colonisation of Oudh. Such were probably responsible for the displacement of the Rajputs calling themselves Bais, Janwar, Dikhit, Raikwar and Gautam, whose arrival, according to the local chronicles of Unao District, dated from the beginning of the thirteenth to the middle of the fifteenth centuries; but newcomers of the Sengur, Gahlot, Gaur, Parihar and other clans continued establishing settlements up to the end of the seventeenth century and later, and these mostly originated with grants of land from the local Muslim authorities or Delhi emperors in return for military or political service.

Once settled, the Rajputs virtually monopolised control of the land of the Province. The nature of their estates varied according to the local political and demographic circumstances. Original settlers, while claiming membership of some recognised Rajput clan, generally started lineages of their own, adopting some title descriptive of their rank or pretensions. For example, lineages in the Bachgoti clan bore the cognomens Rajkumar ('prince'), Rajwar ('monarch') and Khanzada ('nobly born' – applied to Muslim converts) as well as Bachgoti. During the first generation the structure of an estate was simple, with the lineage founder ruling as a petty monarch from his cutchery (*kachahri*) or court house. By prescriptive tradition he had ownership not in the land itself (such a form of property right was unknown in India), but in the 'state share' of its produce and in ferry dues, tolls on carts and beasts of burden, cesses accruing from the use of waste lands, bazaar taxes and general tokens of allegiance from his kinsmen and peasants, such as tribute in times of peace and military service in time of war. Now under certain circumstances an estate would descend undivided to the eldest heir of the next generation. This attribute made it a *raj*, and its owner a *raja*. Under other circumstances it would be divided according to the law of partible inheritance.

The condition of primogeniture was the ability of the lineage to extend its territories as it ramified. This meant that younger sons could acquire estates of their own, where they would found cadet branches of the main lineage. Such cadet branches might also turn their estates into rajes by repeating the process, and thus rajes would continue and even multiply within a lineage and its ramifications so long as it retained the ability to expand geographically. When this process of territorial expansion was prevented, however, or when, having been possible, it suddenly became checked, recourse had to be had to subdivision of the estate (parental or cadet) amongst the male heirs.[13] Further subdivision would follow in the next generation if expansion still remained impossible, and the process would go on until lineage members were actually sharing ownership of single villages and exercising the rights and privileges of lordship as coparcenary communities.[14]

This process increased the independence of the village and turned it into a political unit. The village became a little republic, which the coparacenary community ruled like a Venetian oligarchy. It exercised powers of a judicial and political nature, acting as arbiter in civil and criminal disputes and levying taxes for such public purposes as

> feeding of zemindars [landholders] of other villages on visit or travel; feeding the village's own *muqaddam* [headman] or its zemindars when absent on business of the community; feeding religious persons sojourning ...; payments ... to horsemen and *peons* [messengers] sent by officers for revenue and other purposes; allowances to the village watchmen when ordered to be entertained;

remuneration to individuals for the losses sustained by them in furnishing their cattle and carts when forced by Government . . .; repairing tanks and wells . . .; fines, including those imposed for the value of plundered or stolen property when traced within the boundaries of the village . . .; charity to distressed persons; interest on money borrowed to pay the revenue; expenses of ceremonies to implore rain and favourable seasons; *patwari's* [accountant's] expenses; oil and lights for the village *chaupar* or place of worship; pay to the village faqir attending the village *chapar;* burial expenses of a *muqaddam* or other respected or principal persons and the like; expenses of condolences to the sons of deceased neighbours; festival (as Holi) expenses, etc. [15]

Whether or not a lineage could expand territorially was determined by its military strength vis-à-vis the surrounding population and the local Muslim government. East of the river Gogra conditions were ideal for expansion. There was much waste land, and the authority of the Muslims was continuously weak. They penetrated into Bahraich on their first excursion into Oudh in 1030, but the expedition (led according to tradition by the Apollonian hero Sayyid Salar Masaud) was so disastrous that no further attempt to subjugate the District was made. A few colonies were established here in the fourteenth century; but Muslim political control was never any more than nominal and the field was free for the self-aggrandisement of the various Rajput lineages. Large impartible estates consequently came to characterise the structure of land control in the area, each in the possession of a powerful raja from the Kalhans, Bisen, Janwar, Bandhalgoti or Raikwar clan. It was in this area of Oudh that a form of Rajput federalism resembling that prevailing in Rajputana came into existence. The Raja of Gonda appears to have assumed the status of leader of a federation of lineage rajas, all of whom paid him certain tokens of allegiance and brought their forces into the field at his command.

West of the Gogra, on the other hand, conditions were less favourable for territorial expansion. The number of settlers was much higher, for a start (they were drawn from some forty different clans in the Hardoi District), so the pressure on the land was greater. In the second place, this part of the Province was more easily policed and its revenues more readily secured by the Muslim rulers. The main route linking the Muslim centres of Delhi, Shahjahanpur and Jaunpur with Bengal ran through the cis-Gogra districts of Oudh; and Muslim military garrisons proliferated here during the thirteenth and fourteenth centuries, after the Ghori viceroys in Delhi had extended the rule of Islam across northern India to the Ganges delta. The powerful provincial dynasty of the Sharqi Kings of Jaunpur, who threw off their allegiance to Delhi in 1395, effectively dominated the area for 150 years and put down what appears to have been a general rising of the Rajputs of southern Oudh. But the Muslims were not consistently strong, and when their control slackened a process of territorial aggrandisement similar to that across the Gogra began amongst the Rajput lineage élites. The most remarkable instance of this process was provided by the lineage of the Bais clan calling itself Tilokchandi. The eponymous hero, Tilok Chand, who has one foot in history and the other in legend, established a lineage in Rae Bareli in the period of anarchy which followed the downfall of the Jaunpur dynasty in 1450, and within 250 years this had ramified into six agnate houses with three rajas, whose territories covered the greater part of the District. Several chiefs of Partabgarh and Rae Bareli figure under the title of Raja in the anarchic first decades of the eighteenth century, and this suggests that the effects of partible inheritance were reversed as certain powerful individuals exploited the prevailing possibilities for territorial expansion at the expense either of their own kinsmen or of neighbouring lineages. Only with the strong control of the first Nawabs of Oudh did the practice of subdivision among heirs recommence.

The general situation at the beginning of the nineteenth century, after the strong rule of the first Nawabs of Oudh, again bore the imprint of partible inheritance. The prevailing unit of territorial property was the village share, and the Rajput landlord class, west of the Gogra at least, was a 'yeoman' one, comprising thousands of village coparcenary communities. Even east of the Gogra it seemed that the days of the large impartible estate, or raj, were numbered. The rights and lands of the rajas were already being divided by a process of delegation. Grants called *birts* or *barts,* which entitled the holder to a portion of the state share of the produce and to seigneurial jurisdiction over his village or village portion, were already common and had gone far towards creating a village landlord class. These grants were generally conferred on Brahmins, from motives of piety; but relations and servants often got them too, so the class was similar in composition to that across the Gogra.

During the first half of the nineteenth century the pendulum swung back once more. Territorial aggrandisement again became possible. Circumstances favoured powerful individuals who wished to set up junior heirs on their own. A number of magnates assumed or had conferred on themselves the title of 'Raja' during the last few decades of the Lucknow dynasty – notably the lords of Nigohan in Lucknow District; of Singha Chauda in Gonda; of Amethi in Sultanpur; of Oel, Kaimahra and Mithauli in Kheri; of Mahdauna in Faizabad; of Mahmudabad in Sitapur; and of Rampur in Partabgarh. In each case, as we should expect, the assumption of the title and the impartibility it implied was accompanied by large-scale territorial expansion.

The conditions which facilitated and stimulated this development were two. The first was of course the political and military weakness of the central Lucknow administration. The lack of an effective police ensured free scope for ambitious barons who collected armed followers, built mud forts and proceeded to aggrandise themselves at the expense of weaker neighbours. The British counted 623 forts in the country after annexation, ranging from fortified houses to elaborate fortalices like that of Rana Beni Madho at Shankarpur in Rae Bareli District, the outer circumference of which covered nearly eight miles and enclosed three separate strongholds buried in impenetrable living jungle.[16] The prevailing situation in Oudh during the last decades of the Nawabi was one of constant internecine strife between landholders, in which the stronger waxed mighty and the weaker went to the wall.

The second condition was the system of revenue collection adopted by the later Nawabs. As lords paramount of the province the Muslim rulers in Lucknow asserted their right to its land revenue. This right was not generally disputed, and one of the consequences of the establishment of the Muslim hegemony in Oudh was the loss by the Rajput and Brahmin landlords of a traditional asset. But this did not modify their position in the rural hierarchy. They continued to collect the land revenue (i.e. the state's share of the produce) as before, and the Muslim authorities in turn collected it from them, allowing them to retain a certain percentage (*nankar*) as collector's perquisite. A raja engaged to pay for his complete raj, and his contribution amounted in effect to a sort of feudal tribute. The coparcenary village communities elected representatives to negotiate terms with the royal collectors and generally defend their interests. In Oudh the term *zemindar* (literally, 'landholder') was applied to these delegates, and the village estates they represented were called *zemindaris*.

The later Nawabs adopted the system of farming out collectorships to contractors, and this made for the eclipse of the village communities. The crown revenue farmers were, as has been explained, often lacking in experience and local knowledge, and they consequently subcontracted for the revenues of whole revenue subdivisions (*parganas*) with local lineage chiefs. These subcontractors frequently became the effective landlords of their contracted territories by using their position to dispossess their brethren the village shareholders. In many cases the initiative for a subcontracting arrangement came from the shareholders themselves, who saw in it a means of cushioning themselves against the exactions of the great revenue contractors. They would put themselves voluntarily under some powerful lineage chief (not necessarily their own), and surrender to him their seigneurial dues in return for his protection. Several instances are on record of private estates originating in this way. Local tradition relates that in 1821 the zemindars of three parganas in Kheri District, comprising a ramified lineage of the Ahban clan, went to Khanjan Singh, head of the chief house. They begged for his protection against the grasping royal collector. He stood up to his knees in the river and swore by its sacred waters to the zemindars assembled on its banks that he would preserve their rights inviolate. This made him lord of the three parganas, which descended undivided to his brother and heir, Loni Singh. Loni Singh adopted the title of Raja of Mithauli and reversed the effects of previous generations of partible inheritance by absorbing the rights of lineage communities – Ahban and others – in some 1,500 villages. Another example is provided by the lord of Dera in Sultanpur District, who was the chief of a house of the Rajkumar lineage, in the Bachgoti clan. His estate of six villages expanded into one of 188, mostly as a result of small proprietors' deciding that it would be better for them to enter into a state of protected subordination to the chief than to deal with the crown collector directly. In Sitapur District a raja in a lineage of the Ahban clan, who had been left with little but his title as a result of punitive measures by the Muslim authorities in the seventeenth century, was restored to his ancestral estates by the popular will of his lineage brethren, and he subsequently engaged as revenue subcontractor for the whole pargana of Maholi.

The farming system of revenue collection also made it possible for outsiders, such as bankers and government revenue officials, to acquire private estates. Revenue farming almost invariably meant enhanced demand, and, consequently, the sale of the assets of village communities reduced to bankruptcy. Wealthy men with pretensions to landed status would buy up numbers of these and thus acquire estates in which they would establish new lineages in place of the resident ones. The annals of rural Oudh for the years immediately preceding annexation provide several examples of these 'capitalist' estates. Chandan Lal, head of a banking house at Mauranwan, in Unao District, acquired three scattered villages in 1810, and these formed the basis of an estate which was assessed for revenue purposes at a quarter of a million rupees in 1824. But perhaps the most notable instance of capitalist-turned-landowner is furnished by the Pande family of Gonda. They were bankers to the Rajas of Gonda and adopted the practice of acting as security for zemindars in arrears. In return they took mortgages on the whole or part of the zemindaris or village estates, and, since these morgages generally ripened into sales, the nucleus of an estate, based on Singha Chauda, was soon formed. The family rapidly enlarged this by subcontracting for other villages and by annexation had accumulated a patrimony of over a quarter of a million acres, the third largest in the District. The estate of Nigohan in Lucknow District and that of Mahdauna in Faizabad were formed by government revenue officers. Nigohan was put together by purchase, mortgage transfer and subcontracting by Brahmin bankers who acted as *chakladars* of the division called Baiswara in the days of the Nawabs; while Mahdauna was the name of an estate formed by the powerful revenue farmer and court favourite Bakhtawar Singh, a Singhalese Brahmin.[17] It consisted of 430 villages covering an area of 300 square miles. All the villages composing the estate were acquired by deeds of mortgage or sale from Rajput zemindars, whose ruination was probably systematically engineered by means of exorbitant revenue demands.

Under the operation of the revenue farming system of the later Nawabs, then, large private estates proliferated, formed by either of two ways – subcontracting and purchase – or by a mixture of both. It was the estates so formed that were known as *taluqas*. This Persian term, meaning 'estate' or 'dependency', appears to have been used originally to designate a group of villages held by a revenue subcontractor; but later it became a generic term for all large private estates under a single proprietor dealing directly with the government collector. A taluqa differed from a raj principally in that it was subject to partible inheritance; but, as might have been expected, the strongest *taluqdars* (holders of taluqas) sought to give permanence to their acquisitions by making them rajes, and the fact that so many were thus constituted is an indication of the extent to which the structure of ownership in the countryside had become flexible again. The territorial expansion of ramifying lineages was again possible, and with it re-application of primogeniture to their founders' estates.

The pattern of land control in 1856 in Oudh was thus considerably different from what it had been in 1756. From being a country predominantly of small landholders, the Province had become a country of large ones. Some 23,500 villages out of a total of 37,000 had been absorbed into taluqdari estates. Zemindaris were not everywhere extinguished, it is true. In Lucknow, Unao and Hardoi Districts many remained, and occasionally royal officials succeeded in crushing a powerful magnate and fragmenting his estate into a multiplicity of village zemindaris. It is also a fact that dispossessed village brotherhoods were not invariably depressed to the condition of cultivating peasants and landless labourers. Evidence suggests that they continued to hold their reserved (*sir*) lands at preferential rates and to enjoy 'manorial' rights and local pre-eminence, especially in cases where the scattered nature of his taluqa made it difficult for the taluqdar to exercise constant personal supervision. Their rights in mango groves planted by themselves or their ancestors were furthermore never interfered with. But the general pattern was one of large units, and the prevailing process one of agglomeration.

These were not startling novelties. There was no question of the uprooting of institutions hallowed by centuries' standing, of destroying what Sir Henry Maine claimed was 'the true proprietary unit of India', for in Oudh at least the village coparcenary community was in fact far from immemorial. It had come and gone. Come when circumstances imposed partible inheritance for successive generations; gone when they favoured lineage territorial expansion. The depression of one group of landholders and superimposition of a new one, and with it the erasure of one configuration of land control and the drawing of another, was a process that had been repeated time and time again. It had occurred when the Rajputs first colonised Oudh, as no doubt it had also occurred in response to similar political and social upheavals before that; and it continued to occur during periods of weak government under the Muslims, when strong lineages found they could expand territorially as they ramified genealogically. If it were possible for the land to retain within itself some record of the way property in its fruits has been apportioned, the archaeologist would discover layer after layer of variations on two basic patterns; and he would almost certainly find that the pattern tended to change from collective small-scale to individual large-scale ownership when the central authority was weak, and from large-scale to small-scale when it became stronger.

But if this process of vacillation was constant, its effects were not far-reaching. Indian rural society remained as solid and as slowly changing as the rock beneath the soil itself. No variations in the pattern of land control impinged very much on the existence of the bulk of the rural population, of the ryots and landless labourers. They followed a way of life that might have been laid down for Manu, the first man of Hindu legend. Indian villages were not the immutable atoms that many British administrators believed them to be. Particular villages had come and gone, contracted and expanded, with changes in political or economic circumstances, while only those held in joint ownership by coparcenary communities enjoyed any degree of political independence; but as a sociological and administrative concept the village, meaning a group of hamlets, was undoubtedly very old indeed. The *mauza* of the Muslim revenue records was merely the *deh* or *gaon* of the Sanskrit-based vernaculars under another name. Land revenue and taxes appear to have been collected, public safety regulated and public needs supplied on a village basis for centuries, even millenia. Peasants from epochs a thousand years asunder might have changed places without either noticing very much difference in the organisation of rural life. There would be the same village hierarchy, led by a patriarchal headman. There would be the same caste tribunals or *panchayats*, and the same community of village servants – watchman, blacksmith, carpenter, potter, water-carrier, washerman, tailor, barber, torchbearer, sweeper, pan-grower, leather-dresser – all members of hereditary occupational castes and all remunerated by a share of the grain heap on the village threshing floor. There would be the same village community of traders, including grain dealer, money lender, brazier, a few clothiers and a sweetmeat seller. There would, furthermore, be the same sense of corporateness, born of isolation. Although Oudh was one of the most thickly populated areas of the world by the early nineteenth century, the folk who lived in its villages were probably still as little conscious of and as little affected by the existence of men outside their own communities as they had been a thousand years before. Roads were non-existent, and communications were dependent on cart tracks that were liable to appear and disappear, become flooded or ploughed up, or twist and turn and lead nowhere. Marriage and kin connections were therefore confined to villages within a narrow radius, and contacts with the world at large were uncertain and infrequent. The only visitors were the occasional detachment of soldiers on the march – the sooner gone the better – and members of the peripatetic population of northern India, such as Muslim *faqirs*, Hindu *goshains* and charlatan *jogis*, with their nostrums and magic, performing bears and five-legged cows, all come one day and gone the next. Excursions were reserved for landlords' sons who enlisted as soldiers and for those favoured few among the humbler folk who, the autumn harvest once gathered and the spring crops sown, would sling a pair of baskets from a pole across the shoulders and go off on a pilgrimage to some distant shrine. For the great majority of the villagers the country outside their own fields lay beyond the reach of experience; a hinterland belonging to travellers' tales, legend and the gods.

Within these close-knit communities men pursued a way of life that had remained unchanged not only in its broad design but also in its essential details. The rural economy of Oudh, like that of India generally, was agrarian, for the population were a grain-eating and not a flesh-eating people. The husbandmen followed the behest of nature, retreating from the land when it was baked and powdered by the heats of April and May, and returning with the first cloudburst in June, when it turned black and heavy, and rank vegetation gave the promise of plenty. Then, as soon as the voice of the cuckoo had been heard at twilight, ploughing began for the *kharif* or autumn crop of rice, Indian corn and millet. This was reaped with the onset of the cold weather in November. Ploughing for the second crop, of wheat, barley and pulses followed at once, and the climax of the agricultural year was reached in March, with the cutting of the *rabi* or spring harvest. Soon after the baring of the ground the hot weather set in, the labourer got his first and only rest, and the agricultural calendar came full circle. The fields were irrigated from wells and pools, by means of a system of leather baskets dragged over a squealing pulley on a wooden fulcrum, which antedated even the Persian wheel. The basic agricultural implement was the bullock-drawn wooden plough, which scratched the earth to a depth of four or five inches and which, like the spinning wheel, the flour mill, the curry pounder, the loom and the tools of the blacksmith and carpenter, was of a type that had been used for a thousand and even ten thousand years. Momentous political events and cataclysms of nature; invasion and war, drought, famine and epidemic – all had come and gone without leaving any permanent imprint on the pattern of rural life. There had not even been a change in costume for the historian to chart. Women had worn the same sort of skirt, mantle and bodice, and men the same type of turban, *dhoti* and jerkin, for countless generations. There was no sense of history about Indian rural life, for the present and the past were indistinguishable, and to see it as it was then was to see it as it had always been and as it must apparently always be. If it had moved at all it had moved like a glacier, with a motion made perceptible only by the slower motion of the geological formations around it.

The liberal West, with its tradition of associating change with progress and development with improvement, could not but associate such a state of atrophy with dull apathy and cruel indifference to human suffering. Marx traced it to 'barbarian egotism which, concentrating on some miserable patch of land, had quietly witnessed the ruin of empires, the perpetration of unspeakable cruelties, the massacre of the population of large towns, [and which was] itself the helpless prey of any aggressor who deigned to notice it all'; and he recoiled in horror from 'this undignified, stagnatory and vegetative life', which evoked 'wild, aimless and unbounded forces of destruction and rendered murder itself a religious rite in Hindustan'. 'We must not forget', he warned, 'that these little [village] communities were contaminated by distinctions of caste and slavery; that they subjugated man to external circumstances; that they transformed a self-developing social state into a never-changing destiny and thus brought about a brutalizing worship of nature, exhibiting its degradation in the fact that man, the sovereign of nature, fell down on his knees in adoration of Hanuman, the monkey, and Sabbala, the cow.' [18]

This was not the first time that India had been challenged by the beliefs and values implicit in Marx's judgement. The religion that the Indo-European tribes had brought with them two thousand years before already prefigured that notion of progress through the agency of god-like man which, duly tempered in the confidence generated by the Enlightenment, became the hallmark of occidental civilisation. The religion of the *Vedas* (hymns and formulae) and the *Puranas* (legends and lore) expressed the values of an exuberant, martial, world-affirming, cattle-herding and beef-eating people, and already anticipated, in the worship of anthropomorphic gods, the self-worship of scientific and technological man. The Vedic pantheon, like the Olympia of the Homeric Greeks, contained superhuman male personifications of the forces of nature, who were propitiated and manipulated by a ritual of prayer and sacrifice. But in India these tribes had encountered an age-old philosophy of different hue; a philosophy which, by accepting man as the victim of impersonal forces, precluded the possibility of progress and defined sentient existence as a penance. The indigenous Dravidian systems (Jainism, Yoga, Buddhism) were characterised by atheism, quietism, world-negation, non-violence, vegetarianism, a dualistic view of reality and a notion of transmigration which made it possible for a meritorious soul or 'life monad' to be sublimated as a quasi-divine saint, but which presupposed the highest reward to be complete release from the trammels of matter and personality. These ideas exercised then, as they have continued to do since, a powerful fascination over the Western mentality; and the desire of the Indo-European sages to combine them with their own philosophy led to treatises of great syncretistic subtlety. The Dravidian idea of reincarnation and release was especially influential; though, since the Indo-Europeans linked it to their own monistic concept of a single ultimate reality (*brahman*), they craved for release not from a material, eternal and antithetical universe, but from the illusion of duality or 'otherness' (*maya*). In the *Upanishads* and the writings of the Vedantic school, the mode of release is the Dravidian one of world-renunciation; but in the *Tantras* the old Vedic world-affirmation reasserts itself as a therapy, and the devotee seeks to dissolve the illusion of pluralism in the ecstasy of ritual subjection to the forbidden delights of wine, fish, meat, parched grain and sexual intercourse.

But the Indo-Europeans also encountered indigenous folk beliefs, animistic rites and mother-goddess and ancestor cults that antedated even the oldest doctrines of the Dravidian sages; that were, in fact, almost as old as man himself. These were the untutored responses of men close to nature: the superstitions engendered by the mysteries of mountains, rivers, forests, changing seasons, birth and death, sunrise and sunset. This religion of the Indian countryside always remained beyond the influence of the metaphysical propositions and world-renouncing counsel of the philosophers and priests; though certain elements in Tantrism (notably its eroticism) suggest that the system could be the result of an attempt to bring the rarified religion of the pundits nearer the masses by adopting some of the features of popular cultures.

Western writers long overlooked the essential complexity and diversity of Indian religion, partly, no doubt, because they had been taught by Hegel to expect the reconciliation of opposites in synthesis, and partly because nineteenth-century scholars and officials discovered the Persian ethnic label 'Hindu' and used it to describe virtually everything that was not readily identifiable as Buddhist or Muslim. The term 'Hinduism' thus covers a widely ramified *congeries* of creeds and philosophies. There are a few common denominators, such as adoration of the cow, ancestor-worship, cremation of the dead, reverence of Brahmins (priests) and the concept of retributive metampsychosis; but there is nothing resembling a single system or expressing a single outlook. 'Hinduism' is a paradox. It is at once polytheistic and monotheistic; monistic and dualistic; Bacchanalian and ascetic; militaristic and pacifist – a set of unresolved incompatibilities; a product of juxtaposition rather than synthesis; a mixture rather than a compound.

Traditionally, Oudh was the birthplace of Buddhism. The prince Sakyamuni, the Buddha or Enlightened One, was reputedly born in Kapila, in Gorakhpur District, and it was at the ancient city of Ajodhya, near Faizabad, that he preached, in the sixth century B.C. Buddhism, however, disappeared from the area, as it did from almost the whole of India, after its struggle with orthodox Hinduism in the seventh century A.D. Thereafter Hinduism became the predominant religion; but it was a Hinduism which showed all the features of a complex genealogy.

The cult of Suraj Narayan, the sun god, was prevalent and drew on both Indo-European and Dravidian sources. 'Brahmins are sometimes fed in his honour at harvests', wrote the nineteenth-century anthropologist William Crooke, 'and the pious householder bows to him as he leaves his house in the morning . . . In the chilly mornings of the cold weather you will hear the sleepy coolies as they wake yawning and muttering *Suraj Narayan, Suraj Narayan* as the yellow gleam of dawn spreads over the eastern sky.' [19] The pre-Vedic god Shiva, associated with the inscrutable and complementary processes of birth and death, creation and destruction, was also widely worshipped in a multiplicity of guises and with a multiplicity of consorts. There were various rites connected with the moon, the rainbow, and with different birds and animals regarded as sacred – most especially with the monkey, which enjoyed semi-holy status all over northern India. The monkey-god Hanuman, incorporated into Hindu legend as the lieutenant of the hero Rama, had his shrine in almost every village in Oudh and the adjacent country, and his campaign against the giant Ravana was a favourite theme of dramatic representations at the annual Dasahra festival. 'There Hanuman, in fitting attire, marches along the stage at the head of his army of bears and monkeys; and the play ends with the destruction of Ravana, whose great body, formed of wickerwork and paper, is blown up with fireworks amid the delighted enthusiasm of the excited audience.'[20] In addition to these general cults, each village had its special godlings who resided in the old pipal tree. The pipal was everywhere regarded as sacred, and was preserved from destruction and mutilation. It thrives near old masonry, which its roots invariably destroy, and its age extends often to hundreds, occasionally to thousands, of years. This was the Bo tree, the Tree of Wisdom, under which Gautama Buddha sat in meditation at Bodhgaya, before attaining enlightenment. Like the poplar, it moves a myriad of leaves at the slightest breath of wind, and it was their sighings and whisperings, no doubt, that caused the tree to be regarded as the abode of ghosts and spirits. The banyan tree likewise figured prominently in rural legend and religion, for by a strange inversion of botanical principles its offshoots originate not below but above the ground. Long, thread-like tubers drop from its branches and thicken into new trunks after taking root; and so the tree spreads ever farther like a self-perpetuating grotto, supported by vegetable stalactites whose twisted stems often entomb the dessicated remains of a strangled palm tree. Diseases, especially epidemic ones such as cholera and smallpox, were attributed to demons, and the exorcising of these was the purview of a special group of low-caste 'wisemen' or sorcerers who practised homoeopathic magic and lived in uneasy truce with the high-caste orthodox priests or Brahmins.

Islam had left its mark in every recess of Hinduism. In the north, especially, Muslim saints and heroes were incorporated into the Hindu village pantheons, and it was not unusual to find Hindus paying their devotions at the tomb of some Muslim notable. On a more esoteric level, a movement of synthesis had produced the Sikh sect in the Punjab. Common to Hindus of all sects and all localities was a new mystical awarness of a personal God. Sufis or mystics had formed the spearhead of the Muslim proselytising campaign in India, and their immanentism and peculiar emphasis on direct approach to a personal, compassionate God had produced, either as the result of direct influence or by way of counter-challenge, a parallel development within Hinduism. Devotionalism (*bhakti*) had always had a place in Hinduism as a path of release (*mukti*) from the tramels of illusion and the cycle of death and reincarnation, and it had produced, in the *Bhagavad Gita*, one of the most remarkable works in the canon of mystical literature; but it was not until the full impact and challenge of Islam had been felt that the movement gained prominence and the old Dravidian gods Krishna and Rama came into their own as popular deities. The erotico-mystical cult of Krishna became widespread in southern India and Bengal, while in Oudh and the Ganges valley the puritan cult of Rama predominated. The old Sanskrit epic *Ramayana*, the story of the good and wise King Rama, whose chaste wife Sita was abducted by the King of Ceylon and rescued after many adventures, was translated into Hindi in the sixteenth century by the poet Tulsidasa, and thereafter wove its way inextricably into the fabric of rural culture and religion. Its story became known and loved, and its hero worshipped as a *beau-ideal* by every peasant in Oudh. Wells became sacred by virtue of their association with the wanderings of Rama and Sita, and the fair in honour of Rama which was held every year at Ajodhya, the site of his capital, was the greatest gathering in the kingdom. On occasions in the nineteenth century it attracted as many as half a million pilgrims. The popularity of his cult was so great that orthodox brahminism was forced to accommodate it, and Rama was given official recognition as one of the *avatars* or incarnations of the Vedic god Vishnu.

The fact that the Muslims made so comparatively few conversions in the area of their greatest political significance is an eloquent testimony to the organic, protean and vital character of Hinduism. It had met the Muslim challenge by absorbing the most appealing (albeit heterodox) of the Islamic attributes, and it had done this without breaking its own mould or vitiating its own essential spirit. Islam remained a hothouse religion in Oudh, as in most of India. Outside the artificial atmosphere of the Muslim towns and garrisons, it never established itself as a living growth. Even the few conversions that it did achieve were confined to the Rajput landlord class and these, since they generally had political motives, were skin deep. 'In matters of eating and drinking', wrote Elliot, one of the first British settlement officers in Oudh, 'they [i.e. the Rajput converts] are as particular about their caste as any Brahmin. Many of them wear the Hindu *dhoti* and will greet a Hindu with the idolatrous salutation of *Ram, Ram*! Almost all keep a pundit to fix the auspicious moment of commencing any enterprise, or foretell the nature of its result, and they believe firmly in his predictions.'[21] Patrick Carnegy, one of his colleagues, wrote: 'Between the Khanzadas [converts] and Hindus almost no distinction can be drawn further than that the former say their prayers in a mosque and cut their coats to open from the right. The Khanzadas refuse to eat beef; they plaster their fireplaces before cooking, and very generally use brazen vessels.'[22] The absence of distinct demarcation between the two religious groups made for remarkable communal harmony in the countryside. Only in the large towns, Lucknow and Faizabad, were there occasional conflicts between Hindus and Muslims. The most serious on record occurred in Faizabad, in 1855, when a quarrel arose over an attempt by some Muslims to offer prayers in a Hindu temple at Hanumangarhi. The Muslims insisted, contrary to all documentary evidence at least, that the temple was built on the site of a mosque. The Hindus denied that such was the case and, assisted by Raja Man Singh of Mahdauna, resisted then with force. News of the clash reached Lucknow, and tension rose. A crusading movement began among the Muslims of the city and a march on Faizabad was organised, despite the efforts of the King and leading Shia divines to allay the crisis. The crusaders were dispersed by a force of the King's troops under Captain Barlowe near Rudauli, in November, and their losses amounted, according to some reports, to four or five hundred killed.[23] This affair, however, was truly exceptional, and relations between Hindus and Muslims in Oudh were generally far less acrimonious than those between the Shia and Sunni sects within the Muslim community.

VI

After annexation the British were at last free to apply the remedies that they had cherished for fifty years as a panacea for the ills of Oudh. Revenue contracting was finally abolished and responsible salaried officials set to work to redeem the havoc it had wrought. The erstwhile kingdom was divided into four Divisions (under Commissioners), each of which was subdivided into three Districts (under Deputy-Commissioners). These arrangements were basically akin to those proposed by Minto and Baillie in 1811. The major difference – apart from the fact that British officers now performed the functions origianlly designed for natives – was that whereas the 1811 plan had confined District officers to revenue duties and prescribed the institution of independent courts of justice, the Commissioners and Deputy-Commissioners of 1856 combined both fiscal and judicial authority. Only at the highest level were the functions separated, and a Judicial Commissioner and a Financial Commissioner were appointed to Lucknow to act as supervisory and appellate agents in judicial and revenue cases respectively. This system differed from that adopted in the Ceded and Conquered Provinces in 1831 and in the old Bengal territories in 1859, where the District officer was collector and magistrate, but not judge. The new system had been devised for the Punjab after annexation (1849); and its extension into Oudh ensured that in terms of purview there was not much difference between the new District officer and the *chakladar* of the days of the native monarchy. The Commissioners and their Deputies were allowed wide discretion in the exercise of their judicial powers. They were bound to adhere to the broad principles of policy enunciated in Calcutta, but were absolved from that commitment to the rule of law which had turned their counterparts in Bengal and the Ceded and Conquered Provinces into mere enforcers of the legislative enactments of the Governor-General in Council. This flexibility was in response to public opinion. The British had become sensitive to the popular aversion to the technicalities, delays and inexorable and indiscriminate judgements of courts based on the English model, and in the more recently acquired territories (Sind, Burma and the Punjab) an attempt had been made to obviate this by allowing officers to dispense what Henry Lawrence called 'prompt justice in shirt-sleeves' – that is, justice adapted to local custom and particular circumstances. The object had been to simulate the summary and arbitrary form of authority to which the native population had become accustomed and at the same time temper it with those concepts of disinterest and trust that were the essence of the English attitude to public office. It was the notable success which this, the 'non-Regulation' system, had enjoyed in the Punjab that prompted Dalhousie to prescribe its application to Oudh.[1]

The first months after annexation were a time of feverish activity. Civilian and military officers poured into Lucknow, where they lived temporarily in the Residency while being briefed. Then they were packed off in palanquins to their Districts, where they often had to live under canvas. Many had to leave their wives and families in the capital for lack of suitable accommodation in the out-stations. Once arrived, they plunged into the work of fixing District boundaries, organising courts, jails and police, planning essential roads and postal communications, and gathering the land revenue. This last was the most pressing and most demanding task of all. Pressing because the land was the only source (apart from an excise on liquor and drugs) of revenue; demanding because it postulated two fundamental and complex questions, on the answers to which would largely depend the prosperity and tranquillity of the Province. These questions were: From whom to collect? and How much to collect?

The answer to the first question was really determined by the decision as to what type of landholding class was most desirable. The British, taught by Locke and Blackstone to regard property as the best guarantee of social stability, had brought with them to India the notion of freehold ownership of land and, since they recognised this right in those from whom they collected the revenue, wherever they concluded a settlement they created a landowning class of a sort hitherto unknown. In the 1790s, when a settlement was being devised for those territories (Bihar, Bengal and Orissa) whose fiscal administration had been transferred to the East India Company by the Mughal Emperor, the paramount view had been that big landowners, corresponding to the aristocracy of England, were the most desirable type of proprietor. Faith in large-scale enterprise as a means to agricultural prosperity had been stimulated by the example of the improving landlords of England, so Lord Cornwallis tried to recreate these in Bengal. He made revenue engagements with the hereditary rent collectors (*zemindars*) surviving from the Mughal period, and endowed them with those rights of sale, mortgage and transference by gift which are the characteristics of English freehold property. To perfect the simulacrum and make sure that land would become an attractive investment for mercantile capital (for there was much waste land in Bengal), he provided his new landlord class with an independent judiciary administering property laws of the English type, and assured to them the full fruits of any improvements they might make by fixing in perpetuity the amount that they must pay to the state. A decade later the same principles were applied (though on a temporary basis only) to the revenue settlement of the Ceded and Conquered Provinces, and a landlord class was created out of the individuals who had paid revenue under the native government. These were taluqdars and, where they did not exist, delegates, or zemindars, of village coparcenary communities.[2]

Now had the British been disposed to repeat their experiment with big landlords in Oudh, they would not have had to look very far for candidates. Taluqdars had flourished under the last kings, and most of the land revenue had been collected from them. But as it happened, in 1856 the British were averse to repeating the experiment of 1793. The practical consequences of the Bengal system, combined with wider experience and deeper knowledge of Indian rural society, had convinced them that it had been a bad mistake.

The Cornwallis settlement in Bengal had been a failure. Instead of agricultural prosperity and increased production, it had resulted in social dislocation and distress on a vast scale. Revenue assessments had been pitched too high, and the consequent accumulation of arrears had led to widespread confiscation and sale. The old zemindars had been replaced by capitalist investors who had legal sanction for rack-renting and evicting, for Cornwallis had left the cultivating peasantry to the protection of seigneurial benevolence and competition for labour alone. Much the same sort of thing had happened in the Ceded and Conquered Provinces, and its critics had accused the East India Company of impoverishing the Indian rural population in order to realise money tribute instead of increasing its purchasing power and thus creating a market for English manufactures. They interpreted the failure of the Cornwallis system as a vindication of the theory of rent that had been propounded by Malthus and Ricardo, who, defining rent as the wealth in excess of prevailing profit derived from high quality soils, insisted that it was a just due of the state, a means of obviating other forms of taxation, and not a perquisite of parasitic landlords.

The failure in Bengal was followed by the discovery of the village coparcenary communities of north-western India, and these the British regarded as the missing key, ignorance of which had led them to misinterpret the cypher of Indian rural society. The magnates of Bengal were, it appeared, a modern and alien phenomenon, thrown up by the distorting convulsions of the Mughal empire's death throes. The authentic unit in the Indian system of land distribution was the coparcenary village, immutable and primordial.[3] This theory was of course false. One delusion had merely been replaced by another. But Bengal officers such as Charles Metcalfe, Holt Mackenzie, R. M. Bird and James Thomason became convinced of its historical accuracy and strove to apply its inferences in the Ceded and Conquered Provinces by making revenue engagements on a village basis. The original settlement in the Ceded and Conquered Provinces had been for ten years, and when it expired in 1822 Holt Mackenzie, Secretary to Government in the Territorial Department, devised a successor scheme by which all superior tenures would be abolished and the large landholders converted into mere salaried revenue collectors. The Governor-General, Bentinck, perturbed by the lack of progress made in the minute investigations required to determine the Malthusian 'rent' and alive to the political unwisdom of putting the clock back and depriving big landholders of rights already conceded, caused the plan to be modified; so as finally implemented in 1833 it represented a compromise between the theorists and the pragmatists. Large landlords of the Bengal type were recognised as proprietors in cases where they had already secured revenue engagements; but elsewhere the proprietory right was vested in the village co-sharers or *pattidars*, who were to pay through their headmen a revenue roughly calculated as two thirds of the 'rent' of their holdings.

Although this system developed as a compromise, the spirit which animated its application was unequivocally partisan. Puritanism was adding moral reinforcement to the anti-aristocratic bias already generated by the economic failure in Bengal, the theory of 'rent' and the infatuation with the village communities. An anti-landlord school developed amongst British administrators in the North-Western Provinces (as the Ceded and Conquered Provinces were called after 1833) under the leadership of Robert Bird (Chief Revenue Officer, 1833-41) and James Thomason (Lieutenant-Governor, 1843-53). They taught their subordinates to regard landed magnates as pests and parasites, with the result that, in the words of Sir John Kaye, 'to oust a taluqdar was held by some young settlement officers to be as great an achievement as to shoot a tiger'.

The prevailing climate of opinion being what it was, the chances of the Oudh taluqdars' being allowed to retain their estates were slim. The old Cornwallis system was discredited in the estimation of influential men, and the reports of Sleeman and Outram, which denigrated the taluqdars as usurpers of the rights of the village communities, were obviously not calculated to encourage any form of dispensation in their favour. Dalhousie was therefore content to accept the doctrine of Bird and Thomason and prescribe

Nawab Ghazi-ud-din Haida and
Major Baillie, *circa*, 1814
Collection of A. D. King, Esq

The Residency, Lucknow, before the Mutiny
From Ball's *History of the Indian Mutiny*

Dilkusha Chateau, Lucknow
Copyright India Office Library and Records

Constantia (La Martinière) after bombardment by Sir Colin Campbell, March, 1858
Copyright India Office Library and Records

Rumi Darwaza, Lucknow, before the Mutiny
From John Luard's *Sketches in India*

The Chattar Manzil and Farhatbakhsh Palaces, Lucknow, *circa* 1880
Copyright India Office Library and Records

Part of the Quaisarbugh, Lucknow, showing the dome of the tomb of Saadat Ali Khan
Copyright India Office Library and Records

Reception of Lord Hardinge by Wajid Ali Shah
Copyright India Office Library and Records

the extension of their system into Oudh. 'It must be borne in mind, as a leading principle', Outram was instructed, 'that the desire and intention of the Government is to deal with the actual occupants of the soil, that is, with village zemindars or with the proprietary coparcenaries, which are believed to exist in Oudh, and not to suffer the interposition of middle men, as taluqdars, farmers of the revenue, and such like.' [4]

Such were the general principles enunciated by the supreme government for the settlement of Oudh. They seemed calculated to ensure the death of big landlordism in the province, and many critics of the settlement attributed to their operation just such an effect. 'The chieftains were stripped of nearly all their villages and a settlement made in which they were entirely left out of consideration', wrote one revenue officer in the 1870s.[5] 'The taluqdar class all over the country was thrown into a state of collapse', claimed another, writing in 1858; 'forty years' possession was treated as nothing if at that remote period the occupation could be proved or supposed to be proved unjust.'[6] All this is gross exaggeration. These critics, eager to interpret the revolt of 1857-8 as the nemesis of a revenue policy that they despised, took it for granted that the government's intentions were realised. In fact they never were, because not all the revenue officers in Oudh agreed with the Thomasonian doctrine. The ambiguity of government instructions and the somewhat ill-defined nature of the Financial Commissioner's powers enabled the dissenters to impose their own type of settlement, and so many taluqdars were preserved from the effects of official prejudice.

Martin Gubbins of the Bengal civil service, who was brilliant, disputatious and unstable, was made Financial Commissioner. He was a disciple of James Thomason. In his view the taluqdar was a freakish and baneful phenomenon; a callous turned cancer, produced as a protection against the abnormal pressures of native administration but now corroding the very foundations of rural society. 'The taluqdar', he wrote, 'has aimed not only at grinding the peasant by heavy exactions, but has also endeavoured to rob him of his birthright, the property in the soil ... The great aim of the taluqdar has been to supplant the villager in the property of the soil and constitute himself sole proprietor.'[7] He issued to his revenue officers the instructions which Thomason had drawn up for his own officers in the North-Western Provinces, and he interpreted government directions in a strictly Thomasonian sense. Those directions enjoined that previous to the conclusion of the regular settlement, which was to be made with 'the actual occupants of the soil', a three-year summary settlement, operative from 1 May 1856, was to be made 'with the parties actually in possession'. Gubbins ignored the distinction and directed the Divisional and District officers to make the summary settlement with the 'actual proprietors', by which he meant the village shareholders.[8] He devised a special weapon for use against taluqdars with proprietary rights. He instructed that revenue still due for the current financial year, reckoned at seven and a half instalments out of twelve, be collected at once in a lump sum, and that all taluqdars who defaulted be excluded *a priori* from the summary settlement.[9] This peremptory demand was well calculated to embarrass most of the taluqdars, who had no reserves of capital. They depended on their half-yearly collections from the peasantry, not due again until April or May, when the spring crop ripened, to discharge their obligations to the state.[10] Most, furthermore, were faced by the prospect of a shortfall in their rent collections, since they were now denied the use of the strong-arm methods on which they usually relied to make the peasants pay. Gubbins directed that where rents were 'fairly due' to the taluqdars by the villagers, they should be supported by the police in making distraint; but then nullified the dispensation by adding that in instances where conflict was likely to 'endanger the peace' the taluqdar 'should be set aside without prejudice to any right he [might] possess and engagements made direct with the villagers'.[11]

Gubbins, however, did not get all his own way. Of the four Divisional Commissioners, only one was fully in sympathy with his policy. Two were openly averse to and effectively thwarted it in the territory under their charge.

The man on whom Gubbins could rely was Colonel Philip Goldney, Commissioner of Faizabad Division. He had served his apprenticeship as an administrator under the eccentric and despotic Napier, in Sind. A taluqdar was to Goldney like a red rag to a bull. He was utterly inflexible concerning the payment of the current balances, and demanded seven instalments in full by the end of May. Among those who struggled to find the necessary cash was John Carbery, an indigo planter of Allahabad who had secured the management of an estate near Salon, in Partabgarh District, by advancing money to the taluqdar. 'To pay within the time prescribed', he wrote to General Low, 'was wholly out of [the taluqdars'] power. They remonstrated, they petitioned for an extension of time, but were peremptorily refused. They pawned their jewels; they borrowed where they were able at exorbitant interest; they used every possible exertion to raise the money, but could not succeed.' Some of those who could not pay not only forfeited their right to engage at the summary settlement, but were also imprisoned as debtors.

Unable to meet the demands in full, many great taluqdars, the real nobility of the land, were thrown into the common jail . . . Raja Hanumant Singh of Kala Kankar, taluqa Rampur [in Partabgarh District] was ordered to jail for non-payment. The Raja was dangerously ill at the time, but his eldest son Lal Partab Singh voluntarily went into jail in exchange for his afflicted parent. Jagat Bahadur, an imbecile lad of about eighteen, the adopted son of the Thakurine of the great Bhadri estate [also in Partabgarh District] was incarcerated because the Thakurine could not pay in full the seven-twelfths before the end of May. Many others were treated with the same indignity. [12]

Among these others was Raja Man Singh of Mahdauna, in Faizabad District. The large force of henchmen that he had always kept up had involved him in debt and, unable to meet the demand for instant payment of his outstanding balances, he first resisted and then fled from the British revenue officers. He went to Calcutta, avowedly to seek legal advice but secretly, it seems, in order to consult the ex-prime minister of Oudh, Ali Naqi Khan, who formed part of the deposed King's entourage at Garden Reach. He returned to Oudh in December to find that almost the whole of his villages had been confiscated for default. [13] Goldney applied the

Thomasonian principles with a bigot's intransigence. He encouraged the cultivators to present claims to proprietorship and accepted false criteria as authentication of such claims. 'I have seen Colonel Goldney go outside his cutchery tent, proceed among the crowd and gather the petitions himself by armfuls', wrote Carbery. 'What native would not try his luck when by paying eight annas and giving or promising a few bribes he could not get possession of a landed estate?' Following Thomason, Goldney accepted the planting of gardens and digging of wells as evidence of proprietorship, whereas in Oudh these activities had no such significance; and he disregarded deeds of sale and mortgage on the bare assertion of a claimant that they had been extorted under pressure. His subordinate, Colonel Barrow, Deputy-Commissioner of Salon District, began the summary settlement operations by inviting dispossessed proprietors to submit their claims. Few, however, came forward, so Barrow concluded a settlement with the taluqdars. When this became known to Goldney he at once cancelled the contracts and travelled to Salon to conclude new ones with such of the cultivators as he could induce, by pressing invitations, to present themselves. This importunity called forth a host of imposters, and the village accountants (*patwaris*) and registrars (*qanungos*) did a brisk business in endorsements of spurious claims. Carbery claimed that most of the *soi-disant* proprietors were in fact taluqdars' stewards, who bribed the *patwaris* and *quanungos* to declare them to be legal proprietors. 'The rankest bribery has been almost openly carried on by the countless claimants, and the *qanungos,* with Colonel Goldney's *munshi,* reaped golden harvests.' [14] Under the native government 8,281 villages in the territories comprising this Division had been held by taluqdars. Goldney, by his Draconian summary settlement, reduced this number to 3,575. [15] Even Gubbins thought that he had gone too far and conceded that the taluqdars in the Faizabad Division had been treated with 'undue severity'. [16]

But Goldney's example was not followed by the other Divisional Commissioners. Major Banks, of Lucknow Division, does not appear to have shared the Financial

Commissioner's views on revenue policy. In his case, however, the scope for conflict was diminished by the fact that in the three Districts under his jurisdiction (Unao, Rae Bareli and Lucknow) most villages were already held by coparcenary communities. It was in Charles Wingfield and George Christian, Commissioners of Bahraich and Khairabad, that Gubbins encountered his chief opponents.

Describing his own attitude some years later, Wingfield wrote: 'In the Bahraich Division the proprietary communities had never been very numerous or strong; and the petty zemindari estates had so long been incorporated in the large taluqas that the traces of the original dependent right were very faint, and [I] did not feel [myself] called on to revive it.' In the same dispatch he implicitly condemned the 'strong bias against the taluqdars that pervaded the system' and the prevailing notion that 'extinct and obliterated rights were to be searched out and revived and peasants who had forgotten their origin were to be made proprietors in spite of themselves'.[17] His settlement operations reduced the number of taluqdari villages from 9,003 to 5,614, and of the 3,389 confiscated some 1,300 were included in the two estates of Baundi and Tulsipur. These were distrained *in toto*, the first for default and the second for contumacy. Wingfield did his utmost to save the Tulsipur estate. He allowed the Raja to engage at the summary settlement despite the fact that he was a suspected parricide with no strictly legal title who had defaulted on the current balances; but the Raja was either unwilling or unable to rid himself of his band of unruly followers and had to be incarcerated as a danger to the peace. His villages were settled with cultivators for the remaining duration of the summary settlement, save those which were placed under sequestration in order to realise outstanding dues and the pay of his disbanded soldiery.[18]

George Christian was a thorn in Gubbins's side. He detested the levelling tendencies of the revenue system of the North-Western Provinces and supported the native aristocracy with a fervour that would admit no debate or compromise.[19] He claimed that separate collection of the outstanding balances had not been authorised by the government, and that these should have been carried forward and included in the summary settlement demand. He insisted that Gubbins's estimate of the balances as seven and a half instalments was in many cases at variance with former custom and unrealistic in view of the state of the taluqdars' assets; and he accused him of perverting government instructions in directing that the summary settlement be concluded with the 'actual proprietors'. He took the 'parties actually in possession' of the Governor-General's instructions to mean the taluqdars, where these existed. Christian's position was strengthened by the support of the Acting Chief-Commissioner, Coverley Jackson, who had been appointed in May 1856 to act in lieu of the ailing Outram. Jackson accused Gubbins of throwing the whole settlement operations into disorder and of creating popular discontent by ordering a separate collection of outstanding balances and 'withholding many material points [in government instructions] from the Divisional Commissioners, with the manifest object of inculcating different and impracticable views of [his] own'. Government had directed that the Commissioners be authorised to exercise wide discretion in the realisation of these claims and to waive them in doubtful cases or where they would entail undue hardship; but Gubbins had instead adjudicated them himself, in Lucknow, in consultation with the ex-King's accountant, who had been 'the acknowledged participator in the plunder of the state'. Jackson cancelled this arrangement and tried to get Gubbins dismissed.

The Financial Commissioner [his Secretary reported to the government in July 1856] could not have taken more effectual measures for inducing the native population to believe in his venality than he has done ... Remonstrances and rebuke have not been successful ... His self-esteem is such as to render him impervious to either and [the Acting Chief-Commissioner] is reluctantly compelled to declare that he has no confidence in that officer, and that he does not think that his administration can prosper so long as he is suffered to remain as Financial Commissioner.[20]

The consequence of this dispatch was the removal not of

Gubbins, but of Jackson, whose asperities of temper and intemperance of language the urbane and gentle Canning found intolerable; but by the time Jackson left Lucknow, in March 1857, Christian had completed his settlement work in Khairabad Division and the taluqdars were assured of their respite. Out of 4,243 villages they lost only 916.

As finally implemented, then, the summary settlement of 1856 resulted in something far short of mass dispossession of the taluqdars. Out of some 23,500 villages held prior to annexation, they lost a total of about 10,000, and of these almost half were lost by the taluqdars of Goldney's Division. Here, in the Districts of Faizabad, Sultanpur and Partabgarh, the large landholders undoubtedly did feel aggrieved; yet even here their cause was not lost. The summary settlement was by definition a provisional measure and implied no legal recognition of proprietary rights. One raja who petitioned was informed that his 'exclusion from engagements at that settlement, from whatever cause, could not prejudice his claim to propriety in the taluqa . . . that the said claim was properly matter for judicial suit and that it was in the option of the petitioner to file such suits with the regularly constituted courts of the Province. It would be investigated and decided whenever the operations of the regular settlement might reach that part of the Province in which the taluqa claimed by him is situated.'[21] Nothing irrevocable had been done, therefore; and the probability of reprieve was greatly enhanced by the appointment as Chief-Commissioner of Sir Henry Lawrence, who lost no time in making it known, after his arrival in March 1857, that his mission was to redress whatever wrongs the taluqdars had suffered.

He had long resisted the waves of Westernisation that followed the cyclone of Victorian liberalism. He had opposed the annexation of Sind, of the Punjab and of Oudh; and, as Political Agent in the Punjab before annexation and a member of the Board of Administration thereafter, had fought to preserve native institutions and protect the interests of the Sikh aristocracy. The success of the 'Punjab system' had owed much to his untiring efforts. There was more than a dose of genuine chivalry in all this; but Lawrence's conservatism was more pragmatic than romantic. He never rhapsodised about India and never joined that small band of Europeans who adopted the native way of life. He resisted change less because he was emotionally committed to the old order of things than because he feared the political repercussions of social dislocation. His main worldly concern was the preservation of the British dominion in India, and his spiritual needs were satisfied by fundamentalist Christianity. With his gaunt, grave face, long, grey beard, careless dress and speech weighted with Evangelical earnestness, he was more like some Old Testament prophet than a Hindu *sadhu* or Muslim *faqir*. Dalhousie had disliked him, and had transferred him from the Punjab to Rajputana – a measure which Lawrence found cruel and difficult to forgive. The antagonism had its roots partly in mutual jealousy, for Lawrence had become a veritable 'king of the Punjab' and had an autocrat's impatience of bureaucracy and superior control; and partly in the incompatibility of Lawrence's impulsive, unsubtle and unmethodical mind and Dalhousie's disciplined, intellectual one. But Dalhousie was now gone, and Canning needed someone to replace Jackson.

Although he had felt bound to support Gubbins in his quarrel with Jackson, Canning was far from happy about the policies and the disposition of the Financial Commissioner. 'I am sure it will be necessary for you to keep a close watch and a tight hand upon that officer', he warned Lawrence. 'He has had, as against his late master, a triumph which it would have been unjust and mischievous to withhold from him; but I have good reason to believe that he is overmuch elated by it.'[22] In fact, his victory seems to have chastened Gubbins, and Lawrence found him unexpectedly charming and amenable. 'We have ... sympathies in common', he told Canning, 'and he ... was so tremendously mauled by Mr. Jackson that he, even more than others, has hailed my coming.'[23] Gubbins repented of the treatment meted out to the taluqdars of Faizabad Division, and offered no objection to Lawrence's policy of appeasement. 'The taluqdars have also, I fear, been hardly dealt with', Lawrence wrote to Canning on 18 April; 'at least, in the Faizabad Division they have lost half their villages. Some taluqdars have lost all. Mr Gubbins, however, desires to do justice, and I hope that revenue matters will soon be put on a wholesome footing.'²⁴ Gubbins had in fact begun the work of placation before Lawrence arrived. He made a tour of the Province in the cold weather of 1856-7 and investigated many cases of confiscation. 'I [saw] him at Faizabad in January 1857', he wrote of the taluqdar Rustam Shah of Dera, in Sultanpur District, 'and after discussing his case with the Deputy-Commissioner, Mr W. A. Forbes, it [was] settled that fresh inquiries should be made into the title of the villages which he had lost, and orders [were] issued accordingly.'²⁵ Lawrence was convinced that government instructions had been perverted in the summary settlement operations, and he lost no time in proclaiming this to the landed aristocracy. By means of public durbars and private interviews he made known his intention of restoring to the taluqdars the lands they had held at annexation and of maintaining them in possession pending the fullest investigation of rights and claims. Such promises, delivered in Hindustani with patriarchal dignity and authoritarian assurance, allayed the worst fears of the taluqdari class and induced a mood of reconciliation to British rule. ²⁶

Had the revenue settlement of Oudh involved nothing more than deciding from whom to collect, it would not, then, have created any great resentment. Insofar as there was any threat to vested interests implicit in the policy adopted, it was a threat to the taluqdari class, and this threat was never in fact fully realised. But the British also had to decide how much to collect, and their policy in this regard undoubtedly did create discontent. Ironically, it was discontent amongst the village coparcenary communities – the very class they aimed to cherish and protect.

It was a logical inference from the Malthusian theory that the government might take the whole 'rental' of an estate (that is, the net produce remaining after deducting the cost of labour and the normal profits of capital) without prejudicing agricultural prosperity. Thus the British had believed that they were exercising moderation when they fixed the rate of assessment in the North-Western Provinces at two thirds of the rental. In fact this assessment proved far too high, and the rate was reduced to half the calculated rent in 1855.[27] Such was the standard that Gubbins prescribed for Oudh in 1856;[28] yet this was still oppressive. The authors of the Administration Report of the North-Western Provinces for 1882-3 pointed out that 'the proportion of the rental left to the proprietors by the old assessments in the North-Western Provinces was much less than was absolutely necessary to provide for the support of themselves and their families, bad debts, expenses of management and vicissitudes of season'.[29]

Falling prices and a widening rent differential were long-term causes; but over-assessment was assured from the start by inaccurate information. The rent theory postulated exact knowledge of an estate's liabilities and resources, and this could be obtained only by measuring each field and evaluating every bullock. Such a task was beyond a few dozen European officers, who had only three months at their disposal (in the North-Western Provinces ten years had been insufficient), and they consequently had to rely on accounts and estimates from native informants. Village and estate *patwaris* and *qanungos,* and the newly appointed native sub-collectors (*tahsildars*) were thus in a position to manipulate the assessment rates. There is no doubt that they deliberately caused over-assessment in many instances – either because they wanted to ingratiate themselves with European superiors by securing a handsome return, or because it was in their personal interest to have an estate sold up for arrears. Some, no doubt, simply wanted to punish landholders who had not produced adequate *douceurs*.[30] It was soon apparent that something was wrong, because when the rates of assessment were made known in October 1856 there was an immediate outcry – especially in the Divisions of Lucknow and Faizabad.[31] Lawrence investigated the grievances and reported to Canning in April that reductions to the extent of fifteen, twenty, thirty and even thirty-five percent had been made, thus 'showing how heavy was last year's assessment'.[32] He and Gubbins were confident that the reductions would have a mollifying effect, and Gubbins adduced the fact that the revenue had flowed in without compulsion as evidence of the contented state of the country and the equitability of the new rates. But this was pure delusion. The effect of the reductions was in fact very limited. It was confined to those who had the means and the influence necessary to prefer an appeal – in other words, to the taluqdars and the more powerful among the zemindars. The civil courts of the Deputy-Commissioners were surrounded by venal native acolytes and the vast majority of the petty landlord class were faced with the alternative of either giving large bribes to secure the passage of a petition or selling up their portable assets in order to pay their contributions as assessed. Most chose the second course and many, probably, incurred debts in order to avoid confiscation for default. It can be no exaggeration to claim that by early in 1857 a majority of the village landlord class were facing ruin, and that a situation was fast developing such as seemed invariably to follow British revenue settlements, with arrears, distraint, the creation of a market in land and the supersession of the traditional landholding class by a new one composed of officials, merchants and bankers. Only the taluqdars, it seems, were promised any degree of immunity from the impending catastrophe, for they could circumvent the obstacles surrounding the courts of justice and were besides assured of sympathy from administrators anxious to redeem initial severities. In 1857 Hardeo Bakhsh, the influential taluqdar of Katiari, in Hardoi District, told William Edwards, a revenue officer from the North-Western Provinces, that the native revenue collectors were 'the curse of the country' and that when he had a grievance he always went directly to Christian, the Commissioner, who invariably treated him courteously and promised satisfaction; but a landholder of less consequence with whom Edwards spoke had no such ready access:

> Old Kasuri told me that he had paid a thousand rupees in petitions alone, not one of which ever reached Christian, and more than 6,000 rupees in bribes, notwithstanding which he had lost the villages farmed by him and his ancestors for many generations and had been assessed so highly for those he had left that he had only

been able to pay his rent the preceding year by the sale of some of his family jewels and a mare he highly valued.[33]

The sense of helplessness and frustration induced by the operation of the new British administrative machinery was doubly potent in such men, for during the time of native rule their suits and pleas had obtained direct admission to the highest judicial authorites. These were the men whose sons, brothers and fathers formed the bulk of the East India Company's Bengal army, all the sepoys of which had had the privilege of submitting petitions to the Resident in Lucknow. Now, at a stroke, that privilege had been abolished. Annexation had turned the Resident into a Chief-Commissioner and transformed the inhabitants of Oudh from subjects of a foreign power into subjects of the Company; from a privileged outside group to part of a population whose members were all equal alike before the law and in their despair of ever being able to make use of it.

Ironically, therefore, the British had, within a year of annexation, produced in the Oudh countryside a situation which was the converse of the one they had intended and anticipated. They had reconciled to their rule the class that their policy was calculated to alienate, and provoked to nascent hostility the class they had aimed at propitiating – thereby demonstrating that a mitigated promise is far more prone to antagonise than a mitigated threat. Listeners were not wanting for subversive talk, and subversive talk there was, especially from the men who had lost their livelihood as a result of the disbandment of the old royal army and the taluqdars' forces of henchmen. Fifty or sixty thousand soldiers had been employed by the King, and the British found room for only 15,000 of these in the newly raised Oudh Irregular Force and Military Police. The rest were turned adrift, most with a gratuity amounting only to the equivalent of a few months' pay.[34] The majority lingered in sullen and dissipated idleness on the streets and in the bazaars of the capital; but some took themselves and their grievances to the countryside. In May 1856 the Commissioner of Bahraich reported that discharged soldiers from Lucknow were abroad, spreading rumours to the effect that the deposed monarch was to be restored, which unsettled men's minds, prevented institutions from taking root and inspired doubts concerning the permanency of British rule.[35] A year later it seemed that these doubts were about to be fully vindicated. Detachments of the Bengal army stationed in Meerut mutinied and, after an émeute in which several British officers were killed, marched off to Delhi and proclaimed their allegiance to the old Mughal Emperor. The Indian Mutiny had begun.

As news of this startling development spread into Oudh, signs of an anarchy reminiscent of that of the worst days of the native monarchy began to appear. During the last week in May there were serious riots in Malihabad, in Lucknow District, where the landholders, who were Muslims of Afridi descent, appear to have decided to take the law into their own hands and resume old vendettas.[36] The native troops in Lucknow and the outstations all mutinied during the first ten days of June, and as the reins of authority thus slipped rapidly from the hands of the British, so disorder and confusion increased. It was found impossible to send the European women and children in Faizabad into Lucknow for their better protection, because the intervening District of Bara Banki (then called Dariabad) was in a very disturbed state.[37] 'At present every villain is abroad', reported Sir Henry Lawrence on 26 June, 'and an internecine war prevails in every quarter.'[38] Individuals and communities who had thrived as freebooters under native rule, such as the rulers of Utraula and Tulsipur, in Gonda District, the Kanhpuria Rajputs of Nain, in Rae Bareli, the Raja of Mahona, in Lucknow District and the Gujar tribesmen of Hardoi, resumed their old ways and made themselves the terror of their neighbourhoods. Others, who had been outlawed and banished by the native administration, such as Babu Ram Bakhsh of Dhundiakhera and Shiv Ratan Singh of Pathan Behar, both in Unao District, now returned to claim their own;[39] and men who had scores to settle resumed the feuds that the establishment of British rule had interrupted. Thus the incumbent taluqdar of Roshannagar, in Kheri District, was murdered together with his son and servants by some Ahban Rajputs who had an ancient claim; and Devi Bakhsh

Singh of Bishambarpur, who possessed the proud title of Raja of Gonda, attacked the Pandes of Singha Chauda and Akbarpur, whose estates had been founded in the eighteenth century out of territories traditionally belonging to his ancestors. [40]

The central authority had collapsed; and Oudh rural society reacted in the way that it had always done in response to such a development. It began to change from a small-scale to a large-scale pattern of landed distribution; only in this case, since the weakening of the centre was so sudden, the process was far more rapid than it had ever been before. Almost overnight, the changes effected by the summary settlement in favour of the village landholders were undone, and the taluqdars reoccupied their confiscated territories. In some instances the reoccupation was forcible; [41] but there seems little reason to doubt that in the majority of cases it was the result, just as it had been in the days of the Lucknow monarchs, of zemindars' spontaneously seeking the protection of powerful men. [42]

This relapse the British found it impossible either to forget or forgive, for they interpreted it as an example of flagrant ingratitude on the part of those they had striven to emancipate. In fact it was something quite different. It was less a conscious gesture than a reflex reaction to well-recognised stimuli, for in the British government the petty landholders of Oudh saw not the benevolent despotism that the British themselves saw, but the same combination of potential oppression and actual impotence that they had experienced for generations.

PART THREE: THE CATASTROPHE

Alas! that autumn should come to such a garden!
                                            Ghalib

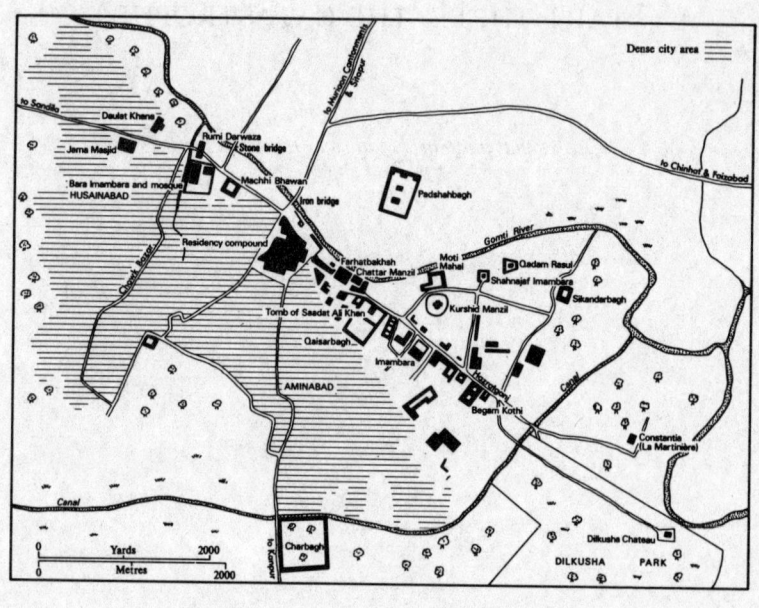

3 Lucknow, at the time of the Mutiny

VII

Seen in retrospect, there seems nothing unduly surprising about the Indian Mutiny. It is surprising, rather, that such a cataclysm had not destroyed the Bengal army much earlier. The poor quality of its regimental subalterns, the incompetence and senility of many of its senior officers and the discontent and indiscipline amongst its native ranks had long been the despair of prescient men. A system of promotion by seniority, coupled with the constant mulcting from regiments of talented officers for General Staff and political posts, had severely impaired its leadership; while the increasing tendency to require their services on distant and hazardous expeditions – inevitable as the bounds of the British empire receded – without adequate compensation in the form of increased pay or prestigious rank had planted a deep sense of grievance in the men from Oudh and Bihar whose families had formed the mainstay of the Bengal army since the days of Clive. The old partnership between European and native had been destroyed by its own spectacular success, for that success had engendered a sense of betrayal in one member and an overweening self-confidence in the other. Long association with the military fortunes of the East India Company had enhanced the sepoys' belief in their own indispensability; but it had brought them no tangible recognition or reward from the British, who were more inclined to attribute their success to their own moral superiority and the Asiatic's innate ineptitude. Thus the sepoys had come to resent a state of affairs that they had themselves helped to bring about, and to be jealous of the men they had elevated from adventurers to potentates and demigods. This mood had already inspired several instances of insubordination and mutiny in the Bengal army before 1857, and it was a commonplace amongst its critics that that army was gravely deficient in discipline. 'The normal state of the Bengal army is such as must appear to an officer of the Royal or of the Bombay army as a state of mutiny', wrote John Jacob, a Bombay officer, in 1850; and Sir Charles Napier, when Commander-in-Chief in India, complained of the 'Augean' state of the Bengal regiments. Sir Henry Lawrence was painfully aware of the declining popularity of the British amongst the sepoys. 'Strange', he wrote, 'that after we have conquered all round we should have lost weight with our own people.' He attributed the growing dissatisfaction partly to the deteriorating quality of leadership, but especially to thwarted and unrequited talent. 'The many are usefully provided for, but honours and rewards, present and future, are still wanted for the few.' The average sepoy was well treated – too well, in fact, for the way in which he had been 'pampered and petted' had contributed to vitiate discipline; but all the 'outlets for restlessness and ability' that had acted as safety valves in the earlier structure of empire were now closing. 'It behoves us therefore, now more than ever, to give legitimate rewards and, as far as practicable, employment to the energetic few, to that leaven that may serve our empire or may disturb, nay, even destroy it.'[1] During the last weeks of his life, at Lucknow, Lawrence watched his prognostications fast moving towards fulfilment and wrote long letters to Canning, urging the retrieval of mistakes which were long past redemption and whose harvest of lives was to include his own.[2]

Dalhousie had worked to improve the quality of the officer cadre, which he had conceded was impaired by the 'abominable' system of seniority promotion; but he failed to appreciate how deeply rooted the sense of grievance was amongst the sepoys.[3] This insensitivity led him into measures which made things worse. He insisted on introducing a standard scale of pay for sepoys throughout the Company's dominions, which meant in effect abolishing the extra allowances traditionally paid to troops serving beyond the Indus river. Such reductions were understandably unpopular. Abolition of their foreign service allowance in 1844 had caused restiveness amounting almost to mutiny in four corps among the troops in Sind, and one regiment had had to be disbanded. Sir Charles Napier, anxious to contain similar unrest among the troops in the Punjab, who were adversely affected by rising prices, restored the old allowances and thereby drew forth a rebuke from Dalhousie which left him no option but resignation. Dalhousie made this policy doubly odious to the troops by decreeing, in his notorious General Service Order, that foreign service would, when required, henceforth be obligatory for all newly enlisted troops, and no longer conditional upon their volunteering.[4]

The annexation of Oudh intensified the prevailing discontent, both because it was so palpably illegal and because it ended the privilege by which sepoys from Oudh could submit petitions for legal redress through the Resident. How highly this sort of privilege was valued had been made obvious in 1805, when a wave of desertions and resignations had followed the abolition of the right of commanding officers to address civil judges on behalf of sepoys from the Company's provinces. The right had been nominally restored in 1816, but it remained in abeyance in effect. Sir George Nugent, the Commander-in-Chief, had complained strongly of the bad effect of its suspension on the morale of the army;[5] yet Dalhousie felt no qualms about depriving the Oudh sepoys of this privilege. Like so many of his contemporaries, he took their loyalty for granted.[6]

The mutinies of 1857 began in February and March, in the Bengal stations of Berhampore and Barrackpore. Sepoys refused to handle cartridges issued for use with the new Enfield rifle. Rumours were current that ritually contaminating animal substances had been used to grease them, and so strong a hold did this pollution complex take on the sepoy mind that soon all cartridges, including those that had already been in use for years, became suspect because of the glaze or stiffness of their paper. In another form the complex was a belief that powdered human bones had been added to the native troops' *atta,* or flour. The trouble had spread to Meerut and Oudh by the last week in April. The 48th Native Infantry, stationed in Lucknow, became mutinous, and the regimental doctor's quarters were destroyed by incendiaries. Whether or not the misgivings of the sepoys concerning the notorious greased cartridges were justified is irrelevant. Men believe what they want to believe, not what they know to be true; and the important fact is that the anti-British agitators who were active around the military stations at this time found many sepoys who had been made willing, by an unarticulated but strong and multifarious sense of grievance, to believe that they were being polluted. These were the men who first uttered defiance and fired the first shots. Most of their brethren probably supported them in response not to deep convictions but to a belief that, since they were implicated anyway by ties of religion, colour and kinship, only by defiance could they forestall their own destruction. Thus it happened that in many places British measures of precaution and self-defence were interpreted as preparations for attack and the sepoys mutinied in panic, compelled by the overpowering instinct of self-preservation. Some fought to the end; but many went to their homes and waited quietly, overcome by disillusionment and by remorse at having proved disloyal to their salt.

Lawrence had long held the view that Sikhs and Gurkhas should be recruited in order to counterbalance the dangerous preponderance of Oudh and Bihar Rajputs and Brahmins in the Bengal army, and he lamented that in Oudh he had been deprived of a second string to his bow as a result of the policy followed by Dalhousie and Outram for the recruitment of the Oudh Irregular Force. This had been formed almost exclusively from the disbanded soldiery of the King, who were kith and kin to the sepoys of the regular army, so there was little chance of its remaining loyal in the event of general mutiny.[7] The sequel proved his fears to be well-founded. On 2 May the regiment of Oudh Irregular Infantry stationed in Lucknow refused to use their newly issued musket ammunition. The following day Lawrence was brought a letter, addressed by the sepoys of that regiment to the 48th Native Infantry, in which they declared their readiness to act as directed for the defence of their faith. Brigadier Gray reported them to be in a very mutinous state, so Lawrence marched north to Muriaon cantonments that same evening and disarmed them with the aid of sepoys still loyal. He tried to restore confidence by restricting punishment to a few dismissals, handing out promotions and re-arming about two hundred of the rebels; but circumstances beyond his control quickly thwarted these efforts. The English papers were full of sensational reports. News of the mutiny in Meerut came in on 13 May, and the seizure of Delhi was reported on the 14th. In the city bloodthirsty slogans were scrawled on walls and doors, and subtle changes in tone and demeanour indicated that men were already shifting their sense of allegiance. Superficially, life went on much as usual for the rest of the month; but nerves tautened as the temperature edged ever upwards and ominous portents accumulated. 'We went out, drove and rode', wrote Dr Fayrer, the Residency Surgeon, 'but always armed and with loaded pistols in the holsters.'

Lawrence, conscious of an ever-stronger undertow beneath the surface calm, prayed for the swift recovery of Delhi and calculated the forces at his disposal. He had only one European infantry battalion, comprising some 600 men, in Lucknow, and this he now moved from its barracks near the Kurshid Manzil and divided, stationing half at the Residency to guard the treasure and the iron bridge, and half at the southern end of the Muriaon cantonments, as to sever communication between the native troops and the city. On a mound to the west of the Residency was the citadel of the early Nawabs, the Machhi Bhawan, now thick with the dust and lumber of disuse. Its position close to the river and the stone bridge, and its dominating aspect, made it an obvious instrument for the control of the city, so Lawrence ordered its refurbishment. Its narrow corridors and doorways were widened and its many levels connected with ramps in order to admit the passage of carts and guns. The walls were loopholed and the parapets heightened. Breastworks, platforms and flanking defences were constructed and one building was fitted up as a powder magazine. Obsolete and worthless cannon were dug out from the old royal arsenal in the citadel and ranged along the higher parapets to give a greater impression of strength. These measures allayed Lawrence's immediate fears of disturbance within the city; but they were no insurance against the danger, which he already foresaw, of attack from outside. The Machhi Bhawan could never stand a siege. Its walls were too weak and its sanitation too primitive. Only in the Residency compound, he judged, would the European and loyal native garrison stand a chance of survival. As soon as his arrangements for the Machhi Bhawan were in hand, therefore, he set to work to fortify the Residency. Soon the trim lawns and parterres had been ploughed up by gun wheels and flattened by sandbags, gabions, fascines and piles of shot and shell; and the one-and-a-half mile perimeter of the compound began to bristle with palisades, *chevaux-de-frise,* caltrops, and gun emplacements. Mountains of provisions were stockpiled and the little garrison church converted into a granary. European civilians were given instruction in gun drill, and officers, civil servants and clerks banded themselves into a body of volunteer cavalry.

Alarming events added urgency to these preparations. On 1 June a detachment of Oudh Irregular Cavalry, sent to reinforce the garrison at Kanpur and dispatched thence on patrol, mutinied and killed one of their four European officers. On the night of 30-31 May there was an uproar in the Muriaon cantonments. About half the men of two Bengal infantry regiments, together with some irregular cavalry troopers, began an orgy of riot and arson. Lawrence, realising that he must at all costs prevent their entering the city, blocked the road with European artillery and infantry and loyal remnants of the sepoy regiments, and in the morning drove the mutineers into the open country to the north. A riot broke out in the Husainabad quarter of Lucknow at the same time, but was quelled by the civil police with the assistance of irregular cavalry. The city was, for the moment, saved – but only at the expense of the out-stations. 'All quiet', Lawrence telegraphed to Canning. 'My anxieties are for Kanpur and the districts.'

The mutineers fled in disarray towards Sitapur, through countryside grilling under a grapefruit-coloured sun. Then they turned west towards the Ganges and made their way to Delhi. When news of their insurrection reached Sitapur, on 3 June, a sepoy shot Colonel Birch of the 41st Native Infantry, an officer whose belief in the loyalty of his men was something like religious faith. Six other officers were killed in the ensuing riot, one of them with his wife and child. Joined by the Military Police, the mutineers then attacked the house of the

Commissioner, Christian, where all the civil officers and their families had taken refuge. Twenty-four out of about thirty Europeans, including Christian himself, were shot or cut down while trying to escape across the river at the rear of the house. On the following day the troops at Muhamdi, a station to the west, in Kheri District, were induced by a party from Sitapur to join the revolt. They allowed the small British party to leave, but then pursued them, shot them up and butchered the wounded. Only one officer escaped, with the aid of a few loyal sepoys.

In the second week of June the native troops posted in the eastern part of the Province revolted, under the influence of news from Azamgarh, Benares, Jaunpur and Allahabad, in all of which towns mutiny broke out during the period 3-6 June. During the evening of 8 June the sepoys at Faizabad, consisting of Bengal native infantry, irregular cavalry and Oudh Irregular Infantry, defied their officers and took over the cantonments according to what appears to have been a pre-arranged plan; but they did not molest the Europeans, and allowed them to leave in boats on the morning of 9 June. Later that same day there was mutiny in the stations of Dariabad and Sultanpur. The Oudh Irregular Infantry at Dariabad prevented their officer from moving the government treasure to Lucknow, and the Europeans fled the station, only narrowly escaping with their lives. The detachment of the 15th Bengal Irregular Cavalry stationed at Sultanpur murdered their commanding officer, and most of the European residents of the station were slaughtered as they tried to escape. Troopers of the 15th Irregulars then galloped off to Salon and consulted the Oudh Irregulars quartered there. Early on the 10th the jail guard released the prisoners and the sepoys absconded, carrying off their property and the six months' pay with which their officers had attempted to buy their fidelity. The officers quitted the station unmolested during the afternoon.

On 10 June mutiny broke out in the stations of Bahraich, Sekrora and Gonda. The three European officers at Bahraich managed to escape from their own men, the 3rd Irregular Infantry, but were massacred later by rebels from Sekrora as they tried to cross the Gogra. Sekrora was used as a temporary headquarters by Wingfield, Commissioner of Bahraich Division. The troops there, all Oudh Irregulars, had been uneasy since learning of the émeute in Lucknow, and Lawrence had summoned all the European women and children in the Division to the Residency on 7 June. A riot broke out in the infantry lines at Sekrora on the night of 8 June but came to nothing because of the prevarication of the native artillery. The following morning his sepoys insulted and upbraided Lieutenant Boileau, and Wingfield, sensing that all discipline was at an end, quietly saddled his horse and rode off to Gonda, telling no one and leaving no instructions. Four officers now remained, of whom three quickly followed Wingfield. Lieutenant Bonham and three European sergeants stayed at their posts until the next morning and then, appreciating the futility of further delay, quitted the station without hindrance from the sepoys. Wingfield did not stay long at Gonda. On 10 June he received a note from Lieutenant Clarke, commanding the detachment at Bahraich, which told him of the disaffection there; and later the same day news arrived of the mutiny at Faizabad. 'I felt satisfied', wrote the Commissioner, 'that to stay any longer must court destruction unprofitably, and therefore gave the civil officers permission to leave.' They went at ten o'clock, and he went with them. Three military officers felt bound to remain until their men, of the Oudh Irregular Infantry, openly foreswore their allegiance; but they too left the following morning, after a native officer had told them that mutiny was imminent.

The mutineers from Lucknow and the western stations, regular troops for the most part, went to Delhi; but those from the eastern districts, who were mainly Oudh Irregulars, joined the rebels from Benares, Jaunpur and Allahabad at Nawabganj, in Bara Banki District. Here they took common counsel and resolved to attack Lucknow.

In that city the Military Police deserted on 12 June; but a group of more than 450 regular and irregular infantry, cavalry and artillery had remained loyal after the disturbance of 30-31 May, and these were joined by six or seven hundred others who returned quietly to their lines when the dust had settled.

Everyone was on edge now, and a controversy developed about the policy to be adopted towards this remnant. Gubbins, whom Lawrence accused of being 'almost insubordinately urgent', wanted to disarm and disband them all and hold the position with the 700 Europeans (infantry and artillery) alone; but Lawrence felt that those at least who had withstood the acid test of recent events deserved to be trusted. Ultimately a compromise was reached whereby the native troops who wanted to leave were granted their discharges and the remainder, amounting to just over 700 men, were allowed to remain. About 230 of these absconded during the siege, but the others, joined by some 120 native pensioners, remained at their posts and by their devoted exertions fully vindicated the confidence that Lawrence had expressed in them.

Reports now arrived almost daily of the gradual concentration of the mutineers to the northeast, and Lawrence, made haggard by the heat, want of sleep and overwork, braced himself for the coming shock. Gubbins, burning with nervous excitement, badgered him with demands for military action and reported that his mind was enfeebled when he refused. Agonised pleas for help came from the British garrison beleaguered in Kanpur, and Gubbins bounded with eagerness to oblige. But Lawrence judged that such an enterprise would be folly. 'I ... grieve that I cannot help you', he wrote to General Wheeler on 16 June. 'Mr Gubbins, who does not understand the difficulties of [that] most difficult of military operations, the passage of a river in the face of an enemy, is led away by generous enthusiasm to desire impossibilities. I write not only my own opinion, but that of many ready to risk their lives to rescue you. God grant you his protection.'

During the last week in June came news that 'some ten regiments with many guns' were collecting eighteen miles off with the avowed intention of assaulting the city. Lawrence did not fear an attack all the while Kanpur held out, and he wrote to Wheeler on the 27th urging him to husband his resources and refuse to treat with the enemy, for help was known to be coming from Allahabad. This letter was never received, for by a supreme irony even as it was being written Wheeler was paying the price of the very policy Lawrence advised him to avoid. After three weeks of excruciating agonies from heat, privation and harassment in an open entrenchment the garrison surrendered on terms to the mutineers on the morning of 27 June and were massacred as they embarked in the boats provided for their withdrawal. No sooner did the mutineers in Oudh hear of this than they began to close in on Lucknow, and early on 29 June scouts brought word that an advance party of some 500 men had arrived in Chinhat, a village only eight miles from the Residency, on the Faizabad road.

If Lawrence had acted immediately in the spirit of Gubbin's recommendations and moved in strength on Chinhat, he might have trounced the mutineers and redeemed the worst consequences of the capitulation at Kanpur. But, inhibited by the uncertainty of his information and by the oppressive knowledge that he would be risking troops who were the garrison's only hope of salvation, he hesitated; and when he suddenly made up his mind to attack, twenty-four hours later, it was too late. By then the rebels were in full strength at Chinhat and his small British and native force of between six and seven hundred men found itself advancing towards a phalanx of five and a half thousand foot and eight hundred horse, with more than a dozen guns. Lawrence faltered; began a retreat; then changed his mind and tried to seize the initiative by attacking what he thought was a weak advance guard in the village. He was misinformed, and his gamble failed. The heat was terrible, the men had had no breakfast and little sleep, and the ground was so unfavourable that he was in danger of being completely encircled. Anticipating defeat, his native artillery and cavalry deserted and he had no option but to order a retreat. His losses were heavy, and amounted to more than 300 in killed and missing alone. The sight of the troops returning in disarray, bloody, dusty and tottering from hunger and fatigue, threw the occupants of the Residency into panic. Native servants ran away. Some women became hysterical; others gathered their children about them and dropped to their knees to pray. Men worked frantically to complete the sketchy defences and roll the guns into position. The victorious rebels crossed the river and moved into the city a few hours later, and by late in the afternoon shells – the first of thousands – began to shower into the Residency compound. Lawrence decided to concentrate his resources and on 1 July contacted the garrison in the Machhi Bhawan by semaphore, ordering them to 'spike the guns well, blow up the fort, and retire at midnight'. The evacuation was carried out successfully, and the whole city shuddered as a charge of 250 barrels of gunpowder, fired by a long train, blew up the old citadel. The Residency was now the refuge of some 3,000 people, of whom almost half were European women and children and non-combatant civilians and servants.

The so-called Indian Mutiny was in fact largely confined to the Bengal army and its effects were hardly felt outside a relatively small area of northern and central India. It never seriously endangered the British position in the subcontinent, for its achievement was essentially destructive. It overthrew British rule, but produced nothing durable to put in its place. None of the rebel elements was capable of assuming the political mantle of the British, so the Mutiny resulted not in the alternative hegemony that was the *sine qua non* of its success, but in a re-creation of that very condition of anarchy which had provided the Europeans with their opportunities in India in the first place. In order to regain their lost position all the British had to do was repeat the role they had already played a century before, exploiting internal divisions and making a vigorous display of military strength. They were assisted by the strategic errors of the mutineers, who directed their offensive not against the heart of the British empire, in the Ganges delta, but against its extremities, in the northwest. Moreover, while the military resources of the rebels were numerically superior to those of the British (there were fewer than 46,000 European troops in India at this time, while the natives of the Bengal army alone amounted to nearly 120,000), one invaluable asset ensured the swift concentration of not only British troops in India, but those in adjacent colonies as well. This asset was the electric telegraph, which linked upper India with Calcutta and Calcutta with Madras and Bombay. It was a recent innovation, and it had revolutionised communications. News which a few years previously would have taken three weeks or a month to travel from Delhi to Calcutta now arrived in a few hours, so within a day or two of the outbreaks in the northwest Lord Canning was summoning reinforcements from Bombay, Madras, Burma, Ceylon and Singapore.

But if the blow to British power was weak, that to British complacency and pride was stunning, and retaliation was immediate and ferocious. Loyal Punjabis converged on Delhi, while companies, battalions and *ad hoc* detachments of Europeans were pumped up from Calcutta to the afflicted stations in Oudh and the central Ganges valley. First as a series of isolated forays of rescue and revenge, and later as a systematic war of reconquest, the British counter-offensive took on a dimension of horror hitherto unknown in the military annals of the East India Company. At Meerut, Delhi and the outstations of Oudh the blood of European women and children had been shed; and with its shedding warfare was suddenly loosed from its customary restraints. The standards of honour and chivalry hitherto more or less scrupulously observed by the British in their Indian wars were forgotten, and a campaign of retribution was waged in which quarter was denied, from which the civilian population was not exempt, and which no obstacles of climate could impede. 'All the hell-passions of our nature have been excited', wrote Sir John Lawrence in 1858. 'It has become a war of extermination against mutineers and, in many cases, even against insurgents. It has become to some extent a war of races.' [8]

When the siege of Lucknow began Brigadier-General Henry Havelock, a Queen's officer recently returned from the Persian War, was already organising the spearhead of the offensive from Bengal at Allahabad, 120 miles away. His mission, as Canning reminded him in frequent and urgent telegrams, was to relieve the garrisons in Kanpur and Lucknow. The odds against his success were at this stage overwhelming. His force was pitifully small – 1,200 assorted Europeans, including two regiments of the Persian force, 150 Sikhs and a couple of troops of irregular native cavalry. It was, besides, the very worst season of the year, for the hot weather had broken and the monsoon was in full spate. For days on end dense rain would fall straight as a plumbline, making the scorched earth hiss, turn to mud and finally disappear under wide sheets of water. Low cloud would deaden the light like a window blind, and provisions become coated with mildew. When the sun broke through the air was filled with stagnant, musty heat. Mud on the fetlocks of horses and cattle became as hard as concrete, metal surfaces stung like a whiplash, leather boots shrank and had to be cut off, exposed skin erupted into blisters, and sweat was crushed out of men's bodies. There were plagues of flies by day, and all through the nights myraids of frogs and insects sounded like the simultaneous winding-up and running-down of a multitude of clocks and watches. But these conditions inspired few misgivings and no inclination to delay in this little, white-haired Baptist general, who always went into battle with the name of Christ on his lips. Havelock's God was the jealous God of the Israelites, of terrible requital and miraculous dispensation; and since no man ever worshipped such a God who did not believe that He was on his side, nor ever claimed that right was might without believing that right was his, Havelock went grimly forward, driving his men to and even beyond the limits of human endurance, terrorising the native population and half expecting the ranks of the enemy to part like the waters of the Red Sea.

He left Allahabad on the afternoon of 6 July and marched up the Grand Trunk Road, the recently completed link between Calcutta and the north-western frontier, through a landscape made nightmarish by the genocidal antics of Major Renaud. Renaud had gone on in advance with orders to lay waste enemy villages and hang every mutineer that he caught, and he had followed his instructions with relish. It was said of him that he was 'rather inclined to hang all black creation'. In two days he had hanged forty-two men on mere suspicion of being rebels and executed a batch of twelve allegedly because they averted their gaze when met on the road. John Sherer, the refugee Magistrate of Fatehpur, who accompanied Havelock, recorded a vivid account of his trail of devastation:

> Many villages had been burnt by the wayside and of human beings there were none to be seen. A more desolate scene than the

country we passed through can scarcely be imagined. The swamps on either side of the road; the blackened ruins of huts now further defaced by weather stains and mould; the utter absence of all sound that could indicate the presence of human life or the employments of human industry (such sounds being usurped by the croaking of frogs, the shrill pipe of the cicada and the underhum of the thousand-winged insects engendered by the damp and heat); the offensive odour of the nim trees; the occasional taint in the air from suspended bodies upon which, before our very eyes, the loathsome pig of the country were engaged in feasting; all these things, appealing to our different senses, contributed to call up such images of desolation and blackness and woe as few, I should think, who were present will ever forget.[9]

Havelock caught up with Renaud early on 12 July, and the combined force engaged a party of mutineers from Kanpur later the same day, before Fatehpur. The enemy were driven back with loss, and no prisoners were taken. Fatehpur was captured, plundered and burnt. Havelock had not lost a single man, despite having been confronted by a force twice the size of his own. He thrilled to the implications of such a victory and attributed it to 'the blessing of Almighty God on a most righteous cause – the cause of justice, humanity, truth and good government in India'. Explained in military terms, the reasons for this astonishing success were the disconcertment of the enemy, who were expecting to encounter only Renaud's advance guard; the excellence of Havelock's artillery; and the demoralising effect of the 78th Highlanders' Enfield rifles, whose effective range was about 900 yards as opposed to the 50 yards of the mutineers' smooth-bore 'Brown Bess' muskets. The enemy attempted twice more to halt the British advance, on 15 and 16 July. Each time they were driven back, though at a higher price in terms of losses. Havelock entered an abandoned Kanpur on 17 July with an exhausted and depleted force.

He had known before he left Allahabad that he would be too late to save Wheeler and the military force; but he had hoped to rescue the two hundred European women and children still held prisoner by the rebels in Kanpur. He now discovered that he was too late for that too. They had been murdered in retaliation for British atrocities, and his men entered the city to find their blood still tacky on the floor of their prison and their butchered remains hardly cold in a deep well.

When it learnt of this ghastly discovery the British public reeled under a sense of outrage. The execration lavished by the London and Calcutta press on Nana Sahib of Bithur, once the darling of Kanpur society but now condemned on circumstantial evidence as the author of the massacre, was probably not exceeded even by that reserved for Kaiser Bill or Hitler. Because the killers were heathen and their victims Christian, the crime seemed not only craven and brutal, but sacrilegious; an affront not only to civilized standards, but to Christianity itself. Revenge thus acquired a religious mandate and suppression of the Mutiny turned into a crusade.

I have often thought whether we were right to think of revenge, [confessed one of Havelock's band of volunteer cavalry] for are we not taught "Vengeance is mine, I will repay, saith the Lord"? And then I eased my conscience by thinking that I was an instrument in His hands . . . No! Never shall a sepoy receive his life at my hands; and had I the power I would never forgive a mutineer. If it took fifty years, I would hang every sepoy that was caught. I would make India feel that England would never forgive such insults and such barbarity as have been heaped upon her daughters.

Men in public life were caught up in this flood of crusading hatred. 'I wish I were Commander in Chief in India', wrote Charles Dickens. 'The first thing I would do to strike that Oriental race with amazement . . . should be to proclaim to them, in their language, that I considered my holding that appointment by the leave of God, to mean that I should do my utmost to exterminate the Race upon whom the stain of the late cruelties rested.' When one member of the House of Commons protested against the British atrocities in India, he was attacked by another for daring to speak in such a way in a 'Christian house of parliament'.[10] The Governor-General, to his everlasting credit, strove to protect the innocent. 'I will not', he said, 'govern in anger.' But 'Clemency Canning' was despised as a sycophant to savages, and could do little to restrain military and civilian officers in the field.

At Kanpur the repaying of evil with evil, of blood with blood, was left to General Neill, a Madras officer who arrived from Allahabad with 400 men on 20 July. He remained to make an example of the city while Havelock crossed the Ganges and pressed on to relieve Lucknow. Neill, after his suppression of mutiny in Benares and Allahabad, was well practised in such work. His name had become a byword for terror, and under his stern authority large numbers of prisoners, mostly civilians, were executed every day. But the pious Havelock was as ruthless, and sadistic besides. It was Havelock who told his artillery officer: 'My dear Maude, I give you leave to hang as many men as you like'; and it was Havelock who prescribed execution by the method of blowing from guns. Two sepoys captured in Oudh were destroyed in this way. 'They were both extremely fine men', wrote Major North, 'in the flower of their age; tall, athletic, graceful, with finely moulded limbs – almost resembling antique statues in bronze.'[11]

Havelock began to move his force across the Ganges on 22 July, in torrential rain. The pontoon bridge had been destroyed, so the troops and supplies had to be ferried across in small boats. These plied back and forth for five days across the river, which was 1,500 yards wide and frothing and swirling like milky coffee. They had to make widely circuitous journeys in order to avoid shoals and currents and compensate for contrary winds, so each crossing involved a trip of some six miles. All but essential baggage had to be left behind. 'No one takes tents – only a change of clothes, and some food and drink', wrote Colonel Tytler. Havelock, misled by ignorance as well as by faith, was confident, and expected to reach Lucknow in five or six days; but later, when information smuggled out of Lucknow had made clear the true nature of the difficulties ahead, and when an encounter with mutineers who had the support of the rural population had revealed the full extent of the enemy's resources, his officers began to realise that he would never make it.

On 31 July Colonel Tytler wrote to the Commander-in-Chief:

We crossed the river on the 28th; encountered the enemy at and between Unao and Bashiratganj on the 29th; took nineteen guns of sorts... We inflicted a heavier loss than usual... Our own loss was 88, reducing us to 1,000 European infantry. We could now only place 850 in line, our numerous sick, wounded and baggage requiring strong guards in this country, where every village contains enemies. We were diminishing daily from cholera, diarrhoea and fighting. The Bani bridge, 120 yards long, strongly intrenched, and said to be destroyed, had to be passed. We could not hope to reach Lucknow with six hundred effective Europeans. We had then to pass the canal and force one and a half miles of street. We found we thrashed the Oudh people easily in the open, but failed to force the small occupied *serais*. The men hung back; and one of our guns was left under fire... Under these circumstances, when asked my opinion as to the possibility of at once relieving Lucknow, I decided against it, for the following reasons. If we failed (and I saw no chance of success) Lucknow was irretrievably doomed and Government in a worse position than ever; while, if we waited for reinforcements, we might still be in time to save it, as the garrison say they can hold out to the 5th August, and longer if necessary, and warn us not to approach Lucknow without less than 2,000 to 3,000 Europeans.[12]

On 2 August intelligence arrived from Neill to the effect that the reinforcements expected from Bengal had been delayed by mutiny in Dinapur. Why Havelock prolonged an offensive now doubly futile is not clear, especially since he had been advised from Lucknow itself not to advance with less than two or three thousand Europeans. His motives were probably mixed. Any delay now must be a long one, and as the garrison were supposed to be short of food a last desperate gamble seemed to offer the only hope of rescue. But Havelock was also fighting for his reputation. He was not well regarded in Calcutta (one newspaper called him 'an old fossil, dug up and fit only to be turned into pipe clay') and he feared that he would be superseded if he did not give Canning what he wanted, for Neill, popularly regarded as the man of the hour, had made known in no uncertain terms his own view that circumstances did not warrant retreat. Havelock was an old man. Only with the relief of Lucknow could he win the glory he had always coveted but which had ever eluded him, and he resolved either to accomplish this himself or prove by Pyrrhic victory that it was impossible. Twice more he threw his wretched troops against the rebels, on 6 and 12 August, and twice more demonstrated the senselessness of further persistence. He sustained battle casualties of only sixty killed and wounded and inflicted a far heavier loss on the enemy; but he now had 300 men stricken with cholera and the remainder were so near to exhaustion that any attempt to exploit his success must have been suicide. If Havelock imagined that he was undermining the enemy's morale by these stinging forays, he was deceiving himself, for he was in fact doing the opposite. In war an advantage not exploited is an advantage conceded. By playing all his cards he had merely revealed the weakness of his hand and inspired the rebels in Lucknow with the elating assurance that they had survived the worst that he could do. They proclaimed his sterile victories defeats and usurped the prestige which he had deserved but had been unable to retain.

The British force recrossed the Ganges on 13 August and then languished, in an open camp, under the alternating effects of pestilent heat and drenching rain. During an expedition against the rebel stronghold at Bithur, on the 16th, twelve men dropped dead from heat apoplexy. On the 19th seventeen officers and 466 other ranks were on the sick list and, after making detachments to guard communications with Allahabad, Havelock could put only 700 men in line. Even Neill was horrified by the condition of the troops. *'Rest they must have'*, he telegraphed to the Commander-in-Chief. 'Nothing can be done towards Lucknow from this until reinforced. An advance now, with reduced numbers (and those nearly used up from exposure and fatigue) would be madness.' Havelock's men had fought and won ten battles in thirty-six days, and they had fought at the worst time of the year against numbers vastly superior to their own; but the fact remained that all their suffering and bravery had been in vain. The Kanpur captives had not been rescued; Lucknow had not been relieved; and the general situation was much worse than it had been when they left Allahabad, six weeks before. Kanpur, Allahabad and Benares were now the only stations held by the British in the whole of the North-Western Provinces and Oudh, and even these were held precariously. A new danger had arisen in the form of the Contingent Force from Gwalior, which had rebelled and was threatening all these positions from the south; while there was no hope of immediate sustenance either from the Punjab and the northwest, whence all resources were absorbed by the siege of Delhi, or from the east, where all available troops were needed for the pacification of Bihar. Furthermore, it was now certain that when the British did ultimately return to take Lucknow, they would find the rebels greatly increased in strength. Hitherto the taluqdars of Oudh had maintained themselves in an uneasy neutrality; but now, faced with evidence of the military bankruptcy of the British, they could hold aloof no longer, and pledged their allegiance to the rebel régime.

Those who had striven to modify revenue policy and conciliate the Oudh taluqdars saw their efforts well rewarded during the first weeks of the Mutiny, for the great majority of the taluqdars made no move to support the rebels. Gubbins reported at the end of June that 'the taluqdars [were] hesitating about joining the mutineers'; [13] and Wingfield wrote that in his Division 'none of the taluqdars had yet shown any indication of revolt'. 'I thought it probable', he added, 'that the mutinous troops would all march towards Lucknow, when I might, with the aid of the well affected rajas, return and re-establish the British authority.' [14] The few large landholders who found themselves in a position to assist the British did not hesitate to do so. Their friendly co-operation enabled large numbers of refugees to escape from the outstations and find their way to places of safety. Some fifteen or sixteen taluqdars in various parts of the Province were approached by fugitives for assistance and shelter, and in only two places – Nanpara in Bahraich District and Oel in Kheri – were these refused. Even then the refugees were not molested. The magnates who actively assisted the rebellion at this stage were seven or eight at the most, though several others took advantage of the prevailing anarchy to rustle and plunder or attack their ancestral enemies. Ten taluqdars put themselves to considerable trouble and incurred danger in order to protect and assist British officers and their families. In Faizabad

District, Raja Man Singh of Mahdauna, who had been put under house arrest for suspected subversive activities, was released after a fortnight and given 5,000 rupees in return for a promise to protect the women and children from Faizabad. He kept his part of the bargain well. He sheltered them and a group of five men who fled from the civil station on the night of 8 June – a total of eight women, fourteen children and seven men – in his fort at Shahganj, and had them conducted safely down the Gogra in a boat when things got too hot for them there. It was entirely owing to his efforts that they arrived safely at Dinapur. Raja Lal Madho Singh of Amethi, in Sultanpur District, gave a courteous reception to three women from Sultanpur, sheltered them hospitably for a fortnight, and then arranged their escape to Allahabad. His neighbour, Rustam Shah of Dera, received the officers from Sultanpur and treated them well until they were rescued by an escort from Benares. Hanumant Singh of Kalakankar, in Partabgarh District, spontaneously offered to protect the Europeans from Salon and, when the offer was taken up, entertained them handsomely in his fort at Dharupur. He personally escorted them to Allahabad and refused all payment for his services. Raja Digvijai Singh of Balrampur received nineteen British fugitives from Bahraich and Gonda in his fort at Pathoangarh for a night and then accompanied them, with an escort of 500 men, to Bansi, whence they made a safe journey to Gorakhpur. Raja Loni Singh of Mithauli, in Kheri District, sheltered and fed fugitives from Muhamdi and Sitapur; and the regent Rani of Dhaurahra, in the same District, received a British party from Mallapur in her fort at Matera. The taluqdar of Murarmau, in Unao District, whose name was also Digvijai Singh, received fugitives from Kanpur and gave them clothes, food and shelter for a month before escorting them safely to Havelock's camp. The taluqdar Ram Sahai of Haraura succoured the Deputy-Commissioner of Dariabad and his wife; and, perhaps most exemplary of all, Hardeo Baksh, the lord of Katiari in Hardoi District, sheltered the Collector of Budaon and the Collector of Farakhabad and his wife and children from 10 June until 30 August, when he sent them down river to Kanpur under the protection of his

The Catastrophe 185

brother-in-law and a guard of eleven matchlockmen.

It is not difficult to understand the motives of these people. Many of the taluqdars had invested in East India Company securities, and most felt that they had nothing to gain from a situation of prolonged anarchy, which promised only to precipitate hordes of self-seeking adventurers committed to the overthrow of the existing rural hierarchy. 'Every person must have observed', wrote Raja Man Singh in a circular addressed to his fellow taluqdars, 'that one sepoy of a mutinous regiment can disturb the whole community ... In each of the villages under every taluqdar there cannot be less than ten *telingas* [sepoys], and consequently there will be as many kings in each village ... When [the taluqdars] find thousands of kings upon their respective estates, it will be difficult for them to save either their estates or their lives.' [15] As Rajputs and Hindus, moreover, they resented the great advantages which the Muslim aristocracy were reaping from the disturbances. 'It is also surprising', wrote Man Singh, 'that people should aid and put into power those very same Muslims who, on invading India, destroyed all our Hindu temples, forcibly converted the natives to Muhammadanism, massacred whole cities, seized upon Hindu females and made them concubines, prevented Brahmins from saying prayers, burnt their religious books and levied taxes upon every Hindu.' It is significant that of the two taluqdars who put themselves at the head of the mutineers and assumed the role of rebel leaders (as opposed to that of merely freebooters) at the outset of the mutiny, one, Nawab Ali Kan of Mahmudabad in Sitapur District, was an influential Muslim, and the other, Raja Jai Lal Singh of Maujadubanspur, in Faizabad, had been a prominent courtier of the ex-King. [16]

But expediency, as well as inclination, induced the taluqdars to hold aloof. They did not for a moment believe that the rebellion could succeed and were understandably reluctant to commit themselves to a lost cause.

They must inevitably be defeated [wrote Man Singh of the sepoy rebels]. They should rest assured that they will never be able to cope with that army and people who defeated ten lakhs of Russians in spite of their discipline, wealth and munitions of war, and finally captured Sebastopol. Three thousand European soldiers have lately dismayed all the Iranis in Persia. Have not the English caused the Emperor of China to make good their losses? There is not a single king in the world who does not fear them.

There is no doubt that the sentiments and arguments which Man Singh expressed in this letter found ready sympathy with most of the taluqdars. If they welcomed the Mutiny at all it was merely for the chance it offered of earning rehabilitation from the British. Sir Henry Lawrence went to considerable trouble to impress upon the taluqdars that the rewards of loyalty would be great. Man Singh was offered a *jagir* (assignment of land revenue) of £25,000 a year, and smaller offers were made to many others. [17] No doubt it was this bait which inspired Man Singh to write: 'If all of you unite and seek for peace, I am sure the Government will remove all your doubts (of whatever kind) and something better will come out of the future.'

But the taluqdars were not in all cases free agents. Many had not only their own inclinations to consult, but also those of military retainers and protected zemindars, whose outlook was far less favourable to the British. When all was said and done, in fact, it was public opinion that determined their behaviour.

There is plenty of evidence to back up this claim. The taluqdars' failure to support the British with active assistance can be largely explained by the restiveness of their kinsmen and retainers, who were motivated by either fear of or sympathy for the mutineers. The followers of Man Singh, for example, did not copy their master's example, and plundered the refugees they were escorting to the boat provided for their escape.[18] Gulab Singh, the taluqdar of Taraul, in Partabgarh District, was hampered in his efforts to protect fugitives from Sultanpur by the reluctance of his retainers to incur the hostility of the rebels. [19] The same was true of Digvijai Singh of Balrampur. 'It was not difficult to perceive', wrote one of his British protégés, 'that our presence was not much liked by many of his followers; nor could his people be depended on to protect us at the risk of their own lives.'[20] When the Sitapur fugitives arrived at Loni Singh's fort at Mithauli, they were at first refused entry by the Raja's retainers. It was only when Lieutenant Burnes, covered in blood after forcing his way through the wicket of the gateway, pleaded personally with the Raja that he obtained asylum for the party. [21] The armed henchmen of Hardeo Bakhsh visibly resented the presence under their master's roof of Edwards and Probyn. 'We were far from being favourably regarded by his people', recalled Edwards, 'who looked upon us as the proximate cause of the mutineers' advancing on Dharupur,'[22] Even so well disposed a taluqdar as this was prevented by his followers from offering more than benign neutrality. He told Edwards and Probyn that his people were quite ready to imperil their lives in their defence and in repelling any attack on Dharupur, but that they would not consent to cross the Ganges and act offensively against the mutineers. [23]

Other influences too were working to pull the taluqdars into the rebel camp. In the first weeks of the mutiny the British found their most active enemies in the Oudh countryside, amongst the village coparcenary class. Major North, who accompanied Havelock in his abortive attempt to reach Lucknow in July, wrote: 'The entire population of Oudh is against us';[24] and Colonel Tytler reported to the Commander-in-Chief on 6 August: 'Every village is held against us, the zemindars having risen to oppose us. All the men killed yesterday were zemindars. We know them to be all around us in bodies of five or six hundred, independent of the regular levies.' [25] The antagonism of these small landholders is not difficult to explain. This area formed part of the division known under the native dynasty as Baiswara, and Baiswara was the cradle of the Bengal army. Villagers in eastern Unao and in the adjoining District of Rae Barcli were kith and kin of some 40,000 of the Bengal sepoys, [26] and their concern to strengthen the rebellion and forestall the sort of vengeance that the British had already perpetrated in Allahabad and Kanpur was only to be expected. Much the same sort of attitude must have been prevalent in Gonda and Bahraich, areas which provided many Brahmin recruits; and the almost universal failure of the petty landholders to oppose the mutineers indicates that sympathy for their cause, generated by a mixture of kin loyalty, detestation of the British revenue system and resentment at the brutality of British reprisals, was felt all over the Province. It cannot be an exaggeration to claim that among the martial and landholding Rajput and Brahmin populace pressure was strong in favour of a general uprising. These elements could command the loyalty of some of the lower occupational castes (the Pasis, who were watchmen, for example) and of many of the cultivators too; but since the motivating grievances belonged primarily to the economically non-productive, socially superior groups, it would be inappropriate to speak of a 'peasant' revolt.

This consensus was a severe embarrassment to the majority of the taluqdars. They were looked to for leadership, for they were the traditional warlords of the country. They still had forts and cannon, for Canning had foreborne to disarm them and they had responded to his demand that they turn their swords into ploughshares no further than by burying them in the ground. That the civil revolt did not occur sooner must be attributed to the hesitation of many taluqdars to dig them up and adopt the role that they were being pressed to accept. But they could resist the mounting pressure only so long as the possibility of British success seemed real, and it seemed far from real after the disaster at Chinhat and Havelock's failure to reach Lucknow. They now felt themselves bound to bow to popular clamour and lead their levies to aid the rebel government in Lucknow. Wingfield, appointed Political Agent with the allied troops from Nepal, wrote from Gorakhpur on 14 July 1857: 'All I see and hear of Man Singh makes me think him staunch up to the moment . . . but we cannot expect him to sacrifice himself for us. He had doubtless already made himself obnoxious to the rebels by his open adhesion to our cause; and if fortune goes against us at Lucknow, instead of being able to render us any assistance, he will himself have to take shelter here.' [27] By the beginning of September he had joined the mutineers in Lucknow. [28] 'As long as he thought the success of the rebellion was but transient', explained Wingfield, 'and that our Government would speedily recover its position, he professed loyalty, and even supported us; but

The Catastrophe

when he heard tht the Gurkhas [allies from Nepal] were not to march through Faizabad, and that Havelock had been obliged to abandon his design of relieving the Residency and retired to Kanpur, he thought our cause hopeless and joined what appeared to be the triumphant side.'[29] In truth, he probably had little choice. Since his championship of the Hindu party in the affray at Hanumangarhi in 1856 he had been regarded as the leader of the Hindu cause in Faizabad and as such could not afford to defy popular opinion once the prospect of British victory seemed faint. Most of the other taluqdars in Faizabad District behaved in a similar fashion. Babu Madho Parshad of Chahora and Raja Udresh Sing of Dhaurwa, both of whom had assisted the flight of the garrison of Faizabad, were compelled, it seems, by their Palwar and Rajkumar clansmen to espouse the rebel cause after the collapse of the British offensive. Babu Madho Parshad attacked Azamgarh in July and then, joined by Udresh Singh and his followers, united with the rebel Nazims of Gorakhpur and Sultanpur in their depredations in Azamgarh and Jaunpur Districts.[30] Raja Rustam Shah of Dera never went to Lucknow and personally remained aloof when all the other taluqdars of Faizabad and Sultanpur lent support to the Nazim of Gorakhpur; but his brother was present with the forces of the Nazim of Sultanpur in November 1857, and there is little doubt that he was following the policy of equivocation adopted by many of his brethren and lending token support to each side in order to insure against both the possible issues of the conflict.[31]

News of Havelock's collapse caused even Hardeo Bakhsh of Katiari to tell his protégés bluntly that he could shelter them no longer. He said that there was strong pressure on him to relinquish his pro-British attitude. The rebel authorities in Lucknow were busy spreading the rumour that the British were bent on ritually defiling the whole population. 'You and I', he told Edwards, 'know that this is all nonsense and folly; but the proclamation is a highly dangerous and inflammatory document, for its contents are implicitly believed by the common people, who are consequently much exasperated against the British.' He went on to say that by harbouring British fugitives he had made himself unpopular amongst his own relatives and tenantry and that this ill-feeling had been aggravated by the rebel authorities in Fatehgarh, who had prohibited people from his villages from crossing the Ganges to get supplies. 'The result of this deprivation is that the people are becoming excited to a degree highly dangerous towards us', wrote Edwards, 'and Hardeo Bakhsh fears he cannot much longer restrain them.' [32]

Hardeo Bakhsh did not, so far as is known, in fact ever lend support to the rebellion, and his example was followed by Digvijai Singh of Balrampur. [33] But of the remaining half-dozen taluqdars who had rendered signal assistance at the outbreak five are known to have followed the lead of Man Singh and associated themselves with the revolt. Madho Singh of Amethi was preparing to join the rebels in early September, and late in October he was stated by native spies to be present in Lucknow with 2,500 men. [34] Hanumant Singh of Kalakankar adopted a hostile stance as early as the second week in July. The guns in his riverside fort opened fire on the *Brahmaputra,* a steamer with a hundred Madras Fusileers aboard which had been ordered up the Ganges for use at Kanpur, and his men harassed the vessel for several days. His son, Lal Partab Singh, was killed opposing the Nepalese allies under Colonel Wroughton in Jaunpur District at the end of September, and in November he was reported to have a thousand troops in Lucknow. [35] Raja Loni Singh of Mithauli sent his agent, Zahur-ul-Hasan, to Lucknow with 300 men in July, and the safety of the English fugitives who were then still under his protection became very precarious. The Raja was unwilling to adopt a decisive policy while the outcome of the contest remained dubious and for two months would neither send them to the British camp nor surrender them to the rebels. Only when it finally seemed sure that the British were vanquished, in October, were they finally sent, shackled, to Lucknow, where the men were executed and the women and children held as hostages until a friendly jailer engineered their escape. But even then, it seems, Loni Singh's hand was forced by Zahur-ul-Hasan, who had returned from Lucknow with instructions to seize the captives. Loni Singh himself afterwards stoutly maintained that he was compelled by the rebel government to give them up and only did so when assured that their lives would be spared.[36] W. Gonne, a Deputy-Commissioner who was one of the refugee party at Dhaurahra, in Kheri District, noted in his diary the effects on his hosts and their neighbours of the British reverses. 'The taluqdars are preparing to go to Lucknow', he wrote on 15 July. 'I think they are persuaded our government is lost.' His entry for 23 July reads: 'The Rani and *Sarbarahkar* [steward] are said to have changed their plans respecting us and to be less favourably disposed.' Again the policy was one of cautious temporising, the Rani being equally reluctant to sabotage her relations with the British by sacrificing her protégés and to antagonise the rebels by refusing to surrender them. 'We are indeed in a dangerous position, for the Dhaurahra estate is coveted both by Esanagar and Bhoor, so the Rani cannot look for sympathy if she boldly takes our part.' Finally she acquiesced in the demands of the local rebel leader, a zemindar called Banda Husain, and allowed them to be taken to Lucknow escorted by her own henchmen. 'The present plan', wrote Gonne on 8 August, 'seems to be to pass some ten days in making pretence of the Raja [her son] taking us into Lucknow himself, by which time something would turn up one way or the other.' The party, suspecting treachery, attempted flight on the way to the capital. They escaped their pursuers, but several died of fever during the subsequent wanderings in the jungles of the Nepal borderlands and only Captain John Hearsey reached Lucknow.[37] A similar line of conduct was adopted by the taluqdar in Partabgarh District whose estate was managed by John Carbery. 'Chattro Pal Singh, the taluqdar, visited me in the zemindar's house where I was in concealment', wrote Carbery; 'and it was only when he saw no chance, as he fancied, of our ever retaking Oudh, that he drove out my servants and set me at defiance.'[38]

Once the prominent taluqdars had yielded, the movement of tergiversation became widespread. It was reported in November 1857 that there were 32,000 men, contributed by some thirty taluqdars, among the rebel forces in Lucknow, as well as large numbers of similar troops with the rebel Nazims of Sultanpur and Gorakhpur in the south-eastern corner of the Province.[39] But there is no reason to suppose that the large majority of these were sent for any reason other than those of popular pressure and calculated expediency. There were, undoubtedly, a few landholders who, inspired by sincere anti-British animosity or genuine loyalty towards the deposed dynasty, were committed *a priori* to the uprising. All the available evidence, however, suggests that most were victims rather than instigators and abettors of the popular rebellion. Nor, seen in the context of the Mutiny as a whole, does this seem unusual or surprising. The Mutiny began as an acephalous movement, undirected and unorganised, and everywhere it spontaneously crystallised around the prominent, but largely unwilling and incongruous remnants of the native aristocracy. Modern research is making it increasingly plain that individuals such as the King of Delhi, the Rani of Jhansi, the Nana of Bithur and the Nawab of Farakhabad, so readily stigmatised by earlier historians as arch-fiends and traitors, were in fact reluctant accomplices in the military and civil revolts, dragged from the ease of pensioned retirement or protected dependence and compelled to conform to ancestral traditions that had long been nothing but a memory.

The reinforcements for which Havelock sat waiting at Kanpur consisted of some 1,400 Europeans recently arrived from Singapore (whence they had been diverted on their way to China), Madras, Ceylon and Burma. They travelled the distance from Calcutta (628 miles by road, 954 by water) with painful slowness, in river steamers that had to battle against monsoon currents in the Ganges and in bullock waggons that moved at three miles an hour. The final driblet arrived in Kanpur on 17 September, and with them came Major-General Outram. This officer, recently returned from commanding the successful Persian expedition, had been reappointed Chief-Commissioner of Oudh following the death of Sir Henry Lawrence early in July, and with the post was linked the command of the two divisions of British forces operating between Calcutta and Kanpur. Squat, swarthy, chain-smoking, punctilious and sober, Outram was, amidst the strong situations and highly coloured characters of the Indian Mutiny, suggestive of someone in a theatre who had wandered inadvertently from the audience to the stage. Sir Charles Napier had called him the Bayard of India; but that was when they were still very good friends. Lady Canning found him 'not the least my idea of a hero'. He was an indecisive general and an uninspired administrator; a man of few ideas, who found action as difficult as he found speech when there was no emotional impulse to drive him. He had caught the popular imagination less by ostentatious prowess than by noble gestures of altruism. He had quarrelled with Napier, a man whom he admired, in order to vindicate the Amirs of Sind; and now, in order to preserve to Havelock the glory of relieving Lucknow he resolved to accompany the army not in his military capacity, which would have involved his superseding Havelock, but in his civilian capacity as Chief-Commissioner. Havelock was therefore spared the chagrin of supersession and, officially at least, remained in charge of the relief operations. In practice it proved otherwise. Once he had become acquainted with Havelock's reckless tactics and callous indifference to the sufferings of his soldiers, Outram regretted his waiver and continually interfered. Havelock was too polite to quarrel, but could not help thinking that the only real effect of Outram's vaunted magnaminity was to saddle himself with responsibility for measures not his own. Relations between the two officers became strained and the campaign marred by the inevitable shortcomings of divided command.

The combined relief force, totalling just over 3,000 men of all arms, crossed the Ganges between 19 and 21 September on a pontoon bridge 2,000 yards long. The first encounter with the enemy took place at Bashiratganj on the 21st, in torrential rain.

We deployed in order of battle and marched onto the enemy's position [recalled one of the cavalry volunteers]. The balls began to fly about as usual, but our line steadily advanced . . . Down, down went the wretches. *Cawnpore, my lads, remember Cawnpore* was the battle cry, and woe to the black skin that came under our swords. At least 250 must have been cut up. Our gallant leader, General Outram, not deigning to draw his sword, kept hitting the enemy as he came up to them with his stick, leaving it to those behind him to kill; and you may be sure they spared no-one. [40]

The rebels were pushed back and on 23 September the British reached the Alambagh, a walled park some 500 yards square on the plain a mile and a half beyond the southern suburbs of Lucknow. The position was taken after a short skirmish and camp established there on the 24th.

Lucknow was surrounded on three sides by water. It was enclosed by the Gomti river to the north and by the unfinished canal to the east and south. The Residency was inaccessible by the most direct route, for the approaches to the south, through the quarter called Aminabad, were bristling with barricades, trenches and loopholed houses. Havelock therefore wanted to circle the city on the outside of the canal, cross the Gomti at its junction with the canal, and approach the Residency from the north, via the stone bridge. It was discovered, however, during a reconnaissance on 24 September, that the recent heavy rain had made the ground too heavy for artillery. Havelock, who never underestimated the value of guns in siege warfare, agreed that the force must instead skirt the city inside the canal, after crossing this at Charbagh, and approach the Residency via the riverside gardens of the Shahnajaf Imambara and Moti Mahal palace.

Two thousand men advanced on the 25th, the remainder being left to guard the field hospital at Alambagh. The Charbagh bridge was desperately defended, and captured only after a recklessly courageous charge by the Madras Fusileers, led by Havelock's son. There was also stiff opposition at the Begam Kothi. Thereafter the route to the Moti Mahal was relatively unimpeded for the main part of the force, but the 78th Highlanders of the rearguard, who took a wrong turning on their way from the bridge and advanced up Hazratganj, suffered heavily before joining their colleagues there. Fire from the Qaisarbagh and the buildings which clustered around the Chattar Manzil and Farhatbaksh was very hot, and many casualties were sustained during the seizure of these riverside palaces. 'A regular fight into Lucknow' is how Captain Willis described the operation. 'At every cross-street guns in position, storming and taking them and running the gauntlet through streets, the houses of which were all loopholed and full of men.'[11] Outram wanted to halt at the Chattar Manzil and enable the column, now greatly extended, to consolidate and re-form; and he planned to minimise further losses by advancing thence through the interiors of the intervening buildings. But in Lucknow in late September the shadows are already long at four in the afternoon, and Havelock had made a fetish of being in the Residency before nightfall. If he calculated he hardly cared how many men must be sacrificed in the attempt. He insisted on an immediate advance through the streets. Outram, exasperated, was on the point of resuming the command; but he bit his lip and said instead: 'Let us go on then, in God's name!' The vanguard pushed on through the dusk into narrow streets echoing and re-echoing with the clatter of battle. Havelock achieved what he wanted, and got the first of the relieving force into the Residency enclosure as the brief Indian twilight was ending; but Outram had the dubious satisfaction of seeing his own misgivings vindicated. Losses were very heavy and the baggage and wounded were stranded for two days at the Moti Mahal. A party had to be sent back for them under cover of night. They lost their way on the return and fifty of the wounded were butchered as they lay helpless in a blind alley. The total losses of the relief operation amounted to five hundred killed, wounded and missing – a quarter of the entire force. General Neill was among the killed.

In the general eagerness to push a force, however depleted, into Lucknow, nobody had given much thought to the question of what was to be done thereafter. Anxiety to prevent another Kanpur had blighted all military judgement. Canning, after telling Outram that his main task was the rescue of the garrison, had made vague suggestions to the effect that he might hold Lucknow if he felt strong enough but that he was to retire if the safety of the garrison would thereby be better secured. It was hardly realistic to suppose that a force of less than two thousand, surrounded by an enemy twenty times their number, could do either of these things; yet the extraordinary fact is that this truth did not dawn upon the British commanders until they were actually inside the Residency. 'In considering the heavy loss at which we forced our way through the enemy', reported Outram to the Commander-in-Chief, 'it was evident that there could be no possible hope of carrying off the sick, wounded and women and children (amounting to not less than 1,500 souls, including those of both forces). Want of carriage alone rendered their transport through five miles of disputed suburb an impossibility.'[42] Seeing no prospect of large-scale relief in the near future, he wanted to strengthen the garrison with a complete regiment of infantry and withdraw the remainder of his force to Kanpur. That remainder, however, was too weak to retire without the assistance of about 300 men from Kanpur, and since Colonel Wilson jibbed at exposing such a small detachment the project had to be abandoned.[43] The embarrassing truth was that having fought their way into the Residency, Outram and Havelock could not get out. All that they had done, and at such great cost, was to boost the enemy's confidence by yet another débâcle and to double the strength of a garrison already, as it was supposed, down to its last crust. Providentially, it was discovered that the stores of grain in the Residency had been miscalculated, so the arrival of the 'relief' force did not entail the prospect of extinction by starvation. But the situation was still serious. 'Our food', wrote Outram, *upon very reduced allowance indeed,* may possibly last till 20th November, but we should have no bullocks left to move the guns.'[44] The relieving force now needed relieving itself, and Lucknow was a bigger headache than ever.

The Commander-in-Chief in India was now Sir Colin Campbell, a Glaswegian veteran of sixty-five who, having neither been born great nor attained to greatness, had nevertheless had greatness thrust upon him. Uneasily it sat, too, upon this shrivelled, hard-swearing campaigner, described by one of the Governor-General's A.D.Cs as a 'nasty-smelling, ugly man'.[45] He had won his laurels as Commander of the Highland Brigade in the Crimea. His men, because he looked after their welfare and shared their privations, adored him; but he had never become much of a popular hero. He was too churlish for London society and the

Horseguards; too diffident and too impatient of incompetence for Anglo-India. 'As a commander I always found him cautious quite to a fault', said Dalhousie, whose dissatisfaction had been the cause of Campbell's resigning his Indian provincial command in 1852. His relations with Canning were cordial; but he made little attempt to conceal his dislike of Outram, whom he could not forgive for having crossed Sir Charles Napier.

Campbell arrived in Calcutta on 13 August and left to take personal charge of the troops collecting at Kanpur at the end of October. He was determined that there must be no more of the strategically unsound policy pursued hitherto. He set his sights on long-term objectives, and refused to be led into dashing but senseless measures by the clamour of public opinion. He wrote to the Duke of Cambridge:

> I have made up my mind not to hazard an attack which would compromise my small force. A road must be opened by heavy guns and the desperate street fighting so gallantly conducted by Sir James Outram and General Havelock – the only course open to them – must, if possible, be avoided in future. Short as the time is, there must be no undue haste on my part. My object is to extricate the garrison from Lucknow. This I will do if it can be accomplished with the ordinary military risk. But I am sure that Your Royal Highness will agree with me in thinking that there are larger interests pending than even that great object and that I must watch over the safety of the small body of troops with which I begin this undertaking as the foundation on which all our combinations for meeting an enemy in the field and the restoration of our government depends throughout the Province ... Whatever the public may say at first, if the devoted garrison were to fall for want of food in consequence of such necessary precaution, I feel certain of the support of Your Royal Highness.[16]

To form such a resolution at a time when prayers for the rescue of the Residency garrison were being offered in every village and cathedral church in Britain, and when the relief of Lucknow was something for which the whole of the English-speaking world was breathlessly waiting, required strength of mind and moral courage of a type in which most

Victorian generals, for all their animal bravery, were sadly lacking.

Campbell operated under circumstances considerably easier than those which had beset Havelock. The recapture of Delhi in the second week of September had released troops from the northwest, and others were available from Calcutta, where British reinforcements from the Cape of Good Hope and Singapore had continued to arrive throughout September and October. By 9 November Campbell, after making detachments for the security of Kanpur and the Alambagh, had some 4,700 men of all arms, half of them British, available for his assault on Lucknow. This was still meagre enough; but it was half as large again as the force which Outram and Havelock had had at their disposal in September and it included, besides, ten sixty-eight pounder naval guns, manned by a brigade of 400 sailors drawn from the warships of the diverted China force. The weather too was now much improved. The rains had ceased and, though the heat was still fierce at midday, a freshness rose with the dawn and returned with the crepuscular parakeets. The country was lush with high crops of millet and sugar cane, and the distances dreamy in tinted haze.

On 12 November Campbell moved forward from his camp in advance of the Alambagh. Following the route recommended by Outram, he skirted the eastern part of the city on the outside of the canal and, after a running fight of some two hours, captured the Dilkusha château. Here he set up his field hospital, commissariat headquarters and baggage dépôt. His personal headquarters he established in Constantia, or La Martinière College as it was now called, which was less than a mile farther north. On 16 November he crossed the canal. The operation presented no difficulty, for the rebels, expected an attack farther to the south, had made a dam which left the canal almost dry near its junction with the Gomti. The first major obstacle was the Sikandarbagh, a walled garden about 130 yards square, with corner bastions.

Hitherto Outram's information, which had been smuggled out of the Residency by an intrepid European called Kavanagh, had proved correct. What he had written concerning the Sikandarbagh, however, was misleading. 'It is said to be occupied by Man Singh', he had reported, 'with some two or three hundred rajwaras [retainers] and two guns. The former are pretty sure to bolt when your guns open upon the place and two or three shells are thrown into it.'[47] In fact it was held by 2,000 rebels who resisted desperately. After a pounding of one and a half hours by heavy artillery a small breach appeared in one of the walls, and through this and adjacent windows Sikhs and 93rd Highlanders poured on a rampage of slaughter. The garrison could not escape, because the gateway was forced by the British, so they made a heroic but hopeless effort to stem the flood with bayonets and muskets. Many were overcome with terror at the sight of the Highlanders' kilts, never before seen in India. A folklore had already begun to accumulate around that strange article of dress and the rumour was current that the Highlanders were the ghosts of the murdered Englishwomen, risen for revenge. No plea for quarter was heeded by these grotesque creatures. Huge, redfaced and besmeared with blood and gunpowder, they stormed into every corner of the garden and its gatehouse screaming *Cawnpore, you bloody murderers!* The tumult of their swearing, hacking, smashing and shooting, and the cries and sobs of their victims, went on for two and a half hours. 'Inch by inch', wrote Lieutenant Frederick Roberts, '[the rebels] were forced back to the pavilion and into the space between it and the north wall, where they were all shot or bayoneted. There they lay in a heap as high as my head, a heaving, surging mass of dead and dying inextricably tangled.' The wooden pavilion caught fire, and the frenzied occupants, who tried to flee, were driven back at bayonet point to be burnt alive. When the attackers were called off, about two in the afternoon, many were sobbing hysterically, for the Sikandarbagh, built for dalliance and pleasure, had become a reeking Alcedema, such as they had never seen before and wanted never to see again. Its gatehouse, pavilion, courtyards and parterres were covered in gore and encumbered with two thousand bodies. But others exulted at the expiation they had exacted. 'From the time of our first opening fire on the Sikandarbagh that morning', wrote Lieutenant Gordon-Alexander of the 93rd, 'to our being mustered outside its walls in the afternoon, we must have been continuously fighting for more than four hours. But we had the proud satisfaction of knowing that in this, our first serious encounter with the rebels, we had done *something* to avenge Cawnpore.'[48] There was neither time nor labour available to bury all the corpses, and many were left to the circling hordes of speckled vultures and the humming millions of irridescent flies.

The avenging army swept on through a heavy flanking artillery fire to the Shahnajaf, which was bombarded and assaulted but not captured until the enemy absconded, after nightfall. All the rebels who failed to make good their escape were slaughtered. 'I was personally occupied till nearly daylight', recalled Gordon-Alexander with great satisfaction, 'in superintending the shooting of belated sepoys, who had evidently been asleep or had been cut off from the back gate in some way when we entered the enclosure.' [49]

The next day, the 17th, the Kurshid Manzil and the Moti Mahal were stormed and captured. With the occupation of the latter communication with the besieged garrison was assured, for Outram had extended his position along the river front to the Chattar Manzil, which was only about 600 yards from the Moti Mahal. The three generals, Outram, Havelock and Campbell, shook hands on the open space between the two palaces that same evening, with bullets whistling about their ears. Total losses for the two days' operations were 550 killed and wounded.

This time, the visitors had not come to stay. Campbell sternly rejected the sentimental reasons advanced for retaining the Residency position, and arrangements for complete withdrawal were made forthwith. The women and children left the compound at noon on 19 November and made their way to the Sikandarbagh through the Farhatbakhsh and Chattar Manzil palaces, dodging fire from enemy guns in the Qaisarbagh and on the northern bank of the river. At midnight on 22 November the long column of the combined military forces, together with 1,000 wounded, filed out of the position in funereal silence. The attention of the enemy had been diverted by a subterfuge which led them to expect an attack on the Qaisarbagh, and the whole convoy, travelling by country lanes along the banks of the Gomti, made its way unmolested to Dilkusha. The only casualty was Havelock, who died of dysentry.

Campbell had done what he had set out to do, and he refused to allow his success to entice him prematurely into more ambitious projects. Outram urged him to attack the Qaisarbagh and then maintain a force there; but Campbell declined. 'I have always been of opinion that the position taken up by the lamented late Sir Henry Lawrence was a false one', he wrote to the Governor-General, 'and after becoming acquainted with the ground, and having worked my troops upon it to relieve the garrison, that opinion is confirmed. I therefore submit that to commit another garrison to this immense city is to repeat a military error, and I cannot consent to it.' [50] Canning, fearing the political effects of total withdrawal from Oudh, had urged the retention of 'a safe position between Lucknow and the Ganges', so Campbell decided to leave Outram at the Alambagh, with 4,000 men and thirty-two pieces of ordnance, pending his own return for a systematic reduction of the city. This position Outram defended for four months, repelling six attempts to dislodge him. Campbell meanwhile hurried back to Kanpur and arrived just in time to rescue the city from the Gwalior Contingent, which had attacked the weak garrison in his absence.

The British thus still had no more than a toe-hold in Oudh; but a turning point in the war had been passed. Their advantages were multiplying and, during the winter of 1857-8, the signs in their favour were clear. Delhi had been recaptured and the northwest was secure. Large reinforcements from England had arrived, and 9,000 troops from Nepal were on their way to join the 3,000 sent down to Jaunpur in July. During the autumn and winter months of 1857-8 the rebels active in Gorakhpur and the southeast of Oudh suffered severe reverses at the hands of the British and their Nepalese allies. Beni Madho, the rebel Nazim of Azamgarh and Jaunpur, was driven out of Azamgarh by Colonel Wroughton, who advanced from Jaunpur. In February 1858 Muhammad Husain, appointed by the Lucknow régime as Nazim of Gorakhpur, was expelled from his District by the Nepalese force advancing from the northeast; and the forces of Mehdi Hasan, the rebel Nazim of Sultanpur, were defeated by General Franks at Nasratpur and Chanda and driven back to Sultanpur. Franks routed them there on 23 February and resumed his march to Lucknow, where he joined the main army on 4 March. Meanwhile, Sir Colin Campbell had been clearing the banks of the Ganges by forays and excursions and gathering strength for a final spring on the capital. By mid-February bodies of troops were crossing daily from Kanpur into Oudh, and strong posts were established along the road to the Alambagh in order to guard communications with Outram and protect the huge convoys of stores.

The small landholders of Unao District were now more friendly towards the British. Sir Hope Grant, in charge of the forces in Oudh pending Campbell's return, made a short expedition into western Unao in in February in pursuit of rebel fugitives and found the civilian inhabitants generally co-operative. At Mianganj he was resisted by 'townspeople and zemindars' men'; but at Bangarmau 'a body of the most respectable inhabitants came out and begged me to spare the place, urging that they were loyal and promising to bring us out whatever supplies we required'. [51] Disillusionment with rebel rule was partly responsible for their change of attitude. 'The rebels committed the error of raising the assessment at least twenty-five percent above what I had fixed', wrote the Deputy-Commissioner of Unao District in March. 'This at once put most of the village proprietors against them.' [52] Rebel taluqdars, such as Jussa Singh of Fatehpur Chaurassi and Babu Ram Bakhsh of Dhundiakhera, had, furthermore, alienated the coparcenery class by their ruthless self-aggrandisement. But fear of nemesis also played its part, for it needed no great perspicacity to see that the British were now set fair to gain ascendency in Oudh.

A fortnight after the retreat from Lucknow [wrote an informant from the Alambagh in December 1857] not a grain of wheat or a wisp of hay could be procured from them, even by force, but the victory [against the Gwalior Contingent] on the 6th of this month suddenly changed the tone of popular feeling. It was then discovered that the English *raj* was *not* over, and the 'sahib log' speedily became much honoured by these servile people. Grain, forage, milk, bread and vegetables poured into the camp with unprecedented abundance, and no difficulty was made in furnishing such supplies as the country round afforded.[53]

In February the sepoys in Lucknow were reported to be openly despairing of being able to resist the coming onslaught, and the taluqdars saw with dismay that the tide was about to turn and leave them, like driftwood, high and dry. Raja Man Sing of Mahdauna hurriedly attempted to re-ingratiate himself with the British. He opened communications with Outram as early as mid-October and excused his conduct by claiming that he had come to Lucknow merely in order to rescue a female relative and had stayed only that he might protect the ex-King's seraglio from dishonour. He returned to Faizabad in mid-January, bringing as evidence of his good intentions the wife and three children of a European merchant of Allahabad, who had been trapped in Lucknow. He made tentative advances to the British authorities at Gorakhpur, delivered over his protégés and promised to rescue more. 'If he sees no hope of mercy', wrote Wingfield, 'he will fight; but if he thinks he has not sinned past forgiveness he will remain neutral now ... His neutrality up to the present time has paralyzed the plans of the insurgents [in south-eastern Oudh] and has made him the object of their indignation.'[54] His behaviour remained equivocal until the British advance on Lucknow in March, since he feared to cut his ties with the rebels until fully assured of absolution from the British. In the majority of the taluqdars, however, the realisation that they had allied themselves to the weaker side produced a different reaction. The prospect of losing everything engendered a new determination and so, paradoxically, it was only now, when the collapse of the rebel cause seemed imminent, that they became committed rebels. They began to sell off their Company bonds at a huge discount and resolved to take themselves off to their forts and jungles, there to cause so much trouble that the British would be glad to purchase their surrender with ancient privileges.[55] It was thus already becoming clear that the fall of Lucknow would not mean the fall of Oudh, and that regaining the lost legacy of the Nawabs might well prove an object of long and costly prosecution.

VIII

The British disliked much of what they saw in the Oudh countryside; but their dislike was tempered by admiration for the virile qualities of the rural population. Their dislike of what they saw in Lucknow was unalloyed. The opulent city offended their moral standards. They consequently felt little compunction about riding roughshod over the sensibilities of its inhabitants, and the changes that the year 1856 had brought about in the way of life of most residents were radical, in some cases even brutal.

Buildings were torn down to make way for the roads, railway lines and other 'improvements' to which Victorian officialdom was much attached but whose purpose was bound to be misunderstood by a population ignorant of the cults of steam, sanitation and slum clearance. When the deposed King, heartbroken at the accounts he received of the piecemeal demolition of the capital of his ancestors, wrote to the Chief-Commissioner to protest, he was curtly informed 'that the officer in charge of public works [was] at liberty to adopt any measure he [might] deem advantageous to the city' and that 'it was therefore inadvisable of His Majesty to trouble writing on such matters'.[1] When Henry Lawrence arrived he was alarmed by what was going on. 'The improvements in the city have gone on very fast – too fast and too roughly', he reported to Canning in April 1857. 'Much discontent has been caused by demolition of buildings etc., and still more by threats of further similar measures; also regarding the seizure of religious and other edifices and plots of ground as *nazul* or Government property.'[2] One particularly tactless instance of the appropriation of religious buildings was the conversion of the Qadam Rasul, a shrine containing a stone supposed to bear the Prophet's footprint, into a powder magazine.[3]

The luxury market of the city collapsed like an arch without its keystone when the court was abolished, and many merchants and craftsmen were faced with poverty. Other members of the trading community were threatened with the burden of double taxation, for the Judicial Commissioner insisted on his right to impose a *tah bazari,* or market ground rent, in addition to the *cungi,* or town rate levied on grain dealers, which had been inherited from the native administration. When Coverley Jackson opposed the tax, he was overruled by the Calcutta government; but Lawrence was so disturbed by the outcry that it had caused that he suspended its application on his own authority, pending further inquiry.[4] The new tax on opium caused even greater distress. In the Regulation Provinces, where almost all the opium for the China market was grown, the cultivation and marketing of the poppy were government monopolies. In the non-Regulation Provinces, whose output was mostly for domestic consumption, its cultivation was free, but all the crop had to be sold to government agents for testing and processing, and it was allowed to be retailed only by licensed vendors, who had to pay a heavy excise. The non-Regulation system was applied in Oudh, and although this meant that no restriction was placed on cultivation it did mean a sharp rise in price. So sharp, in fact, that many of the numerous addicts of Lucknow could not obtain their habitual doses, and were driven insane. [5]

Popular discontent with the new régime reached a climax in the early months of 1857, when there was a dramatic rise in the price of food grains. Millet, barley, peas and wheat all reached famine prices. Wheat, for example, retailed at sixteen and a half seers the rupee, as opposed to an average rate of nearly twenty-four seers. [6] Native petitioners attributed the increases to the wholesale pre-emptions and corrupt practices of the government corn contractors; but prices reached similar levels in Allahabad and Benares at this time, so it seems that they were rather a reflection of general shortage or prevailing political uncertainty. It is quite likely, however, that the large purchases made by government agents in Lucknow, when Lawrence was preparing for a siege, did make the situation worse.

These specific grievances were magnified by a prevailing revulsion against the crudity of British manners. The irritability, and the loud, ungracious demeanour of the new officials, together with their daemonic energy and supercilious disdain for the art and life-style of the city, jarred all the more painfully on the citizens of Lucknow because they had hitherto been shielded from contact with the British.

As it was the court that had epitomised the worst vices of Oudh society, so it was the court that bore the brunt of British resentment. Wajid Ali Shah, together with his closest relatives and advisers, left Lucknow for Calcutta soon after his deposition in order to plead the cause of his restoration; but he left behind him nearly a thousand relatives and dependents whose means of support was stipends from the interest on the various loans made by the sovereigns to the Company. Payment of these was suspended by the British pending an inquiry into the rights of each individual and the drawing up of a pension list; and since it was reckoned that the settlement of the claims of the discharged soldiers must have priority the investigation was deferred for a whole year, during which the stipendaries had nothing to live on save what they could get by selling their trinkets and begging under the cover of dark. By February 1857 Coverley Jackson was so perturbed by their miserable plight that he telegraphed for permission to make good at once six months' arrears of all substantiated claims. Permission was granted and Jackson began payment. Lawrence continued it after his arrival and speeded up the investigations; but even so, it was not until the beginning of June that the greater number of the stipendaries had received what was owing to them up to 31 December 1856.[8] *Jagirdars*, or holders of assignments on land revenue, suffered a reduction in income as a result of a new ruling which decreed that, in keeping with British revenue policy, they were henceforth to receive only half the rental of their assigned lands and that the zemindars were to keep the remainder.[9] The *mahals*, or queens, housed in the Chattar Manzil were humiliated and distressed by a hamfisted blunder on the part of Coverley Jackson. This building was among those set aside for the use of the ex-King's family, but the Acting Chief-Commissioner, apparently unaware of this, told the occupants to leave so that it could be used for government purposes. According to reports received by the King, the ladies were ejected when they refused to go, and their belongings thrown after them into the street. Canning insisted that the King had received a 'very greatly exaggerated' account of the incident, but admitted that there was a 'true foundation for the complaint'. Jackson, he reported, had been reprimanded and the building placed again at the disposal of the royal family; yet it appears from Martin Gubbins' narrative of the Mutiny that officers of H.M. 32nd Regiment still had their quarters in the palace at the time of the outbreak. [10]

The hostility of the court aristocracy was further deepened by the way in which royal custodians were pushed aside and the property under their charge confiscated and auctioned. Canning said that the complaint related to state property such as arms and the King's military stores; but he could not deny that the King's stud and menagerie had been sold without his consent and that his English library had been removed from the Qaisarbagh to La Martinière College both without his permission and in spite of the protests of his appointed guardian. [11]

Most of the civil, like the military servants of the native government found themselves unemployed after annexation. The displacement of ministers of state and important revenue officials, such as *nazims* and *chakladars,* was deemed inevitable, since they had been so closely associated with the iniquities of the old régime; but Outram, during his first term as Chief-Commissioner, felt that efforts should be made to retain the services of the host of minor officials and clerks who were threatened with loss of livelihood by the change of government. The policy was not a success. Many functionaries refused to serve under the British, and those that were employed soon had to be dismissed for corruption or incompetence. The Calcutta authorities had prescribed pensions for those with more than seven years' service to their credit; but it appears that very many were excluded from this benefit on technical grounds. [12] When Lawrence arrived in Lucknow he found it swarming with redundant human debris, the sight of which filled him with foreboding.

The city is said to contain six or seven hundred thousand souls [he wrote to Canning in April 1857] and does certainly contain many thousands (20,000 I was told yesterday) of disbanded soldiers and hungry, nay starving, dependents of the late government. There *must* be intrigue and disaffection in such a mass. I know of no incivility; but I observe angry looks. This very morning a clod was thrown at Mr Ommaney and another struck Mr Anderson while in a buggy with myself. [13]

When the mutinous sepoys poured across the Gomti on the afternoon of 30 June, they therefore entered a disaffected city. Some elements in the population were no doubt deeply dismayed by their advent. The capitalist and banking classes had no quarrel with the British, and many had invested in British securities; but the court aristocrats, unlike their counterparts in the countryside, were quick to welcome the revolt for the possibilities that it offered of retrieving lost power and privileges; and the lower classes, once the collapse of the British administration was a *fait accompli,* saw the continuation of the rebel régime as the lesser of two evils. 'Telegraph to the Governor-General', Outram instructed one of his staff officers a few days after his entry into Lucknow on 25 September, 'that my hopes of a reaction in the city are disappointed. The insurgent sepoys have inspired such a terror among all classes and maintain so strict a watch beyond our pickets, that we have not been able to communicate with one single inhabitant of Lucknow since our arrival.'[14] It is more likely, in fact, that this reticence derived from dread not of the rebels, but of the British. There is no evidence to suggest that there was any large-scale exodus of frightened citizens at the outset of the mutineers' domination, but plenty to indicate that vast numbers forsook the city as the prospect of the reassertion of British authority, and with it the perpetration of reprisals, became more certain. [15]

The first few days of July were a time of confusion. When the sepoys found themselves checked at the Residency their discipline and morale began to disintegrate and they turned to looting, drinking and hunting out the civil police, who were reckoned to be collaborators of the British. Two aspirant generals quickly recognised the necessity of giving direction to these dissipated energies, and remained throughout the struggle rival contenders for the leadership of the rebel army.

One was Raja Jai Lal Singh, a court taluqdar with lands in Faizabad District. He emerged as spokesman for the army in the first days of July and acted as medium of communication between the rebel headquarters in the Kurshid Manzil and the royal harem in the Qaisarbagh. In Lucknow, as elsewhere, bewilderment and doubt had followed the first reaction of elation at the rapid and surprising success of the revolt, and the sepoys and their native officers wanted the reassurance which only a leader qualified to bear the burden of both their allegiance and their guilt could give. The only authentic candidate was their King; but since he was in exile they had to find a substitute. This was the mission of Raja Jai Lal, and it was not without problems. The cavalry, predominantly Muslim, advocated the enthronement of Sulaiman Qadr, a brother of Wajid Ali Shah; but this plan was dropped – either because, as one report has it, the candidate declined the proferred honour, or because, according to other evidence, the Hindu infantry sepoys insisted that the throne must remain with the progeny of the deposed King.[16] Raja Jai Lal's own wishes seem to have played their part in determining the final choice. He drove a bargain with Hazrat Mahal, the only concubine in the zenana willing to commit herself to the rebellion, and agreed to present her young son to the soldiery as a child of Wajid Ali Shah in return for the recognition of himself as military leader. The boy, who was called Birjis Qadr, was accepted by the army and duly enthroned early in August; but there is evidence to suggest that not all the soliders were completely happy with the choice. Conditions were imposed which indicate reservations on their part, notably that all orders from Delhi must be obeyed and that there must be no interference in military affairs.[17] That many felt their first allegiance to be due, under the circumstances, to the Mughal Emperor is demonstrated by the arrival in Delhi, in the weeks before its recapture, of several contingents of troops from Lucknow.[18] It was probably at the army's behest, too, that tokens of allegiance were sent to the old Imperial capital by the revolutionary government of Oudh.[19]

The Catastrophe

Doubts exist about the paternity of Birjis Qadr. The royal zenana contained some five dozen concubines, so Wajid Ali Shah's children must have been numerous; but it was common gossip in Lucknow that Birjis Qadr was the son of Mammu Khan, *darogah* and paramour of Hazrat Mahal. These two certainly cohabited during the short reign of Birjus Qadr, and Mammu Khan showed great eagerness to have the boy selected for the honours of royalty; but as the date of the start of their liaison remains among the many mysteries of the harem there is no means of estimating the worth of the rumour. Probably the King himself did not know who the boy's father was. He had shown enough interest in him to grant him a *jagir*, [20] but not enough to take him to Calcutta.

Hazrat Mahal was acknowledged as regent during her son's minority and she at once made Mammu Khan her partner in power by creating him chief of the *diwan khana* or high court. This made him subordinate in rank to Sharf-ud-daula, the Kashmiri Sunni who had been minister during the days of Muhammad Ali Shah and Amjad Ali Shah, who was now made *naib*, or chief minister; but it was generally acknowledged that Mammu Khan, while far from the most able of the male triumvirate, was certainly the most powerful. The busiest was undoubtedly Raja Jai Lal Singh. He remained president of the council of state, a body composed of about twenty army officers and civilian ministers, and when this was not in session was fully occupied with the conduct of the siege of the Residency, the raising of new levies and the search for money to pay his troops. He was reported to have spent most of his time going around digging up treasure from the houses of prominent merchants and nobles, including that of the absent ex-minister, Ali Naqi Khan; [21] and his obsession with measures for the reduction of the Residency was probably caused by his knowledge that treasure worth a quarter of a million sterling was buried there.

His rival contender for the allegiance of the army was a *maulvi*, or Muslim priest, called Ahmad Ullah Shah. He was thought to hail from Multan and had been arrested in Faizabad in February 1857 for forcibly resisting the efforts of a British officer to disarm him and his followers. His belligerent behaviour, and the seditious papers found in his possession indicated that he was a *ghazi* or Islamic crusader, whose mission was the promotion of a holy war (*jihad*). Muslim militants such as this were not uncommon in northern India at that time. A movement was afoot for the regeneration of Indian Islam, inspired by the puritanical and fundamentalist doctrines of Shah Wali Ullah, a divine of eighteenth-century Delhi, and his disciple, Sayyid Ahmad of Rae Bareli. The followers of Shah Wali Ullah regarded northern India as *dar-ul-harb* ('hostile territory') as opposed to *dar-ul-islam* ('Islamic territory'), and preached that a *jihad* of the type prescribed by the Prophet was consequently incumbent on all Indian believers. They called themselves *mujahidin*, which means 'fighters of a *jihad*'.[22] In 1826 Sayyid Ahmad had embarked on a crusade to liberate the Muslim tribes of northwest India from the Sikh rulers of the Punjab, and it was his ambition ultimately to free the whole of Hindustan from *kafirs* ('infidels'). He was killed in battle against the Sikhs in 1831; but his followers remained active after his death and eagerly joined the revolt against the British in 1857. Of these the Maulvi of Faizabad was one. There is evidence that he had joined the disciples of Sayyid Ahmad at Patna, in 1821, and his connections with Multan reinforce the supposition that he had in the meanwhile been involved in the *jihad* in the northwest. His mission to Faizabad appears to have been anti-Hindu rather than anti-British, for he came to visit the tombs of the Muslims who had been killed in the religious riots of 1856 and to avenge the death of one of their leaders, a *maulvi* called Amir Ali;[23] but when the Faizabad mutineers broke open the jail and set him free he responded to the situation with true political opportunism and made his way to Lucknow to place himself at the head of both Hindu and Muslim rebels and wage a campaign of eradication against the British.

His exhortations were sound. He urged a strict prohibition on looting, an expansion of the rebel offensive to the east and a scientific reduction of the Residency by concentrated battery fire.[24] But he went largely unheeded in the early stages of the revolt. As a Muslim extremist he was naturally suspect to the

Hindu sepoys, while his Sunni beliefs precluded any ready sympathy between him and the Shia Muslims of the city and the army. Raja Jai Lal therefore managed at first to retain control of military operations and keep the Maulvi out of the council of state.[25] At one time he was ejected from the city altogether and obliged to live in the suburbs.[26] Later, however, as rebel reverses increased and the troops grew dissatisfied with the conduct of the court party, his forceful personality, holy character and military judgement commanded increasing support from all sections of the army. Jai Lal Singh and Hazrat Mahal were forced to agree to his return to Lucknow, where he began to style himself Viceregent of God and to pose a serious threat to the pre-eminence of the court faction. The Maulvi of Faizabad is a mysterious figure. The obscurity from which he emerged remains unpenetrated, and the records offer only fitful glimpses of this 'tall, lean, muscular man with thin jaws, long thin lips, high aquiline nose, deep-set, large dark eyes, beetle brows, long beard and coarse black hair falling in masses over his shoulders'. Yet he is historic, for he was almost the only individual to leave his imprint on the Indian Mutiny who was neither born great nor favoured by the great. He was, in fact, the only character approximating to a popular leader that that momentous struggle produced. His rise to power changed the character of the revolt in Lucknow. The court faction had striven to turn it into an aristocratic reaction, concerned primarily with the redress of grievances resulting from the abolition of legal, social and economic privileges. 'The honour and respectability of every person of the higher orders are considered by [the British] as equal to the honour and respectability of the lower orders', runs one of the proclamations of Birjis Qadr. 'Nay, comparatively with the latter they treat the former with contempt and disrespect, and at the instance of a Chamar [a man of one of the lowest castes] force the attendance [at court] of a nawab or a raja and subject them to indignity whithersoever they go.'[27] The Maulvi gave a different colouring to the revolt. He appealed to popular religious susceptibilities and popular fears, and under his leadership the rising briefly assumed the character of a mass movement. 'The war is now fully believed throughout Lucknow to be a religious crusade', reported a native informant in the pay of the British in November 1857, 'and crowds of people are flocking into the capital from the districts to take part in it.' [28]

The stubborn resistance of the British garrison in the Residency had, as the Maulvi was quick to realize, little military significance. It deprived the rebel leaders neither of important position nor, apart from the treasure, of important resources. Their control of the city was complete in spite of it. The defence of the Residency was a mere fight for survival. The garrison could not hope to recapture the city and whether they survived or succumbed was irrelevant in the military context of the rebellion. Yet the symbolic importance of this defence was great. For the rebels it represented a vestige of that British intrusion whose eradication was the only ambition common to them all. By providing a focus for the multifarious and often conflicting energies released by the Mutiny it imposed a semblance of direction on a phenomenon whose tendency was centrifugal. This aspect of the siege became especially important after the fall of Delhi, when the cause of Birjis Qadr attracted the fleeing cohorts of the vanquished Mughal. For the British, on the other hand, it was a symbol of tenacity and heroism; a comfort in their tribulations and a stimulant to their extraordinary dynamism. The abasement at Kanpur and Allahabad had so checked their complacency that a call for a Day of Humiliation was heard in Calcutta. Critics of the British administration in India reinforced their indictment by interpreting these events as evidence of divine retribution.

> Not without God [wrote the Christian Socialist J. M. Ludlow] have we been stricken in our dearest affections and in our bosom sins – in our domestic relations and in our national pride. Tremendous must have been the faults which needed so tremendous a chastisement ... Surely, the more we scrutinize our own English conduct the more we shall feel that the blessed English martyrs of Delhi and Kanpur have fallen victims of our own sins and our own vices, of which the passions of our rebellious Indian slaves have been but the instruments. [29]

But if the massacre at Kanpur was a sign of divine displeasure, how otherwise could the triumphant defence in Lucknow be interpreted, save as a portent of divine favour? The glory of that achievement threw into shadow the shame of Kanpur and Delhi and shone forth as a holy mandate for the continuation of the British *raj* in defiance of popular will. If the rebellion in Oudh destroyed the notion that British rule was preferred by the population, the successful defiance of that rebellion by a mere handful suggested that this rule had its sanction elsewhere than in popular consent, and reinforced that notion of themselves as an elect people which the British had imbibed with the Calvinism of their Protestant heritage. 'Not without God, surely', wrote Ludlow, 'has the fabric of that marvellous empire been upreared – the vastest, strangest ever possessed by a small people at the other end of the earth. Not without God has this marvellous struggle of the present year been maintained, by a scattered handful of Europeans, as few amidst the surging masses of an alien race as men shipwrecked on the face of a vast ocean.'[30] The plight of the Lucknow garrison provided the archetypal example of the 'few amidst the surging masses of an alien race', and it helped to ensure that the shattered liberal vision of popular Indian gratitude for the blessings of British rule would be replaced by a notion even more remarkable for its stamp of self-assurance – the high Imperialist notion of the White Man's Burden of heavenly mission and earthly ingratitude. The little band in the Residency did more than make history. In a sense they made scripture, for their refuge became one of the holy places of British Imperialism and their struggle, reiterated and glamorised in verse and prose, re-enacted on the stage and refought in spirit, summarised the Imperial ethos and furnished the Imperial dogma with all the apparatus of miracles and martyrs.

The position which the garrison defended for the first nine weeks of the siege covered an area considerably larger than the Residency compound. The northern part of the Residency grounds, which lay low beside the river, was abandoned; but to the south houses and offices of the city, including a slaughter house, a native bank and the King's Hospital, were occupied, and their inclusion increased the perimeter of the position to 2,300 yards. Apart from a ridge to the north, there were no natural features to define the enceinte. It was marked in part by the outer walls and fortified verandahs of houses, but elsewhere barriers of palisades, sandbags and mud parapet had been constructed across intersecting roads and alleys. The defences were in many places very sketchy and there were no flanking salients; but they mounted thirty pieces of artillery, in four batteries, and these compensated in large measure for their weakness. After the entry of Havelock's and Outram's force on 25 September the position was more than doubled in area. The abandoned river front was reoccupied and the eastern boundary extended to include the Farhatbakhsh and Chattar Manzil palaces and their adjacent buildings. Thirteen extra pieces of ordnance new reinforced the defences.

The rebels brought about two dozen guns, including some of large calibre, to bear on the position – from a distance of only fifty or sixty yards in several places. Their fire was generally precise, and British attempts to disable them by daring sorties and spikings were largely unavailing. The rebels had expert workmen who would drill out the spike or bore a new touch hole.[31] The rebels' infantry reserves were moreover enormous, especially after the arrival of troops from Kanpur and Delhi. Yet they were unable to adopt the obvious tactics of cannonade and assault, for they were very short of artillery ammunition and the buildings that cluttered the approaches to the Residency position – deliberately left standing by the British – deprived them of a clear field of fire. They therefore tended to use high elevation fire and aim their missiles at the interior of the British works, while the buildings that were a hindrance to their artillerists were turned to good account by their marksmen, who used them as cover for an unremitting and deadly accurate musketry offensive against the defenders at the barricades and batteries.

The rebels pinned all their hopes of breaching the British defences on mining operations, but their skill in this art was far outmatched by that of their adversaries, who promptly retaliated with countermines that destroyed their most elaborate efforts. During the first stage of the siege the rebels started no fewer than thirty-seven mines, of which twenty-five were foiled by the British engineer officers and the ex-miners of the 32nd (Cornish) Regiment. After burrowing like moles towards the tell-tale clinking and chipping of the rebels' pickaxes, they would either break through into the gallery and put the occupants to flight or lay a charge and blow them up. On two occasions the British even took the offensive in this tactic and scored remarkable successes. One of their mines, sprung on 21 August, blew up a house opposite the southern face of the defences, whence the fire of enemy marksmen had been particularly lethal, and killed, it was estimated, between eighty and a hundred men. The second mine was exploded slightly to the east of the first and eliminated all the buildings facing one of the British batteries. Eleven of the enemy mines failed through lack of expertise. In some cases the galleries were too close to the surface and caved in; sometimes the charges were insufficiently tamped, with the result that the force of the explosion travelled not upwards but back along the gallery and up the shaft, literally hoisting the miners with their own petard; and on other occasions a mine exploded only to show its dismayed contrivers that they had misjudged their underground distance or direction. The very first enemy mine gallery, which was aimed at the British north-face battery, was both wide and short. The heavy charge was sprung with great visual effect on 20 July and a party rushed to storm the expected breach; but when the smoke cleared they found that the only damage was a large crater in the ground thirty yards from their target. Two mines, one at the southern face and the other at the south-western corner, were exploded as a prelude to an assault on 5 September; but these also failed to have the desired effect, through their galleries' being too short. Their only really successful effort of this nature was made by the rebels against the southern face of the position, near the cavalry stables, where the noise of the horses prevented the detection of subterranean activities. The mine was sprung on 18 August and it made a gash thirty feet wide in the defences; but as no full-scale attack had been prepared the rebels failed to exploit their advantage. Their assault was repulsed and the breach repaired with little loss of time or men. By the middle of September the destroyed mine shafts and galleries around the Residency position had created a sort of no man's land where further digging was impossible, so the danger from mining more or less ceased. [32] It revived, however, with the extension of the position after the arrival of Outram and Havelock. During this, the second stage of the siege, the struggle was almost entirely an underground one, because artillery was of very limited use at the long range now imposed. British countermeasures were renewed with increased daring and vigour and thwarted all but a few of the enemy's efforts. By the time the siege ended British countermines extended to an aggregate of over 3,000 feet, at a depth of some 200 feet. 'I am aware', wrote Outram, 'of no parallel to our series of mines in modern war.'

The British suffered a steady toll of casualties throughout the siege. 'Harris, the chaplain', wrote Dr Fayrer in his journal on 8 July, 'has very hard work, and he does it nobly. He has five or six funerals every night in the Residency churchyard, and as these take place under fire it is a service of great danger.'[33] When the siege began the combatant defenders were about 1,600 strong, of whom some 750 were natives. This number had been reduced by about half by 25 September, but the casualties were not so heavy as this seems to indicate. Of the losses, 230 were due to desertion of sepoys, and of the 564 remaining only 228 were deaths. Many of these, moreover, were caused not by the enemy's fire but by the inadequacies of contemporary surgery. These were the days of pre-antiseptic medicine. Gangrene or tetanus would make a scratch fatal, and amputation, which the surgeons in the Residency regarded as essential in cases even of slight bone damage, invariably resulted in death. The casualties were heaviest among the European gunners, and by the end of the first stage of the siege only twenty-four out of the original seventy-three remained alive and fit for duty. 'The number of our artillery men was so reduced', reported Brigadier Inglis, 'that on the occasion of an attack the gunners – aided as they were by men of H.M. 32nd Foot and by volunteers of all classes – had to turn from one battery to another wherever the fire of the enemy was hottest, there not being nearly enough men to serve half the number of guns at the same time.'[34] Nevertheless, during the middle two weeks of September the garrison was probably as secure as it had ever been. The rebels, convinced that the whole of the defences were undermined, made no more assaults. The weather was getting cooler and provisions were still sufficient to last for weeks and even months. Poor diet and fatigue had caused a general debility among the defenders; but it was quite erroneous to suppose, as Havelock and Outram were supposing, that inanition had by this stage pushed the garrison almost to the point of surrender.

The misconception had originated with none other than Brigadier Inglis, in command of the garrison since the death of Major Banks, Lawrence's successor, on 21 July. In a letter smuggled out of the Residency on 16 August, Inglis had written to Havelock:

> Our provisions will last us ... until about 10th September. If you hope to save this force, no time must be lost in pushing forward. We are daily being attacked by the enemy, who are within a few yards of our defences. Their mines have already weakened our post and I have every reason to believe that they are carrying on others. Their eighteen-pounders are within 150 yards of some of our batteries, and from their position, and our inability to form working parties, we cannot reply to them and therefore the damage hourly is very great. My strength in Europeans is 350 and 300 natives and the men dreadfully harassed ...

It was the message of a man whose disappointment had mastered his judgement. Things were in fact not nearly so bad as he claimed. His figure for native troops implied a loss of more than 450, whereas the return of battle casualties as at 26 September showed a total of 203, which, added to the desertion figure of 230, indicates an aggregate loss, during the first stage, of only some 430.[35] When computing his European force, he obviously took no account of his civilian volunteers, who still mustered 123 effectives on 26 September and many of whom had proved good soldiers during the siege.[36] The mistake concerning food supplies appears to have been genuine, for the force was put on half rations at this time; but it could have been avoided by consultation with the commissariat officers. Gubbins and others insisted that the estimate must be false, and were proved right after the arrival of Outram and Havelock. The remaining stores were then found to be adequate to feed the combined forces for eight weeks and excess wheat had to be carried away at the time of the evacuation.[17] Water was never in short supply, because there were several good wells in the compound.

The non-combatants in the Residency, consisting of European women and children, civilian men who had not enrolled as volunteers, native servants and fifty boys of La Martinière College, totalled about 1,400 at the beginning of the siege. Their casualties were considerably lighter than those sustained by the combatants, and very few were caused by enemy fire. At the beginning of the investment the wives of the high-ranking officers appropriated the upper rooms of the Residency, reckoning that these alone afforded the airiness and comfort suited to their status. But after Miss Palmer had had her leg carried off by a round shot on 1 July and Sir Henry Lawrence had been fatally wounded by an exploding shell on the following day, they were happy to make do with more lowly quarters. The wives of the European privates, non-commissioned officers and uncovenanted civil servants took refuge in the *taikhana,* or cellar, of the Residency, where they were completely beyond the reach of the enemy's shot, shells and bullets. Of a total of 500 women and children in the garrison, only sixty-six died during the siege, and of these fifty-one were children who succumbed to the effects of malnutrition and disease.[38]

Mosquitoes, hornets, heat, rain, evil smells, lack of exercise, body vermin, poor food, disturbed sleep, dysentery, pyaemia, scurvy, ecchymosis and – loathsome above everything – the swarming, clustering flies, all made life acutely uncomfortable for the non-combatants, and some of them were afflicted in a more terrible way, by cholera, smallpox, wounds, bereavement or painful death in the overcrowded and foetid hospital. But there was no such mass suffering, no such torture of privation and wholesale destruction of the recognised pattern of life as there had been at Kanpur. High-ranking members of the garrison, in fact, lived well, with the aid of private hoards of culinary luxuries and the assistance of native servants or, where these had absconded, boys of La Martinière College seconded to domestic duties. Martin Gubbins refreshed himself with a bath and change of linen every day and treated his guests to a fare which could not by any standards be called scanty.

One glass of sherry and two of champagne or of claret [he wrote] was served to the gentlemen, and less to the ladies, at dinner. One glass of light Sauterne was provided at luncheon . . . A cold luncheon only was served, and we made an early dinner at four. By these timely precautions the supplies which we had were husbanded and the wants of our numerous guests were provided for during the whole siege . . . At dinner our chief luxury was rice puddings, of which two daily appeared on table. The eggs for these were derived from a few poultry which we had managed to preserve; and the milk from goats and two cows belonging to our guests, which were half-starved during the siege. Occasionally a plum pudding or jam pudding was made and always caused great excitement at the dinner table . . . One cup of tea was made for each person in the morning, our English maid, Chivers, presiding at the tea table; another cup of tea at the ten o'clock breakfast, and another at night. We enjoyed both sugar and milk in our tea, a luxury which few possessed besides our garrison, and this often attracted friends. [39]

Not many lived as comfortably as this; but most, it appears, had some share of extras to supplement their meagre commissariat rations. The British soldiers got their usual issue of rum throughout the siege, and their wives had tea to drink – with milk, it seems, for when they arrived at the Sikandarbagh after the evacuation they declined the tea offered them by the 93rd Highlanders because there was no milk in it. This somewhat impaired the compassion of the Highlanders, who had expected to find them starving. Nor, if we are to judge by a letter written by Outram to his wife shortly before the evacuation, did the clergymen have to renounce all comforts of the flesh. 'Tell the good Bishop', he wrote, 'the Catholic priests are well, with the exception of the usual gout.'

At first the emotional shock caused by the horrors of their situation was great; but constant exposure to danger and the sight of death soon bred an antidote of indifference, and a sense of perspective reasserted itself in which punctilios and proprieties had all their customary salience. The rituals of British Indian society survived even as their practitioners were falling, and no reaction was so strong as that provoked by an affront to its values. Class distinctions were carefully maintained, and 'ladies' held aloof from 'women'. As soon as the enlargement of the position made movement possible visits were paid and received with all the elaborate etiquette of cantonments in peacetime. 'Ladies' who had to wash their own clothes or cook their own food evoked as much compassion as those who had lost a husband or a limb, and the garrison went without bread because the native bakers had deserted and it was reckoned unsuitable that European 'ladies' – or even 'women', apparently – should get their forearms covered in flour. Martial law was supposed to prevail, but this meant little more than that when Major Banks died overall command passed to the senior military officer and the civil office of Chief-Commissioner remained unfilled. There was never any question of rigid discipline or putting the needs of the community before the interests of the individual. The various officers whose houses were within the entrenchment supervised their territory as best suited themselves, and when someone died without heirs his possessions were sold by auction. Anyone prepared to pay enough could occasionally acquire fresh supplies of sugar, tobacco, brandy, beer, ham and pickles.

As the ordeal of the Residency garrison ended, so that of the rebel government began. After the successful operations of Sir Colin Campbell in November Hazrat Mahal, Mammu Khan, Sharf-ud-daula and Raja Jai Lal Singh had to guard themselves not only against an eventual British counter-offensive, but also against the mounting hostility of an army demoralised by failure and riven with jealousies about unequal pay. The rebel troops, especially those from Delhi, now responded with increasing eagerness to the messianic promises and pretensions of the Maulvi Ahmad Ullah Shah. On 15 February he took the field in person, leading the rebel cavalry in an attack on Outram's position at the Alambagh; and when Sir Colin Campbell launched his final assault on

Lucknow in March 1858 it was the Maulvi who was the animating spirit of the resistance. The Begam worked hard to retain the leadership of the revolt by fiery personal exhortations to the troops, but, sensing that she was losing control even of the sepoys who had put her son on the throne and seeing that the taluqdars were leaving the capital for the safety of the countryside, she began to contemplate treating with the British.[40] This was a move which the Maulvi had, however, foreseen and forestalled. In November he had used his influence to secure the execution of the male prisoners brought in from Mithauli, so the court party were now both without hostages with which to bargain and deeply implicated in the one type of crime which the British were known to regard as beyond redemption. The Begam did not therefore dare to trust her adversaries; and since there can be no treaty where there is no trust she felt compelled to put such thoughts from her mind.

Anticipating that the third British onslaught would come from the same direction as the first two, the rebels constructed three enormous lines of defence across the eastern approaches to the Qaisarbagh, whose 400-yard-square enclosure they made their citadel. The first, or outermost, which was the longest, lay inside the canal from its junction with the Gomti to the Charbagh bridge. William Russell described it as 'a great railway-looking embankment'. The second subtended the angle formed by the river and Hazratganj and incorporated the eastern walls of the Kurshid Manzil and the Moti Mahal; and the third was formed by a rampart round the north-eastern face of the Qaisarbagh itself. Each of these lines consisted of earthen parapets with bastions and natural or artificial wet ditches; and a total of 127 pieces of ordnance, including several eighteen-pounder guns and large-calibre mortars and howitzers, reinforced them at strategic intervals. The rebels were, however, still short of artillery ammunition, and during the operations had to pay old women a high price to bring in expended roundshot. In addition to the three main lines of defence, barricades were erected in all the main streets and the major buildings were loopholed and fortified. It was determined that, should the principal works fail to stem the attack, resistance must be carried into the depths of the city, so houses well within the western and southern commercial quarters were defended with mud parapets and furnished with guns and supplies of gunpowder. The number of defenders is uncertain. The official British estimate of a hundred thousand is probably an exaggeration, for it is known that most of the taluqdars and their henchmen had left Lucknow by this time; but it is quite likely that the city contained fifty or sixty thousand sepoys and some few thousand untrained volunteers and levies.

The decision to attack Lucknow early in 1858 was a political one. Military wisdom, as Sir Colin Campbell pointed out to the Governor-General, was against it, because British positions to the west of Oudh, in the Doab and Rohilkhand, were still insecure and a diversion of strength elsewhere would invite a repetition of the tragedy at Kanpur. But Canning could not rest while Lucknow remained in rebel hands. Now that Delhi had been recaptured the reassertion of British power in Oudh was in his view of paramount importance.

Every eye in India [he wrote to Campbell in December 1857] is upon Oudh, as it was upon Delhi. Oudh is not only the rallying point of the sepoys ... it represents a dynasty. There is a King of Oudh seeking his own. Few people care for him, it is true; but his existence and the position he has assumed give to our success or non-success in Oudh an importance in the eyes of the native powers which they do not attach to our measures in other districts.

Campbell urged that he could not subdue the Province with fewer than 30,000 men. Canning therefore compromised and suggested that he should concentrate on Lucknow and leave the rest till later. 'I grant that, as with Delhi, so with Lucknow, we may find ourselves disappointed of a very widespread and immediate effect from its capture. We may find that the revolt in Oudh will not collapse because Lucknow is taken. Still, I hold that the active mischief which will result from leaving it untaken will be incalculable and most dangerous.' [41]

This decision was doubly vexatious to the Commander--in-Chief, because it meant that he had to spend the greater part of the campaigning season of 1857-8 relatively idle. He could not move on Lucknow immediately after his victory against the Gwalior Contingent in December, first because he did not then have at his disposal the 20,000 men and the siege train that he reckoned necessary for the operation, and secondly because he was required by the Governor-General to wait for Jung Bahadur and his Nepalese troops, who might feel aggrieved if they were denied a share in the glory and the loot. The Nepalese were delayed in their progress from Gorakhpur by lack of carriage and by commissariat mismanagement, so Campbell was forced to sit twiddling his thumbs at Kanpur while the Indian press, ignorant both of his objectives and his impediments, chafed at his inactivity and lampooned him as 'Sir Crawling Camel'. Small wonder that, as William Russell noted, Jung Bahadur was 'the present *bête noire* of our General's life'. When he finally received Canning's permission to begin operations without the Nepalese allies the harvest ripening around the camp before the Alambagh and the heavy dew of the mornings were already signalling the departure of the cold weather.

The delay did, however, enable the Commander-in-Chief to collect a formidable army – the most formidable, in fact, that the British had ever put into the field in India in a single line. Soon after he had captured Dilkusha and made it his base of operations, on 4 March, General Franks joined him from the east and brought his force to a concerted strength of over 25,000 men of all ranks, with eighty pieces of artillery. Yet the originality of this army lay less in its size than in its composition. It included over 5,000 horsemen, a cavalry proportion unprecedented in the annals of British India, and no fewer than sixteen battalions of British infantry. It was, indeed, a predominantly European force, composed in the main of regiments forming the 'army of retribution' sent out by the home government to save the Indian empire. The native contingent (comprising Sikhs, Nepalese and irregular cavalry) was outnumbered by the British, a disproportion unheard of hitherto and calculated to send a chill of fear into sepoys persuaded that British military might was a myth.

The Commander-in-Chief surveyed his army with a mixture of professional pride and paternalistic fondness and promised himself that he would on no account expose it to the destructive ordeal of street fighting. He therefore rejected Outram's plan for an attack from the west and taking the enemy lines of defence in reverse. The western end of Lucknow was a warren of lanes and alleys, many of them unmapped. 'I thought it safer to keep to the open', he wrote, 'and ... avoid all street fighting. I have always been strongly impressed with the danger of that sort of struggle.'[42] He chose instead to penetrate again by the gardens and palaces of the eastern end of the town, leaving it to the ingenuity of his engineers and the power of his artillery to overcome the obstacles that the enemy had so laboriously prepared. 'The most earnest endeavours were made,' he wrote later, 'to save the infantry from being hazarded before due preparation had been made'; and his guiding principle throughout was 'the absolute necessity for holding troops in hand, till at each successive move forward the Engineers reported to me that all which could be effected by artillery and the Sappers had been done'.[43] He decided to do what all the textbooks said a general in command of a small army should never do – divide his force and advance along two lines separated by an unfordable river. The enemy works abutted on the Gomti and, convinced that the British would never fly in the face of convention and cross the river, the rebels had not bothered to construct flanking defences on its northern bank. It was this omission that Campbell determined to exploit, by sending Outram to the northern bank to enfilade and turn their main positions preparatory to a parallel onslaught south of the river by himself.

It was a daring plan, but it worked beautifully. Outram crossed the Gomti by a pontoon bridge on the morning of 6 March with 7,000 men and an array of heavy artillery. Then, driving enemy pickets before him, he moved west along the Faizabad road. During four days and nights he gradually shifted his position up the Gomti to the accompaniment of a fortissimo chorus of artillery, sending a cascade of shot and shell across the river in advance of the main British thrust on the southern bank. On the 8th he established a battery of twelve guns which enfiladed the first line of defence so effectively that on the following day the enemy abandoned all their positions near the Gomti, leaving a way clear for the spearhead of Campbell's main advance. A further two batteries were established opposite the Shahnajaf and the Chattar Manzil, and on the 9th he reached the Padshahbagh (now the site of the University), whence he commenced bombarding the Qaisarbagh on the following morning. On the 11th he moved forward again and set up three smaller batteries to destroy the enemy works at and about the iron bridge.

South of the river, the main force began its operations on 9 March. La Martinière was bombarded and captured with little loss, and as soon as Outram's guns had compelled the enemy to evacuate the river end of their first line of defence a party was sent forward to seize the abandoned position. The attack was then pushed south and by nightfall the whole embankment had changed hands. The penetration of the city proper began on 10 March with the bombardment and assault of the Begam Kothi. Campbell reckoned that this was 'the sternest struggle which occurred during the siege', for although most of the immense garrison of 5,000 men fled when the walls had been breached in two places, a small and determined band of about 700 barricaded themselves in the dark rooms around the various courtyards and inflicted some sixty or seventy casualties before being blown up or shot through the roofs. Many were burnt alive, and their flesh emitted a nauseating bluish vapour as it crackled and roasted in its own fat.

The Begam Kothi once secured, all the important positions between the middle and outer lines of defence (the Sikandarbagh, the Shahnajaf, the Qadam Rasul and the European barracks) were seized, and preparations made for an advance into the heart of the city.

Hazratganj provided the obvious route, since this was the main thoroughfare of the eastern part of Lucknow; but, true to his resolution to eschew street fighting, the Commander-in-Chief determined to knock his way through the buildings ranged along the southern side of the avenue. The heavy guns of the artillerists and the pickaxes and crowbars of the sappers pierced the walls and partitions, and the advance was pushed forward building by building, compound by compound. 'Fancy getting into a house in Park Lane, only twice the size, with gardens and courtyards', explained Edmund Thackeray of the engineers, 'and knocking a hole in the next with sixty-eight-pounders, then bringing up the guns and knocking a hole in the next and rushing in and so on. The rebels did not understand it. They had prepared the street with batteries and loopholes etc., while we went into the houses themselves and broke through from house to house.' [44] After blasting and delving in this way for two days the British reached a small imambara. Here the middle line of defence abutted onto Hazratganj. The gunners threw up a battery — their fourteenth — and throughout the night of 13 March this building and those adjacent were bombarded by roundshot, shells and grape. A party of a hundred Sikhs led the assault at nine o'clock on the morning of the 14th, followed by British infantry and sappers with scaling ladders, crowbars and axes. The occupants offered little resistance and the Sikhs and British were able to seize, with slight loss, not only the imambara but all the buildings between it and the Qaisarbagh. The Sikhs, driven by lust for plunder, could not be restrained until they had penetrated the courtyards of the Qaisarbagh itself; so by nightfall Campbell's forces had not only turned the middle line of defence but also captured the guns of the third line and secured a lodgement within the very citadel of the enemy. Meanwhile troops from the Sikandarbagh seized the main positions on the middle line of defence and occupied all the buildings along the river as far as the Chattar Manzil; while Jung Bahadur's Nepalese, who finally arrived in camp on 14 March, threw themselves into sundry minor engagements on Campbell's left, in the southern suburbs of the city.

Events had moved fast — too fast, in fact, for the Commander-in-Chief, whose notorious caution now played him false. That afternoon Outram had wanted to capture the iron bridge and thereby block the escape of the rebels across the river. Campbell, not expecting the Qaisarbagh to fall that day, saw no reason to incur casualties by a frontal attack on the bridge defences, which he intended to seize later in reverse. Outram was therefore told that he might do as he wished only if he could be sure that it would not involve the loss of a single man. This order tied Outram's hands. The bridge remained open, and more than 20,000 rebels escaped across it that night. Sir Colin's attempts to rectify his mistake merely made it worse. On the 15th, expecting the enemy to flee towards the north or the west, he sent cavalry forces to block the Sandila and Sitapur roads; and on the 16th, in order to prevent further egress from the city, ordered Outram to recross the Gomti by a bridge of casks and take the iron bridge in reverse. The fugitives aimed for neither the north nor the west, but for the very route – the Faizabad road to the east – which Outram's manoeuvre left open. All thus escaped, to continue the war in the countryside.

Outram, now operating on the southern bank of the Gomti, drove the enemy from their riverside positions beyond the Chattar Manzil. He captured the ruins of the Residency, took the iron bridge and then continued up the river to secure the Machhi Bhawan, the stone bridge and the Great Imambara. Batteries were set up in the Residency and the Great Imambara, and these shelled the remaining enemy positions throughout the night. Thus driven ever further towards the west, the remnants of the rebel army, with the Begam and Mammu Khan at their head, took refuge in the Musabagh, a pleasure garden by the Gomti beyond the suburbs of the city. The last major engagement took place on 19 March, when Outram assaulted this stronghold, killing four or five hundred of the enemy and capturing all their twelve guns. Only the British cavalry, directed to move round from the Alambagh, south of the city, and intercept the fugitives, failed to play its part. Brigadier William Campbell lost his way amidst ravines and forests and, to the bitter disappointment of the British officers, five or six thousand rebels made their escape. [45]

Only the Maulvi, Ahmad Ullah Shah, ensconced with a band of his crusaders within a fortified serai in the south-western corner of the city, now lingered to defy the awful reality of defeat – inspired perhaps, by God's message to Muhammad: *Yea, if you are patient and Godfearing and the foe come against you instantly, your Lord will reinforce you with five thousand swooping angels.* With him was the rebel minister, Sharf-ud-daula, who was first his prisoner and then, when the Highlanders stormed their way into his position on 21 March, his scapegoat. The Maulvi fled; but Sharf-ud-daula's mutilated body remained to show the heathen and the faithful that the foe had prevailed not because of divine forsaking, but because of human treachery.

In their own estimation they had prevailed because of their powerful artillery. 'Though [the rebels] had prepared for the most desperate resistance', wrote General Napier, 'their opposition was crushed by the irresistible power of artillery directed against them from all quarters, for which they were not prepared.' This is an analysis which the casualty figures fully vindicate. The conquest of Lucknow, a city twenty miles in circumference, containing half a million inhabitants and defended by a force perhaps three times the size of their own, had cost the British 127 men killed and 595 wounded. Together these amounted to less than half the casualties incurred during the recapture of Delhi, which, although a much smaller city, was a more densely constructed one, with none of those spacious approaches that had enabled Sir Colin Campbell to avoid street fighting and bring up all his guns.

So Lucknow, Babylon of India, lay prostrate before her vanquishers, condemned to a chastisement doubly severe now that she had added the sin of defiance to those of luxury and vice. Not even from Kabul, scene of the murder of a British envoy and symbol of the most crushing humiliation that British arms had ever suffered in India, had the British exacted an atonement such as that which they now exacted from Lucknow. As it advanced, the army of conquest turned into a plundering mob, which sacked the city and carried away its vast wealth piecemeal. Palaces, houses and shops were pillaged by hordes of soldiers, camp followers and human predators from the surrounding countryside. For days they roamed the streets, smashing their way into locked buildings and digging under the floors of stifling rooms. Often they turned up nothing but trinkets and worthless lumber; but elsewhere dingy chests and boxes were broken open to reveal, like shattered flint matrices, heaps of mineral splendour. Gems were gouged from sword hilts, caskets, pipe stems and saddlery, while exquisite muslins, shawls, brocades and cloths of gold and silver, impregnated with the scent of musk and sandalwood, were dragged from the recesses of boudoirs and zenanas and swathed grotesquely round grimy, sweating bodies. Few of the plunderers had any notion of quality or value. They threw aside jade vases, reducing them to smithereens, and grabbed brass pots thinking they were gold. They sold emerald bracelets as chandelier chains and offered chandelier crystals in the belief that they were diamonds. The native camp followers carried away all they could, and after the capture of the Qaisarbagh the dusty road back to Dilkusha was thronged with twenty thousand of them, all staggering under the weight of assorted loot, while Gurkhas and Sikhs, wild with greed, struggled against the tide in an attempt to reach the source of the flowing stream of riches. The Europeans wantonly destroyed what they could not remove, and within hours of their capture the courtyards and apartments of the imambara and Qaisarbagh were ankle deep in fragments of looking-glasses, girandoles, vases, crockery, furniture, glassware and alabaster figurines, all smashed and scattered amongst the grisly debris of the recent combat. The value of prize captured in Lucknow was officially estimated at £134,000; but this represented only a tiny fraction of the true worth of the property seized or destroyed. Nothing like its real value was obtained for the property sold by the Prize Agents, since they auctioned it in Lucknow at a time when there was hardly anyone in the city save camp followers and soldiers. Valuable items were knocked down for a few rupees. Unofficial estimates put the value of the auctioned loot alone at higher than one and a half millions sterling; and there is little doubt that the greater proportion of what was captured was never surrendered to the Prize Agents but disposed of privately. The British troops were deeply suspicious of the official way of handling loot, and Outram later claimed that the orgy of wrecking in Lucknow was partly due to the determination of the soldiers that what they could not remove themselves should not fall into the hands of the government.[46]

How much booty was carried back to Nepal by the Maharajah Jung Bahadur and his men will never be known, but it is said that when they began their return journey in April they were so heavily encumbered as to be incapable of defending themselves in the event of an attack.[47] The total value of property destroyed and seized certainly amounted to many millions of pounds; but even when this is said the full extent of the damage is not stated, for much was destroyed on which it was impossible to put a price. All the records of the native administration perished, for example, a sad loss to historians.

When the din and dust of conquest and pillage had settled, Lucknow was a city of death and silence. The terrified inhabitants had fled to the countryside and the streets were empty, save for domestic fowl, pariah dogs and a few old women. In the palaces and pleasure gardens vultures gorged on decomposing corpses, and the blue sky was smudged with smoke. Slowly and cautiously, as the stench cleared and the fires burnt out, the citizens returned, to pick over their blighted homes and test the sincerity of the British assurances of peace and protection. The wreckage was cleared, the thoroughfares filled, the shops opened and the worst physical ravages of the rebellion were repaired; but Lucknow was never the same again. Its essential spirit of frivolity and pleasure had received a shock from which it could not recover. The King, the court, the spendthrifts, the patrons of music and letters did not return; and the qualities of life and art that they had nourished and that had made the city what it was, languished beyond resuscitation. The new masters cared for none of these things, and Lucknow survived the trauma of the Mutiny only to become aware, like an abandoned, ageing courtesan, that time had moved on and made her a relic; a city of shame without even a past of which she might be proud.

IX

The Governor-General was right in his prognosis that the fall of Lucknow would not mean the fall of Oudh. The struggle in the countryside continued for the better part of a year after the conquest of the capital and only after a full-scale campaign during the cold weather of 1858 was the pacification of the Province finally assured.

Yet he was also vindicated in his estimate of the political importance of retrieving the capital, for there is no doubt that, after the débâcle suffered by the rebel régime in Lucknow, the revolt lost much of its 'yeoman' character. The small landholders, seeing that the wind was changing, began to trim their sails, and the various British columns that made forays into the interior in the early part of the year encountered little hostility from them. General Walpole, for instance, making for Bareilly in Rohilkhand, reported in April from Sandila, about thirty miles west of Lucknow, that the general temper of the rural population was now friendly. 'Since the fall of Lucknow the influential people have become fully aware of the hopelessness of the struggle and their chief object now is to make the best terms they can.'[1] To the east of the capital, the road to Faizabad was reported open and safe in July. The country folk were 'decidedly not hostile' and the inhabitants of Faizabad 'manifested their joy' at the return of the British officials and their release from the oppressive yoke of the rebels.[2] The revolt had ceased to be a 'national' one and was kept alive only by exceptional circumstances and the strenuous efforts of three minority groups, one of whom derived its support from outside the Province.

The circumstances were those created by the Governor-General's insistence that Rohilkhand must be dealt with after the fall of Lucknow. This diverted troops from Oudh, and the Commander-in-Chief refused to undertake the systematic subjugation of the Province with the reduced forces remaining – much to the chagrin of the new Chief-Commissioner, Montgomery, who reckoned that Sir Colin showed too much respect for the 'rabble forces' opposed to him.[3] The reassertion of British authority in the interior was therefore delayed, and confusion reigned throughout the hot and monsoon months; but this portended no uncertain issue to the struggle. The three groups who kept alive the semblance of rebellion were the nucleus of the rebel government, the remnants of the mutinous Bengal army, and the freebooters and bandits who had sprung up during the anarchy of the revolt like weeds in a neglected cabbage patch. The simultaneous activities of these three elements created much alarm; but the situation was in fact much less serious than it seemed. Since their efforts were not, until the very end at least, co-ordinated; and since they did not feed on any large measure of popular support, they were sustained less by intrinsic strength than by the temporary British distraction, and as soon as the British confronted them in earnest they disappeared like fireflies in the morning.

After their escape from Lucknow, the court faction, headed by the Begam Hazrat Mahal (who was later joined by Raja Jai Lal Singh) and the crusaders, under the leadership of the Maulvi Ahmad Ulla Shah, at first went their separate ways. The Begam and her crowd fled northeast and ensconced themselves at Bithauli, while the Maulvi made his way towards the northwest and encamped at Bari; but neither lingered to encounter the troops of General Hope Grant, from Lucknow, and both made off towards the north-western border, where they appear to have sunk their differences and joined forces. They skirmished with detachments from the army of the Commander-in-Chief, then operating in Rohilkhand, at Muhamdi, Pali and Shahjahanpur during the early part of May; but their main intent was to gather strength for an attempt to recapture Lucknow. Their efforts to enlist the aid of Jung Bahadur of Nepal failed,[1] but they did succeed in gaining the support of the rebels of Rohilkhand, under Khan Bahadur Khan, and of Prince Firoz Shah of Delhi. It is probable indeed, that Afghans from Rohilkhand, rather than Rajputs from Oudh, now formed the mainstay of their forces.[5] By early in June the allied rebel troops, amounting to some 16,000 men, had congregated at Nawbganj, not more than twenty miles from the capital, and the inhabitants of Lucknow, fearing the worst, began to decamp in large numbers. General Hope Grant moved out to give battle with 5,000 men on 12 June, and succeeded in driving them back only after a stiff engagement. The resistance of the enemy was not, however, the only obstacle that Grant had to encounter. Thirty-three of his men were killed outright, and 250 prostrated, by the smothering heat. [6]

The rebel force fell back on Bithauli to lick its wounds, and then withdrew farther north to Baundi, in Bahraich District, where it remained inactive for the remainder of the rains. The Maulvi, however, who does not appear to have taken part in the affair at Nawabganj, continued his campaign of disruption on the north-western frontier area. On 15 June he appeared with about 500 horsemen before the stronghold of the Raja of Pawayan, near Shahjahanpur in Rohilkhand. The purpose of his visit is not known; but whatever its motive, it was the last that Ahmad Ullah ever made. A quarrel began, which developed into a military engagement. The Maulvi was shot and killed – during the combat according to one account; during a parley according to another – and as soon as he fell his head was struck off. The Raja's brother brought the dripping trophy to the British Magistrate at Shahjahanpur and claimed the £5,000 in cash and the free pardon that were the price it carried. [7]

After the fall of Lucknow the mutineers of the Bengal army and the Oudh Irregular Force rejected the leadership of the court faction and the Maulvi and went off in a mood of mingled desperation and despair to their homes in Gonda, Bahraich and the Districts in the southeast of the Province. [8] Here alone the revolt continued to be a popular one, led by taluqdars such as Lal Madho Singh of Amethi, in Sultanpur; Jyoti Singh of Charda and Hardat Singh of Baundi, both in Bahraich; Raja Devi Bakhsh Singh of Gonda; and Raja Ghulam Singh of Rampur Khasia, in Partabgarh. The revolt continued to be particularly active in the southeast, the area known as Biaswara, which was the home of so many sepoys, and it produced here a new popular leader in Rana Beni Madho

Bakhsh, of the Bais clan, paragon of Rajput valour and chivalry, whose deeds are to this day sung by village bards at the time of the Holi festival.[9] His pedigree was long and proud. It included the renowned Raja Satna of Kakori, one of the leaders of the fifteenth-century Rajput revolt against the Sharqi Kings of Jaunpur, and the eponymous hero Tilokchand, father of a line of many kings. It appears that his anger had been roused against the British at the outbreak of the Mutiny by the severe and unjust punishment of one of his kinsmen by the Commissioner of Fatehpur, and he sent 700 men and two guns under his brother to Lucknow in October 1857.[10] After the defeat of the rebel government he ensconced himself in his strong fortress at Shankarpur, in Rae Bareli District, and it was around this focus that many of the sepoy mutineers congregated after their ejection from Lucknow. The forays and excursions that they made under Beni Madho's leadership kept the country in this part of the Province in a state of anarchy for some seven months and constituted a serious threat to communications along the Lucknow–Kanpur road. But there is enough historical evidence to tarnish the shining image that Beni Madho and his followers have bequeathed to folklore. At one stage there was dissension in his camp, and a section of the sepoys rejected him and returned to the Begam;[11] and it is known besides that he was in two minds about continuing the revolt. In May he was reported to be contemplating surrender on terms, since he was prepared 'always to obey those who [were] in power'; and by the end of the month he had in fact submitted a tender of allegiance to the British.[12] By July, however, he had thought better of this. He reverted to his old guerrilla activities and in September led a contingent of 12,000 men in the defence of Sultanpur, a city which Grant attacked and finally captured. It was reported that his flirtation with the loyalist cause had been nipped in the bud by 'fears that Government [would] as before make a summary settlement for three years and then take his estates as a punishment for his offences'.[13] In fact, Beni Madho was something of an unwilling rebel, compelled to act against the dictates of prudence and inclination not only by fear of punishment, but by the peremptory canon of Rajput pride and the intransigent insistence of his Rajput followers. The same was true of Lal Madho Singh of Amethi, who found the 1,500 sepoys who attached themselves to him a severe embarrassment. He made it clear on several occasions early in the year that he wanted to declare his allegiance to the British; but he was inhibited until the last minute by fears lest the sepoys would murder him if he did.[14] It is likely that such pressures played a part in determining the attitude of many of the rebel taluqdars of the northeast and southeast. It was sepoys of the Bengal army who kept the revolt alive, just as it had been sepoys who began it, for even when other rebel elements had been conciliated or defeated, many of them still bore a guilt which could not be expiated by surrender. Men from regiments that had murdered their European officers were never offered the amnesty that was eventually extended to all other rebels,[15] and they therefore felt assured of life and liberty only so long as they eluded the British.

The predatory element endemic in Oudh society was doubly active under the conditions that obtained throughout the hot and rainy seasons of 1858. Many of the so-called mutineers of the countryside were in fact buccaneers of the perennial sort, whose malefactions had little to do with either the sepoy mutiny or the popular revolt, and whose tenuous association with these was never anything more than a marriage of convenience. Babu Ram Bakhsh, the taluqdar of Dhundiakhera in Unao District, a proscribed outlaw who had returned to Oudh at the outbreak of the disturbances, took advantage of the power vacuum to rustle and plunder at the head of a band of freebooters. Others of the same ilk were Bhagwan Bakhsh, one of the notorious Kanhpuria Rajputs of Nain, in Rae Bareli; the bloodstained Rani of Tulsipur; and, most infamous of all, Raja Digvijai Singh of Mahona in Lucknow District, whose lust for plunder had been an embarrassment even to the rebel government.[16] After the retaking of the capital he became a scourge of the countryside. 'I receive daily reports of the excesses committed by Raja Digvijai Singh', reported the Deputy-Commissioner of Lucknow District in May. 'He has armed himself to the teeth at his own fort and daily commits depredations in the country. At one time he plunders a whole bazaar ... and at another he lays waste a village and establishes a *thana* [police post] of his own.' [17]

The decisive influence in this phase of the rebellion was that of the taluqdars, the great majority of whom, outside the northeast and southeast, were now reconciled to British rule. It has often been claimed that a taluqdars' revolt occurred at this time. The threat of such an eventuality had certainly been real; but there is no evidence to suggest that it actually took place. If it had, the reconquest of the Province would have been impossible.

A taluqdari revolt seemed likely because most of the large landholders were in a desperate mood at the time of Colin Campbell's assault on Lucknow, and Lord Canning did nothing to help reassure them. He prepared for issue to the 'taluqdars, chiefs and landholders of Oudh' a proclamation which declared all the soil in the Province to be confiscated, with the exception of the estates of six chiefs mentioned for their loyalty [18] and those of any others who could prove a similar qualification. The only terms guaranteed to others who submitted (provided that they had had no part in the murder of Europeans) were life and honour, though it was promised that their claims to former rights would be considered on their merits. Canning wanted to appear lenient and was so convinced that the proclamation was conciliatory (since it absolved self-confessed rebels from death, transportation and imprisonment), that he required its publication to be delayed until after the fall of Lucknow. It might then appear a concession of strength and not a ruse of weakness. The document raised a storm of protest, and led to a ministerial crisis in London. Everybody except Canning realised that it was impotence masquerading as power, since it implied a threat that the British could not implement. The Chief-Commissioner of Oudh, Outram, predicted that its effect would be disastrous. There were 'not a dozen' landholders who had not associated themselves with the rebel régime, so it must lead to the confiscation of almost all the soil of the Province, and thus antagonise the taluqdars, many of whom were reluctant rebels, at a time when their assistance or at least their passivity was essential. He wanted to promise restoration of their lands to all taluqdars not guilty of heinous crime. Canning rejected this proposal with some indignation, claiming that it would indicate 'nothing short of capitulation to every recusant taluqdar' and 'concede a victory to rebels and . . . put a premium on insurrection'; but he did authorise the Chief-Commissioner to promise a 'large' indulgence and a 'liberal' review of their claims to all who capitulated without delay. Outram made the most of this permission. When sending the proclamation to taluqdars whom he considered uncommitted rebels, he enclosed a private circular of his own. 'The Major-General, Chief-Commissioner of Oudh', he wrote, 'in sending you the proclamation, wishes to inform you that if you act at once and come in ready to obey his orders – provided you have taken no part in the atrocities committed on helpless Europeans – none of your lands will be confiscated and your claims to lands held by you prior to annexation will be reheard.' He was telling them, in other words, to take no notice of the Governor-General. Robert Montgomery, who succeeded Outram as Chief-Commissioner in April, adopted a similar policy and 'spared no pains to make kown to the people that timely submission and faithful obedience to the paramount power would stay the execution of the sentence of confiscation'. [19]

At the same time he inaugurated a new land settlement. Its object was to reverse the effects of the summary settlement of 1856 and restore to the taluqdars the lands they had held at the time of annexation. Canning approved, for he had always intended that the lands of the Province, once confiscated, should ultimately be restored to the taluqdars. This was not because he thought that they had been hard done by in 1856. In his view the majority of them were usurpers, 'distinguished neither by birth, good service, or connexion with the soil', and had been justly dispossessed. His concern was not to redress the grievances (which he reckoned ill founded) or even reward the services (which he considered minimal and unimportant) of the taluqdars; it was rather to punish the village proprietors, who had let down the government that had stood forth as their champion. The events of 1857-8 had made it sadly clear, in Caning's view, that the Government of India had acted 'with more of chivalrous justice than political prudence' in its land policy. 'Not an individual', he wrote, 'dared to be loyal to the Government which had befriended him ... The endeavours to neutralize the usurped and highly abused power of the taluqdars by recognising the supposed proprietory rights of the people, and thus arousing their self--interest and evoking their gratitude, had failed utterly.' Canning, like most of his contemporaries, misjudged the reaction of the village communities because he failed to appreciate the difference between the intentions and the achievement of the British authorities.[20] By the time the new land settlement had been completed in 1859 the taluqdars again held over 22,000 villages in Oudh, which was only 900 fewer than the number they had held at the time of annexation.[21]

Thus neutralised by counter-proclamations and settlement operations, Canning's proclamation had little, if any, influence on the behaviour of the taluqdars. Most of those outside Gonda, Bahraich and the southeast, now that they were relieved of the popular pressure that had caused them to maintain a posture of rebellion, were content – glad in fact – to accept the terms offered by the Chief-Commissioner. The few who had remained loyal throughout could not but be encouraged to remain loyal now, and among the others there was a general movement of self-rehabilitation. It was, as usual, Raja Man Singh of Mahdauna who set an example for the majority to follow. Late in April he co-operated with the British authorities and supplied transport across the Gogra for the returning Nepalese force. The rebels from Gonda and Bahraich set upon him as a renegade and besieged him in his fort at Shahganj from the end of June until the end of July, when General Grant came to the rescue. Thereafter Man Singh worked actively in support of the British, and other taluqdars began to follow suit. The Raja of Murarmau, in Unao District, tendered his allegiance in April, and Rustam Shah of Dera, in Sultanpur, wrote to the officer in charge of the Jaunpur Intelligence Department offering to re-establish British rule if he would but come to Dera.[22] Prominent taluqdars in Kheri District were reported to be refusing to co-operate with the rebels in April,[23] and two of those in Sitapur District (Bari and Biswan) took up arms against the rebel Amil of Khairabad in June.[24] All the taluqdars of Lucknow District save two had tendered their allegiance by the beginning of May,[25] and the Raja of Tiloi in Rae Bareli was fighting against the forces of Beni Madho the following month.[26] Udresh Singh of Dhaurwa, leader of the Faizabad Rajkumars and one of the most powerful landholders in the District (as well as one of the most inveterate rebels), made his submission in July, and letters from three other taluqdars followed in August.[27] It was reckoned that most of the more powerful taluqdars had signified their willingness to submit by the end of May. By the end of June it was calculated that only about three dozen chieftains and rebel officials, holding twenty-five forts, remained actively hostile.[28] When it is recollected that the Province contained 623 strongholds and that the number of taluqdars officially recognised after the Mutiny amounted to some three hundred, it will be appreciated just how small was the number of impenitents. Even among these there were men who were not prepared to defy the British with force and who were kept in the rebel camp only by intimidation. 'There is no doubt', wrote the Chief-Commissioner, 'that there are many zemindars who are friendly to our cause and would show themselves such if they could but be sure of protection. But when they see that to proclaim themselves on the side of the British Government, without being prepared for the consequences, is to subject themselves to the immediate attacks of the rebels, the best affected amongst them are obliged to dissimulate.'[29] The truth of this assertion was demonstrated during the cold weather campaign, when all the hostile taluqdars of Bara Banki District surrendered without firing a shot.

It has been a common criticism of the British that, in making the Oudh land settlement of 1858-9 with the taluqdars, they surrendered to the very forces of feudalism that they had defeated. Such an argument is at variance with two important facts. First, the confrontation between the British and the forces of feudalism (that is, the taluqdars) that had threatened at the beginning of 1858 never occurred. There was therefore no defeat. Second, if that confrontation had taken place, outright British victory would have been impossible. The resources of the British would not have been adequate to reduce the hundreds of strongholds in Oudh, and the mere attempt must have cost thousands of lives. The taluqdari settlement averted this confrontation. It was not, therefore, a redundant concession made in the hour of victory, but a political bargain that was an essential condition of success.

The cold-weather operations of 1858 were marked by few encounters and pitched battles. They consisted of a series of pursuits, with frequent detachment of small columns. There were early stirrings in cool, Corotesque mornings; mad dashes of cavalry across fields saddle-high in corn; forced marches through boggy rice plantations, sandy wastes and uncharted forests; and Christmas dinners in tamarind groves. The brisk air, the balmy sunshine, the abounding game and the excellent provisions made the whole affair seem like a prolonged picnic after the horrors of the hot-weather operations, and officers and men revelled in it, like giants refreshed. It was a strange-looking army that the Commander-in-Chief put into the field. Scarlet and pink had almost completely disappeared from the dress of the English and Scottish corps, and in their place were the various shades of slatey grey that were the original khaki.[30] The officers had changed beyond recognition from parade-ground swells in broadcloth and lace to swaggering brigands with sola topis swathed in gaudy scarves, khaki jerkins with chain-mail shoulder pads, pistols and swords stuck casually through broad coloured cummerbunds, and baggy trousers tucked into high leather boots. The sixty-five-year-old Commander-in-Chief, hardly ever out of the saddle until injured late in December by a fall from his horse, rode at the head of his men in a frock coat and high pith helmet, with a common sabre tucked under his arm.

Sir Colin's plan was to drive all the rebels remaining in Oudh northeast across the Gogra into the triangle of territory between that river and the Nepalese hills. Here those who refused to surrender could more easily be cornered and decisively dealt with. As the troops moved ahead, the country in their rear was to be garrisoned and pacified by detachments of the newly raised Oudh Military Police, a corps which had been carefully recruited from Jats, Afghans and Sikhs.

The western side of the cis-Gogra districts was cleared by two columns penetrating from the west: one from Shahjahanpur, under Brigadier Troup, the other from Farakhabad, under Colonel Hall. Hall's main achievement was the capture of Ruia, a fort near Rudamau in Hardoi District whose owner, a Raikwar Rajput called Narpat Singh, had achieved an undeserved notoriety earlier in the year by repulsing an ill-planned assault by General Walpole. He rejected terms, claiming that he was a powerless instrument in the hands of the mutinous troops.[31] This may well have been true, because he was paralytic and therefore relatively helpless. It is even possible that he was under the thumb of a renegade European. The evidence for the presence of such a rebel amongst his men appears conclusive, though the strength of his influence may well have been exaggerated by sepoy informants anxious to mitigate their own guilt.[32] Plans were laid for a concerted attack by several columns on 28 October, but Narpat Singh fled across the Gogra with all his men and treasure under cover of dark, leaving his stronghold empty save for a few prisoners and a flock of geese. Almost equally painless was the seizure of Mithauli, the fort of the taluqdar Loni Singh, in Kheri District. This chief exchanged gunfire with Troup on 8 November, but absconded before an assault could be delivered. His fort was found to be immensely strong. It was nearly a mile square and surrounded by a ditch 40 feet deep and 30 feet wide as well as by a 40-foot belt of bamboo forest. Cannon shot made no impression at all on this living wall, which bent and blunted even hatchets of Sheffield steel. But the evacuation of this fort had not been caused by faintheartedness. The unexpectedly accurate vertical fire of Troup's mortars had wrought havoc amongst the garrison, and they left more than 400 dead to prove it. Loni Singh provides a rare instance of a taluqdar who, having began as an equivocal rebel, was turned by circumstances into a committed one. He sent no reply, made no excuses when summoned by Troup to submit under the terms of the Queen's Proclamation, doubtless because he felt himself excluded, for having surrendered his European fugitives, from the benefits of the amnesty.[33]

Most of the rebels from these western Districts were successfully herded across the Gogra by Troup and Hall, acting in conjunction with Brigadier Barker from Lucknow, who supported their operations by ejecting the enemy from Sandila and Birwa, two strongholds in Hardoi District. The only rebel leader who slipped the net was Prince Firoz Shah. With about 1,500 men, he doubled back to the Ganges, crossed it and the Jumna, and joined the enemy in central India.

The flushing operation in Baiswara, or the southeast, was under the immediate supervision of the Commander-in-Chief, who had about 20,000 men, 11,000 of them British, for the purpose. Brigadier Wetherall, acting in advance of the main force, entered Oudh from Allahabad late in October and on 2 November captured Rampur Khasia, in Partabgarh District, a fort held with 4,000 men, most of them sepoys, by Ram Ghulam Singh, the Kanhpuria leader. But Wetherall lost over a hundred men in the assault, a toll which well indicates how severe a strain on British resources widespread taluqdari resistance would have imposed. On joining Wetherall Sir Colin Campbell – or Lord Clyde, as he had now become – prepared to deal with Amethi, the stronghold of the long prevaricating Lal Madho Singh. This chief, on being sent a peremptory demand for surrender, appeared in person in the British camp; but his men, whom he had eluded by slipping out of the fort under cover of darkness, were, he said, preparing to resist. Dispositions were made for an assault early on 11 November; but the garrison decamped during the night and when Lord Clyde took possession of the fort he could find no trace of the thirty guns it had been reported to contain. He flew into a rage, and accused Lal Madho of having tricked him. The trembling culprit revealed the hiding places of sixteen cannon, but there was no trace of the others, which the fugitives had clearly removed.[34]

Most of the sepoys who fled from Rampur Khasia and Amethi took refuge with Rana Beni Madho at Shankarpur. He was probably less than delighted with the compliment. It seems that he was personally still inclined to surrender, for on 13 November he sent a *vakil* to the British camp to inquire what terms the Commander-in-Chief offered. But Lord Clyde had already made it clear that his submission must be unconditional. 'He must . . . come out at the head of his sepoys and armed followers and with them lay down his arms in the presence of Her Majesty's troops.'[35] There is no doubt that, even if he had been prepared to comply, his followers, now amounting to some seven and a half thousand men, would never have allowed him to do so. This was the very heart of Baiswara and the still potent animosity of the population was clearly visible in the 'beclouded countenances of the villagers around, who receive us with distrust and dissatisfaction'.[36] Beni Madho abandoned his fort during the night of 15 November and, agile and slippery as a fish in water, darted away across the countryside no one knew whither. 'We have "certain" intelligence that he is at all points of the compass at exactly the same hour of the same day', wrote William Russell, 'and we have not thirty-one columns to verify these reports.' Finally authentic news came that he was making for Dhundiakhera, the lair of the outlaw Babu Ram Bakhsh, near the Ganges in Unao District. Lord Clyde caught up with him there on 24 November and engaged and defeated the combined rebel forces; but the remnant dispersed, the main part making a frenzied attempt to flee across the Ganges, while Beni Madho himself disappeared in a cloud of dust towards the north. He was next heard of on 6 December, when he was reported to be encamped close to the Gogra. At once the Commander-in-Chief was in the saddle and off to catch him before he crossed the river. Hooves pounding and gun limbers bouncing, the cavalry and horse artillery tore mile after mile through villages, over water courses, across stony fallow and new-ploughed arable land. They covered ten miles in forty-five minutes, and arrived foaming, steaming and too late. The calm river lay before them, a ribbon of water in a belt of silt three miles wide, and Beni Madho was already on the other side.

All the most refractory of the Oudh rebels, amounting to about 30,000 sepoys and 20,000 assorted levies and retainers, led by the Begam, Raja Jai Lal Singh, Mammu Khan, various rebel officers and perhaps a dozen taluqdars, now lay pent up in the north-eastern corner of the Province. This was the time for Lord Clyde's decisive blow. For two weeks he stalked them, and they retreated ever farther, beyond Sekrora, beyond Bahraich, into the desolate waste of grassland, marsh and tropical jungle that lay under the Himalayan foothills. Here, amidst the wandering herds of wild deer and nilgai, chilled by winds from the mountains and drenched by winter rain, the sepoys began to feel very far from home. Large numbers decided at last to risk the perfidy which their leaders had assured them was the hallmark of the British character, and surrendered under the terms of the amnesty. Within a month or two only 20,000 oddments from the vagrant and mutinous populations of the Province remained to provide an army for the rebel generals and a court for the rebel queen. Again Hazrat Mahal and Beni Madho sent to know what terms their adversaries offered. But it was as if they were trying to escape the trammels of their own destiny. Lord Clyde would promise them no more than their lives, and demanded that they come forth with all their followers and lay their arms at his feet. Pride, and the unwavering recalcitrance of those sepoys who knew themselves precluded from pardon, made surrender on such terms impossible. They turned their thoughts instead towards Nepal, an independent state where the British could not follow them and whose ruler might perhaps be moved by the plight of a fallen queen and her ailing son. The hope was faint, but it seemed the brighter for the extinction of all the rest. Lord Clyde guessed their intentions and groped his way grimly through a moonless night in an endeavour to defeat them at Banki before they crossed the border.

They were sighted on the morning of 31 December in a position not far from the Rapti river, with jungle behind and to their left and a wide swamp in their front. The British infantry turned their left under cover of the jungle, and captured three guns, while the cavalry turned the swamp to their right. The rebels withdrew into the jungle to the rear, turned and replied with a few shots, then fled on again into the plain beyond. Hotly pursued, they divided into two parties. One made for the Nepal hills, startlingly near, to the northwest; the other for the river Rapti, a few miles to the east. Impelled by a furious momentum, the British cavalry pursued the second party to the banks of the river and, in a cascade of spray, plunged in headlong after the frantic fugitives. The swift and icy waters frothed, swirled and turned briefly red around a struggling mass of men and horses. But the British troopers had just ridden thirty miles, and were in no condition to keep up the chase. Large numbers of the rebels were killed or drowned; but the majority escaped to the northern bank of the river, where they joined the remnants of the first party and withdrew into the hilly fastnesses of Nepal.

That, dramatic though it was, was not quite the end of the story. Maharaja Jung Bahadur, the prime minister of Nepal, hesitated to commit himself on the issue of the rebels' extradition. He was reluctant to offend the British by granting them asylum; but he feared to antagonise his own troops by seizing and surrendering them. So the Begam and her followers lingered for months in the borderland, occasionally making forays into the territory that was once their homeland, but invariably forced back into the inhospitable hills and jungles of the country of their exile. A few, including Mammu Khan, Loni Singh of Mithauli and Raja Jai Lal Singh, ultimately gave themselves up to the British authorities, and Digvijai Singh of Mahona and Babu Ram Bakhsh of Dhundiakhera were captured. The others, comprising the Begam herself, the Raja of Gonda, Beni Madho, the Rani of Tulsipur and perhaps half a dozen taluqdars, remained outlaws, and finally died of exposure or disease. The Begam appears to have been a virtual prisoner of the sepoys, and in her mortification she heaped invective on their heads, complaining that they had made goats of herself and her son, who had never sought their support and patronage.

Jai Lal Singh and Babu Ram Bakhsh were tried and hanged for complicity in the murder of Europeans; Loni Singh and Digvijai Singh were transported to penal settlements in the Andaman Islands. These sentences were exceptional in their severity. Penitent rebels were generally treated with leniency. Confiscation of their lands plus removal on a small state pension to some centre outside Oudh was the typical punishment. A total of 364 people were brought to trial for rebellion in Oudh. Of these 23 were executed, 115 transported, 13 imprisoned for less than three years, 27 flogged, 47 fined and 139 acquitted.[37] About fifty individuals, ranging from powerful taluqdar to petty co-sharer, had their lands confiscated.[38]

This reprisal was mild indeed in comparison with the mass executions that took place after the recapture of Delhi, Kanpur, Benares and Allahabad. The hysterical screams for vengeance had subsided with the fear that had inspired them, and as the British reasserted their strength and repaired their damaged pride their attitude grew more constructive and magnanimous. The old rancour and hatred disappeared, and rebel leaders who had fought with bravery and honour were not denied the final accolade of the admiration of their enemies. If the British were in the end forbearing victors it was, in part at least, because they felt, like Shakespeare's Mark Antony, that they would rather have such men as their friends than enemies.

PART FOUR: EPITAPH FOR A PRINCELY STATE

*No tawdry rule of kings,
But toil of serf and sweeper —
The tale of common things.*
                    Kipling

X

Most of the taluqdars of Oudh had, as we have seen, entered into the rebellion at the behest of their retainers and the petty landlords under their protection; yet the view which prevailed after the Mutiny (and which has prevailed ever since) was that these lower classes had followed the taluqdars, out of 'feudal' loyalty and an overriding sense of attachment to the old order of things. This interpretation strengthened the conservative view of Indian society as an organic whole in which the territorial aristocracy had its essential function. The Mutiny was seen as an awful warning to those who had spurned the taluqdars as an anachronistic and baneful encumbrance with no place in the affections or the loyalties of the people. 'Whatever the abstract idea of justice', wrote Montgomery, the new Chief-Commissioner, 'the fact remains important and incontrovertible that the superiority and influence of these taluqdars form a necessary element in the social constitution of the Province.'[1] Canning, who was really motivated by pique against the village landholders, enunciated this view as the rationale behind the new land settlement with the taluqdars. He claimed that the village proprietors had shown themselves indifferent towards their own rights and in favour of the taluqdari system. It therefore behoved the government to restore that system and to acknowledge the general importance of the native territorial aristocracy. 'The maintenance of a territorial aristocracy in India', he wrote, 'wherever we have such an aristocracy still existing, is an object of so great importance that we may well afford to sacrifice to it something of a system which, while it has increased the independence and protected the rights of the cultivators of the soil and augmented the revenue of the state, has led more or less directly to the extinction or decay of the old nobility of the country.'[2]

Those taluqdars of Oudh who had not put themselves beyond redemption by heinous crime or stubborn recalcitrance thus emerged from the Mutiny much stronger than they had been even during the days of the native government. Men of the class that had but a few years previously been reviled as an incubus now found themselves, to their own amazement, regarded as a pillar of the British Raj. Their lands were restored and confirmed to them by legal guarantees, and those conspicuous for services to the British were loaded with honours and rewards. Man Singh of Mahdauna, Digvijai Singh of Balrampur and Hardeo Bakhsh of Katiari were all made Knight Commanders of the Star of India and granted the title Maharaja; and vast additions transferred to their estates from the confiscated territories turned them into princes in more than name. Thirty taluqdars were vested with the powers of either Magistrate and Collector or Assistant Magistrate and Collector within their estates, and full-scale durbars were held by the Governor-General in Lucknow and in Calcutta for the formal investiture of this new order of nobility.[3]

The members of the first generation wore their newly acquired plumage gauchely. They remained illiterate, churlish Rajputs, more at home in the fields and jungles than in the perfumed chambers of the great. But by the time their grandsons had inherited their lands and titles an extraordinary cultural metamorphosis had taken place. The typical taluqdar was no longer a spare and dusky robber-baron but a portly, tawny imitation of an English country gentleman; an old boy of the Colvin Taluqdars' College, dressed in English suit and patent leather shoes, who would show his guests the family album, offer them champagne and cigars and chat with them about estate management and world affairs. The crude mud fort with its farmyard population had disappeared, and in its place had risen up a mansion of solid masonry, with stuffed tigers, mock baronial fireplace, potted aspidistras, ormolu clocks, mezzotints of the Lake District and portrait of Queen Victoria.

The court aristocracy, however, enjoyed no such rehabilitation. All the hopes which Wajid Ali Shah had cherished of eventual restoration were dashed by the Mutiny. How serious those hopes had been is indicated by the fact that he continued to refuse to sign the treaty of abdication, thereby sacrificing a pension of £120,000 a year. In June 1856 a deputation led by his brother, his mother and his eldest son, and comprising a total retinue of 140 people, set sail for England in order to lay his case before the British Parliament and Crown. It was an ill managed pathetic affair. Soon after their arrival the leaders of the royal party were received by Queen Victoria; but then came news that rebellion had broken out in India and, even more calamitous, that Wajid Ali Shah had been arrested as a suspected sympathiser. Few people in Calcutta seriously believed that he was an instigator of the Mutiny; but on 13 June 1857 a Muslim from the King's large entourage at Garden Reach had been caught trying to seduce from his allegiance a sentry at Fort William, whom he assured that the King's followers were preparing to seize the fort. Canning decided to incarcerate Wajid Ali Shah to save him from his own friends, and every effort was made to spare him indignity and undue discomfort. In England, however, the finer shades of his motive were lost and the stigma attached to imprisonment and suspicion destroyed what sympathy the plight of the deposed monarch had aroused. [4] The petition for the redress of his grievances which was laid before the House of Lords on 6 August had to be withdrawn on a technicality. The climate of opinion at this time was so obviously inauspicious that the royal party finally abandoned their mission and sought permission to leave the country and proceed on a pilgrimage to Mecca. The queen mother died in Paris in January 1858, *en route* for Egypt, and was buried with Islamic rites in the Muslim cemetery of Père Lachaise. The King's brother returned to London, where he also died, leaving substantial property which an English court awarded to Wajid Ali's eldest son. This prince, a youth of seventeen or eighteen years, moved to Paris and then to Calcutta, where he passed the remainder of his life in idle socialising and poetasting. [5]

On his release from confinement after the Mutiny Wajid Ali Shah found he had lost the taste for martyrdom. He agreed at last to withdraw the petition still pending in London and accept his pension. [6] His crown jewels, worth £60,000, which had been preserved in the Lucknow Residency throughout the siege, were also restored to him,[7] and thus fortified with means to support his clamouring dependents and courtiers he installed himself again in his palatial mansion at Garden Reach. Here he enjoyed the wealth, the leisure and the prestige tinged with pathos that are the perquisites of the more fortunate monarch in exile, waxing even fatter and growing even more prodigal now that he had no Resident to sermonise him. His vast, tax-free wealth was frittered away on all the pleasures to which he had become addicted – women, wild animals, music, dancing and poetry – and until he died in 1887 something of the spirit of old Lucknow lingered on in this exclusive residential quarter of Calcutta. Wajid Ali never abandoned his posture of grief and melancholy, and in his verse he continued to pine for lost loves and joys; but even he must have appreciated, in the brief moments when he ceased from self-pity, that history is not always so generous to fallen princes.

Lucknow city underwent many changes in the post-Mutiny years, alike of destruction, reconstruction and decay. Much of the old town was swept away to make room for new military defences. The Machhi Bhawan, the iron bridge and the Residency were strongly fortified, and all the buildings between and around them levelled to make a clear field of fire. Husainabad quarter, by the river to the west, was thus cut off from the city and turned into a separate village, and the riverside palaces to the east were left isolated and exposed in a wilderness of rubble and weeds. Three broad, straight avenues were driven through the heart of the city from the west, the south and the southeast to converge on the Machhi Bhawan; and the site of a spacious new military cantonment was marked out beyond the canal to the southeast, absorbing most of the park of Dilkusha. A new suburb began to grow up around Charbagh, which became the site of the Lucknow railway station.

While the British remained in India, Lucknow was assured of a certain prominence. It was a Provincial capital until 1877, when Oudh was amalgamated with the North-Western Provinces; and then revived in importance in 1921, when it became the seat of the government of the North-Western Provinces, re-named the United Provinces in 1902. The city, because of its memorials of the Mutiny, meant much to the British, and the flag which they hoisted over the ruined Residency in March 1858, and kept flying night and day for ninety years, acquired an almost mystical significance. The pock-marked Residency ruins were preserved with religious care, and the Residency grounds, where hundreds of the victims of the siege lay buried under lawns and flower beds, became something of a shrine to which, as a battered, weather-worn notice to this day sternly warns, 'motor lorries, buses, carts, ekkas, elephants and persons with head loads' were not admitted.

But by the time the British left the subcontinent, in 1947, Lucknow had long ceased to be the major city of northern India. All the incentives to revival and growth had passed it by. Industry had gone to Kanpur, the 'Manchester of India'; Muslim learning and letters to Deoband, Hyderabad, or the new Muslim university at Aligarh; metropolitan wealth and society back to Delhi, re-created the Imperial capital in 1911; and later the European and American tourists concentrated on Delhi and Agra, whose architectural monuments had found more favour with those Western writers who formed popular taste. After 1947, moreover, with the creation of the separate Muslim state of Pakistan, Muslim energies and preoccupations in the subcontinent were largely devoted to the consolidation and defence of the new homeland, and those of the faith remaining in India felt, as a minority existing under Hindu domination and by Hindu sufferance, neither encouragement nor inclination for the self-advertisement of cultural efflorescence.

Thus Lucknow, a Muslim creation, has never regained its old commercial and cultural importance, and it is doubtful that its population today is much larger than it was in the last days of the native dynasty. It continues to be the capital of the largest province in India (now called Uttar Pradesh); but the new Hindu rulers, with their incongruous cultural values and Sanskritised speech (aggressively promoted as an official language) have taken possession in the manner of cuckoos or hermit crabs. They do not belong.

The few foreign visitors who go there today find a large but quiet town beside a pretty river, still served regularly by the northern and north-eastern railways, but only infrequently and incidentally by the domestic airline. The fascination of an old Indian market town remains, for the commercial quarters are relatively untouched by alteration and decay. Here time, instead of conquering, has itself been conquered. The bazaars in Aminabad and Chowk come alive at evening, and only the ubiquitous cycle rickshaws seem to belong to the present century. In the main Chowk Bazaar, a street scarcely wide enough for a man to walk down with his arms extended, everything is much the same as it was a hundred and fifty years ago – the open-fronted shops, with displays of embroidered shirts and waistcoats, hookahs, condiments, perfume, shoes, paper kites, enamel étuis and silver jewelry; the smell of spices and fresh jasmine; the sound of silver being beaten to making wrappings for sweets. Prostitutes still tout for custom from the carved balconies above the shops, just as von Orlich described in 1843. But there is little that is now recognisable as the painted, fairy city of the princes. The new Indian rulers' attitudes towards the Nawabi period and its culture are hostile ones, largely inherited from the British, and they have made no attempt to preserve the architectural heritage of the city. The Kurshid Manzil and Constantia still stand, assured by the posthumous liberality of Claude Martin of a flourishing life as La Martinière Girls' and Boys' Schools; but many of the old edifices, including the Daulat Khana, most of the Qaisarbagh, the Farhatbakhsh and the Moti Mahal palaces and both the original bridges, have disappeared without trace, while the others lie crumbling and neglected, unrescued from the ravages of monsoon, flood and earthquake and unprotected from the slow but inexorable reclamation of time. The Chattar Manzil, once the United Services Club and now the Central Drugs Research Institute, has lost its roof kiosks and domes. The slender pillars that used to flank the central archway of the Rumi Darwaza have snapped off, and vegetation has begun its insidious work of destruction in the higher masonry. The once gleaming *chunam* façade of the Bara Imambara has become blistered and blackened, and from a distance the building is now suggestive of a row of decaying teeth. The domes of the adjacent mosque are disfigured by weather stains, excoriation, sprouting vegetation and broken finials. The riverside entrance of the Shahnajaf Imambara has been washed away. Dilkusha is a ghostly ruin. The yet splendid tomb of Saadat Ali Khan lies locked up and untended in an overgrown garden. These monuments ill sustain scrutiny by day, but still repay a visit on a spring or autumn evening, when the light is kinder to their blemished complexions and the glowing western sky sets off their magnificent profiles. At evening too they teem again with life, for then among their cupolas and parapets thousands of parakeets gather, verdigris-green and vermilion-beaked, whose cachinnation would persuade you that all the dead of Lucknow had awakened, and joined in a frenzied recapitulation of ancient revelry.

APPENDIX 1

Treaty between the Honourable the East-India Company and his Excellency the Nawaub Vizier-ool-Mumaulick Yemeen--ood-Dowlah Nazim-ool-Moolk Saadut Alee Khan Behauder Mobaurez Jung, for ceding to the Company, in perpetual Sovereignty, certain Portions of His Excellency's Territorial Possessions, in Commutation of the Subsidy now payable to the Company by the Vizier.

Whereas, by the Treaty now subsisting between his Excellency the Vizier and the Honourable the East-India Company, the Company have engaged to defend His Excellency's dominions against all enemies; and to enable them to fulfil that engagement his Excellency is bound by the aforesaid Treaty to pay to the Company, in perpetuity, the annual subsidy of seventy-six lacs of Lucknow sicca rupees, and is further bound by the said Treaty to defray the expense of any augmentation of force which, in addition to the number of troops stipulated in the Treaty, shall be judged necessary to enable the Company to fulfil their engagement of defending his Excellency's dominions against all enemies: and whereas it is advisable that the funds for defraying these charges be established on a footing which shall admit of no fluctuation of either increase or decrease, and shall afford satisfaction and security to the Company in regard to the regular payment in perpetuity of all such charges, the following Treaty, consisting of ten articles, is concluded, on the one party, by the Honourable Henry Wellesley and Lieutenant-Colonel William Scott, on behalf and in the name of his Excellency the Most Noble the Marquess Wellesley, K.P., Governor-General for all Affairs Civil and Military of the British Nation in India, by virtue of full powers vested in them for this purpose by the said Governor-General; and on the other part, by his Excellency the Nawaub Vizier-ool-Mumaulick Yemeen-ood-Dowlah Nazim-ool-Moolk Saadut Alee Khan Behauder Mobaurez Jung, in behalf of himself, his heirs, and successors, for ceding to the Honourable the English East-India Company, in perpetual sovereignty, certain portions of His Excellency's territorial possessions, in commutation of the former and augmented subsidy, and of all other sums of money now chargeable to his Excellency on account of the Company's defensive engagements with his Excellency.

Appendix 1

Article I. – His Excellency the Nawaub Vizier hereby cedes to the East-India Company, in perpetual sovereignty, the under-mentioned portions of his territorial possessions, amounting in the gross revenue to one crore and thirty-five lacs of rupees, including expenses of collections, in commutation of the subsidy, of the expenses attendant on the additional troops, and of the Benares and Furruckabad pensions.

Statement of Jumna Chuckla Corah Kunah and	Rupees	A	P
Chuckla Etawah	55,48,577	11	9
Rehr and others	5,33,374	0	6
Furruckabad and others	4,50,001	0	0
Khairaghur and others...............	2,10,001	0	0
Azimghur and others: Azimghur Mownan Bunjun	6,95,624	7	6
Goruckpore and others, and Butwul	5,49,854	8	0
Goruckpore	5,09,853	8	0
Butwul............................	40,001	0	0
Soobah of Elahabad and others	9,34,963	1	3
Chucklah Barellie, Asophabad and Kelpory	43,13,457	11	3
Nawaub Gunge Rehly and others	1,19,242	12	0
Mohoul and others, with the exception of the Talook of Arwul	1,68,378	4	0
Total Jumna ... Lucknow Sicca Rupees ...	1,35,23,474	8	3

The above-mentioned muhals being ceded to the Company as held by the Aumils in the year 1208 Fusly, no claims are to be hereafter made on account of villages or lands which in former years may have been added to, or separated from, the said muhals.

Article II. – The subsidy which, by the second Article of the Treaty of 1798, his Excellency engaged to pay to the Company (now that territory is assigned in lieu thereof, and of the expenses of the additional troops) is to cease for ever, and his Excellency is released from the obligation of defraying the expenses of any additional troops which at any time may be required for the protection of Oude and its dependencies whether of the countries ceded to the Company, or the territories which shall remain in the possession of his Excellency the Vizier.

Article III. – The Honourable the East-India Company hereby engage to defend the territories which will remain to his Excellency the Vizier against all foreign and domestic enemies; provided always, that it be in the power of the Company's Government to station the British troops in such parts of his Excellency's dominions as shall appear to the said Government most expedient; and provided further, that his Excellency retaining in his pay four battalions of infantry, one battalion of Nujeebs and Muwatees, two thousand horsemen, and to the number of three hundred Golandauze, shall dismiss the remainder of his troops, excepting such numbers of armed Peons as shall be deemed necessary for the purposes of the collections, and a few horsemen and Nujeebs to attend the persons of the Aumils.

Article IV. – A detachment of the British troops, with a proportion of artillery, shall at all times be attached to his Excellency's person.

Article V. – That the true intent and meaning of the first, second, third, and fourth articles of this Treaty may be clearly understood, it is hereby declared, that the territorial cession being in lieu of the subsidy and of all expenses on account of the Company's defensive engagements with his Excellency, no demand whatever shall be made upon the treasury of his Excellency, on account of expenses which the Honourable Company may incur, by assembling forces to repel the attack, or menaced attack, of a foreign enemy, on account of the detachment attached to his Excellency's person, on account of troops which may occasionally be furnished for suppressing rebellions or disorders in his Excellency's territories, on account of any future change of military stations, or on account of failure in the resources of the Ceded Districts, arising from unfavourable seasons, the calamities of war, or from any other causes whatever.

Article VI. – The territories ceded to the Honourable Company by the first article of this Treaty shall be subject to the exclusive management and control of the said Company and their officers; and the Honourable East-India Company hereby guarantee to his Excellency the Vizier, and to his heirs and successors, the possession of the territories which will remain to his Excellency after the territorial cession, together with the exercise of his and their authority within the said dominions. His Excellency engages, that he will establish in his reserved dominions such a system of administration (to be carried into effect by his own officers) as shall be conducive to the prosperity of his subjects, and be calculated to secure the lives and property of the inhabitants; and his Excellency will always advise with, and act in conformity to, the counsel of the officers of the said Honourable Company.

Article VII. – The districts ceded by the first article of this Treaty shall be delivered over to the Company's officers from the commencement of the Fusly year 1209, corresponding with 22d September Anno Domini 1801, and his Excellency will continue to pay the subsidy and expense of the additional troops from his treasury, in the same manner as hitherto observed, until the Company's officers shall have obtained complete possession from his Excellency's officers of the countries so ceded. The Company will not claim any payments of subsidy from his Excellency's treasury, after their officers shall have obtained possession of the said districts from the officers of his Excellency.

Article VIII. – The contracting parties, with a view of establishing such a commercial intercourse between their respective dominions as shall be mutually beneficial to the subjects of both States, hereby agree to frame a separate commercial Treaty. In the meantime it is agreed, that the navigation of the Ganges, and of all other rivers where they may form the mutual boundary of the two States, shall be free and uninterrupted; that is to say, that no boats passing up and down the Ganges or other rivers, where they form the mutual boundaries of both States, shall be stopped or molested for duties, nor shall any duties be exacted from boats which put to, in the possessions of either of the contracting parties, without intention of landing their goods. It shall, however, be in the power of both Governments to levy such duties as they may think proper on goods imported into, or exported from their respective dominions, not exceeding the present usage. It is further stipulated, that no exemption from duties on articles purchased in his Excellency's reserved dominions, for the consumption of the troops stationed within the Ceded Territories, shall be claimed after they shall have been delivered over to the Company's officers.

Article IX. – All the articles of former Treaties, for establishing and cementing the union and friendship subsisting between the two States, are to continue in full force; and all the articles of the Treaty concluded by the late Governor General, Sir John Shore, on the part of the Honourable the East-India Company, and his Excellency the Vizier, in the year 1798, not annulled by this Treaty, are to remain in force, and continue binding upon both contracting parties.

Article X. – This Treaty, consisting of ten articles, having been settled and concluded in the city of Lucknow, on the 10th day of November in the year of our Lord 1801, corresponding with the second of the month of Rujeeb of the year 1216 Hijjuree, the honourable Henry Wellesley and Lieutenant-Colonel William Scott have delivered to the said Vizier one copy of the same in English and Persian, sealed and signed by them; and his Excellency the Vizier has delivered to the Honourable Henry Wellesley and Lieutenant-Colonel William Scott another copy, also in Persian and English, bearing his seal and signature; and the Honourable Henry Wellesley and Lieutenant-Colonel William Scott engage to procure and deliver to his Excellency the Vizier, within the space of thirty days, a copy of the same, under the seal and signature of his Excellency the Most Noble the Governor-General, when the copy under their seals and signatures shall be returned.

A true copy:
(Signed)   N. B. EDMONSTONE,
 Secretary to Government.
(Signed)   C. R. CROMMELIN,
 Acting Chief Secretary to Government.

APPENDIX 2

A List of the Nawabs and Kings of Oudh

Mirza Nasir

1. Saadat Khan (Burhan-ul-Mulk) 1720-39 — Another son
2. Safdar Jung 1739-56
3. Shuja-ud-daula 1756-75
4. Asaf-ud-daula 1775-97
5. Wazir Ali 1797-98
6. Saadat Ali Khan 1798-1814
7. Ghazi-ud-din Haidar 1814-27
8. Nasir-ud-din Haidar 1827-37
9. Muhammad Ali Shah 1837-42
10. Amjad Ali Shah 1842-47
11. Wajid Ali Shah 1847-56

Notes

Abbreviations

Blue Book	Parliamentary Papers, House of Commons, 1856, no. C2086 (vol. 45, pp. 341ff.)
Freedom Struggle	*Freedom Struggle in Uttar Pradesh* (ed. Rizvi and Bhargava)
Gazetteer	*Gazetteer of the Province of Oudh* (1877)
Home Misc.	Home Miscellaneous Records
I.O.L.	India Office Library and Records
Mins of Ev., 1832	*Minutes of Evidence taken before the Select Committee of the House of Commons on the Affairs of the East India Company* (1832)
Oudh Papers	*Papers Respecting a Reform in the Administration of the Government of His Excellency the Nawab Vizier* (1824)
Pol. Cons.	Political Consultations
Pol. & For. Cons.	Political and Foreign Consultations
Pol. Letter	Political Letter
P.P.C.	Parliamentary Papers, House of Commons
P.P.L.	Parliamentary Papers, House of Lords
1832 Report	*Report on East India Affairs from the Select Committee of the House of Commons* (1832)
Sec. Cons.	Secret Consultations

Section I

1 In the vernaculars the name is Awadh. These satraps also ruled Rohilkhand and Allahabad for many years.
2 The so-called Mughals (or Moguls; the word means Mongol) were in fact Chagatai Turks. Their homeland was Transoxiana in central Asia. They invaded India in 1398 under Tamerlane but did not set up permanent dominion there until 1526, when Babur, fifth in descent from Tamerlane, seized Delhi from the last of the Sultans of the Lodi dynasty.
3 Pol. Letter from Bengal, 13/xi/19.
4 Bengal Pol. Cons. 20/xi/19, no. 58. See also Bengal Pol. Cons., 24/iv/19, no. 59.
5 Bengal Pol. Cons., 22/iv/20, nos. 23-5.
6 India Pol.& For. Cons., 11/xii/47, no. 192; 6/x/49, no. 130.
7 Pol. Letters from Bengal, 21/x/20, paras. 103-36; 22/ii/28, paras. 5-19, 46-64; C. J. Brown, 'The Coins of the Kings of Awadh', *Journal and*

Proceedings of the Asiatic Society of Bengal, vol. VIII, no. 6, 1912.
8 Heber *Narrative of a Journey*, II, p. 45; Archer, *Tours in Upper India*, p. 21.
9 'An Account of Lucknow', *Asiatic Annual Register*, vol. II, 1800, p. 97.
10 There seem to be two theories concerning the origin of this symbol. One is that it derived from the fish which was the vehicle of Khwaja Khizr, a prophet who, according to Islamic legend, drank of and presided over the well of immortality sought by Alexander the Great. The other is that it derived from the order of Mahi-o-Maratib, instituted in pre-Islamic times by Khusru Parviz, King of Persia and bestowed as a high honour by the Mughal emperors.
11 Pol. Letter from Bengal, 17/iii/20; Kaye, *Sepoy War*, III, p. 435n.; von Orlich, *Travels*, II, p. 96; Abu Talib, *History of Asaf-ud-daula*, pp. 72-3. The bridge was designed by John Rennie, whose work included Waterloo Bridge.
12 India Pol. Cons., 27/ii/37, nos. 34-5. The canal is known as Ghazi-ud-din's canal, presumably because Nasir-ud-din intended it as a memorial to his father.
13 *Asiatic Annual Register*, vol. VI, 1804, pp. 9-10; Abu Talib, *History of Asaf-ud-daula* pp. 30-1, 57.
14 The old elaborately contrived, rhythmical and rhyming Persian was still the principal medium for prose works, but Urdu prose was produced too. The most notable examples are Insha's tale *rani kethi ki kahani* (1809) and Sarur's *fasana-e-ajaib* (1842). The significance of the former depends less on the exclusively Hindi content of its vocabulary than on the fact that it is straightforward prose written at a time when Amman's *bagh-o-bahar* was regarded as revolutionary because of its idomatic, non-literary flavour. It was in fact disparaged as such by Sarur.
15 In 1828 the King decided to extend the period of observation of Moharram from ten to forty days: Bengal Pol. Cons., 22/viii/28, no. 12.
16 Ibid., no. 11.
17 *Travels*, II, p. 104.
18 India Pol. & For. Cons., 8/ii/50, no. 150.
19 According to sources quoted by Masud Hasan Rizvi Adib in *urdu drama aur istej*, part II, pp. 45-50, Amanat was commissioned to write the drama by Wajid Ali Shah, whose interest in opera had been stimulated by the performances of a French courtier. Adib discredits the story on the grounds that Wajid Ali Shah (1847-56) had no European courtiers and that Amanat, owing to a speech impediment, never went to court. The first claim is quite untrue and the second, while substantiated, does not necessarily rule out court influence. Indeed, Adib himself points out, *indar sabha* was modelled on the *rahas* made popular by Wajid Ali Shah; but the idea of operatic influence, even indirect, via the *rahas*, does seem far-fetched. Save during the reign of the Anglophil Nasir-ud-din, European music of the non-military kind was not appre-

ciated at the court of Lucknow. In the time of Ghazi-ud-din Mr and Mrs Lacey, professional singers from Calcutta, were engaged, but failed to please; and Wajid Ali Shah engaged a European singer called Mario only to require him to give up vocalising and beat a drum for himself to dance to. For the Laceys see Bengal Pol. Cons., 24/iv/23, nos. 16-19, 7/xi/23, nos. 48–50; for 'Mario', Hare, *The Story of Two Noble Lives*, II, p. 153. Rosen (*Die Indersabha des Amanat*, p. 6) calls the play 'a Vishnuite *yatra* [mime play] in Islamic form'.
20 *Narrative of a Journey*, II, pp. 92-3.
21 *Voyages and Travels*, I, p. 164.
22 India Pol. Cons., 27/ii/37, no. 31.
23 India Pol. Cons., 6/iii/37, no. 95.
24 Pol. Letter to Bengal, 25/x/20, para. 88.
25 Pol. Letter to Bengal, 6/iv/25, para. 120.
26 Pol. Letter from Bengal, 10/vi/31, para. 199; India Pol. Cons., 23/i/37, no. 31: 27/ii/37, nos. 32-3; 13/iii/37, no. 29.
27 India Pol. Cons., 23/i/37, no. 31; 13/iii/37, no. 29. Abraham Roberts was also the father of Lord Roberts of Kandahar, but all published material relating to the family omits mention of the liaison which resulted in this Eurasian progeny.
28 Pol. Letters from Bengal, 1/viii/31, paras 33-4; 11/xi/31, para. 12; Bengal Pol. Cons., 5/iii/32, nos. 47, 48. Gardner left Lucknow in 1833 and never returned. He died in 1835 (Bengal Pol. Cons., 9/v/33, no. 32).
29 India Pol. & For. Cons., 16/vi/49, no. 89.
30 Bengal Pol. Cons., 28/x/31, nos. 31-2. Captain Herbert was later succeeded by Colonel Wilcox. Herbert's diary of his stay in Lucknow is printed by D. B. Diskalker, 'Foundation of an observatory at Lucknow', *Journal of United Provinces Historical Society*, July 1937.
31 *Asiatic Annual Register*, vol. III, 1801, pp. 34-9; Valentia, *Voyages and Travels*, I, pp. 163-5.
32 Bengal Pol. Cons., 2/ix/31, nos. 95-6; 16/ix/31, nos. 51-4; India Pol. Cons., 27/ii/37, no. 31; 6/iii/37, nos. 92, 95.

Section II

1 Pol. Letter from Bengal, 13/vi/23, paras. 153–3.
2 Bengal Pol. Cons., 30/ix/31, no. 19; 5/iii/32, nos. 54, 55; Pol. Letters from Bengal, 1/x/32, para. 216; 31/x/32, para. 225; Herbert's diary in Diskalker, 'Foundation of an observatory', *Journal of U.P. Historcal Society*, July 1937, pp. 23-4.
3 Bengal Pol.Cons., 19/ii/30, no. 33; Mundy, *Pen and Pencil Sketches*, p. 17; Fanny Parks, *Wanderings of a Pilgrim*, I, p. 182; Fayrer, *Recollections*, p. 87.
4 Bengal Pol. Cons., 14/x/29, nos. 77, 78, 81, 82.

5 Pol. Letter from Bengal, 30/xi/16.
6 Pol. Letter from Bengal, 15/iii/22.
7 Ibid.
8 Stocqueler, *Memoirs and Correspondence of Major-General Sir William Nott*, II, p. 175.
9 Bengal Pol. Cons., 19/v/20, nos. 18, 19.
10 Low's personal circumstances are explained in his letter to Bentinck dated 18/xi/33: Home Misc., vol. 828.
11 Stocqueler, *Memoirs and Correspondence*, II, p. 332.
12 It was Warren Hasting's failure to honour this pledge of protection, and his instigation of Asaf-ud-daula to plunder his mother, that constituted the matter of one of the articles of his impeachment. The pledge was renewed in 1784 and again in 1798, on the accession of Saadat Ali Khan.
13 Pol. Letter from Bengal, 1/i/17, paras. 100-46.
14 See below, section III, for details of all these loans.
15 P.P.L., 1859, Sess. 2, no. 74, p. 47.
16 Paton, *Abstract*, p. 120.
17 *Oudh Papers*, pp. 268-9, 274-5, 280, 286, 321-2, 411-13, 425, 434, 444, 476. Tahsin Ali Khan was regarded with special favour by the British since, as a result of his confidential relationship with Asaf-ud-daula, he had been able to provide the evidence necessary to disqualify Vizier Ali Khan from the succession in 1797: ibid., p. 596.
18 Pol. Letters from Bengal, 8/v/29; 3/x/30; 1/viii/31; 21/xi/33; Emma Roberts, *Scenes and Characteristics of Hindustan*, II, pp. 152-3. Aga Mir died in Kanpur in 1833. Investigations of claims against the property left in Lucknow dragged on over several years.
19 Pol. Letters from Bengal, 22/ii/28; 3/x/29.
20 Paton, *Abstract*, pp. 121-2, 126-7, 130.
21 Pol. Letters from Bengal, 3/vii/28; 10/vii/34; India Pol. & For. Cons., 21/xi/46, no. 287; 11/xii/47, no. 202; Paton, *Abstract*, pp. 114-18; Sleeman, *Journey*, I, pp. 282-3, 286, 288-94, 297-304.
22 Paton, *Abstract*, p. 143.
23 Bengal Pol. Cons., 27/xi/29, no. 18.
24 Pol. Letter from Bengal, 26/xii/29, para. 77.
25 Pol. Letter from Bengal, 22/ii/28.
26 See Ricketts to Amherst, 25/viii/23; I.O.L. MSS EUR/F/140, no. 95.
27 Pol. Letter to Bengal, 1/x/28, paras. 21-39; Pol. Letter from Bengal, 9/x/30.
28 Documentary sources for this affair are voluminous. The most important are: Bengal Pol. Cons., 27/xi/29, nos. 18, 19; 26/xii/29, no. 16; 29/i/30, nos. 20, 24; 18/ii/31, no. 71; 6/v/31, no. 16; Pol. Letters from Bengal, 9/x/30, paras. 40-63; 29/iv/31; 1/viii/31; 'Memorandum' bound in Pol. Letters from Bengal, vol. 27, after folio 189. There is a reference to the affair in Trevelyan, *Life and Letters of Lord Macaulay*, II, pp. 153-6.

29 See Mrs Mir Hasan Ali, *Observations on the Musulmans*, p. 28.
30 Bengal Pol. Cons., 29/viii/31, no. 15.
31 For Low's integrity see Ursula Low, *Fifty Years with John Company*, p. 141; Low to Metcalfe, 25/iv/35: Home Misc., vol. 738, ff. 363 et seq.

Section III

1 See Appendix 1.
2 Article 6 of the treaty reads: 'His Excellency engages that he will establish in his reserved dominions such a system of administration ... as shall be conducive to the prosperity of his subjects and be calculated to secure the lives and property of the inhabitants; and His Excellency will always advise with, and act in conformity to the counsel of, the officers of the said Honorable Company.'
3 Bengal Pol. Cons., 30/ix/31, no. 3; Spry, *Modern India*, I. p. 237; P. P. L., 1859, Sess. 2, no. 74, para. 317. The number of *chaklas* appears to have been reduced to twelve at some time between 1831 and 1839: see Varma, *Wajid Ali Shah*, p. 34; Butter, *Southern Districts of Oudh*, pp. 97-8. Of the three lists available, no two are the same.
4 This is the figure given by Sleeman for the ten years 1838-48 and adopted by Outram: see *Blue Book*, p. 90. An assessment of the revenues for 1830 appears in a report from Maddock, Bengal Pol. Cons., 30/ix/31, no. 3, which gives total income as 128 lakhs. But it is not clear whether this figure, which is adopted by Spry, *Modern India*, I, p. 237, refers to the estimated revenues or to the net amount realised.
5 India Pol. Cons., 12/ix/36, no. 73.
6 Najm-ul-ghani Rampuri, *Tawarikh-e-Awadh*, cited by Varma, *Wajid Ali Shah*, p. 34.
7 India Pol. Cons., 6/iii/37, no. 92. See also Bengal Pol. Cons., 30/ix/31, no. 3; Sharar, *Guzashta Lakhnau*, pp. 57–8.
8 India Pol. Cons., 23/x/38, no. 48; 1/ii/43, no. 77; Sleeman, *Journey*, I, pp. 61, 65. See also Mirza Rajjab Ali Sarur's description of Amjad Ali, cited in Varma, *Wajid Ali Shah*, p. 62.
9 Benett, *Gonda Settlement Report*, p. 36.
10 Elliot, *Chronicles of Oonao*, p. 132; *Gazatteer*, I, pp. xlix-lii; III, p. 417. The term *nizamat* was an old one, but it was Saadat Ali who first used it in this sense. The number of *nizamats* varied according to the demand for large revenue contracts; and the failure of a *nazim* to fulfil his obligations could result in the break-up of the farm into smaller units. This happened to the extensive tracts farmed by Almas Ali Khan after his death. See *Oudh Papers*, pp. 118-19.
11 Pol. Letter from Bengal, i/viii/31, para. 36.
12 E.g. the case of Shah Behari Lal. See Bengal Pol. Cons., 26/viii/31, no. 21.
13 Paton, *Abstract*, p. 92.

14 Sleeman, *Journey*, I, pp. 139-40; P.P.L., 1859, Sess. 2, no. 74, paras. 97, 126-9; Bhatnagar, *Awadh under Wajid Ali Shah*, pp. 160-1; India Pol. Cons., 12/ix/36, no. 73.
15 *Gazetteer*, III, pp. 438-9.
16 See below, section V, for a more detailed account.
17 *Oudh Papers*, p. 71. See also ibid., pp. 68, 94-5, 100-10, 118-19.
18 Bengal Pol. Cons., 30/ix/31, no. 3.
19 P.P.C., 1852-3, no. 692, p. 38.
20 See, for example, Heber's testimony in *Narrative of a Journey*, II, pp. 88-9.
21 India Pol. Cons., 12/ix/36, no. 73.
22 India Pol. Cons., 20/ix/41, no. 40.
23 Bengal Pol. Cons., 30/ix/31, no. 3.
24 Sleeman, *Journey*, II, pp. 42-3.
25 India Pol. Cons., 20/ix/41, no. 40.
26 Ibid.
27 Irwin, *Garden of India*, pp. 138-9; Benett, *Gonda Settlement Report*, p. 32; *Gazetteer*, III, pp. 38-9; Sleeman, *Journey*, I, pp. 152-3, 163-5.
28 Metcalf, *The Aftermath of Revolt*, p. 190.
29 *Oudh Papers*, p. 13.
30 Pol. Letter from Bengal, 10/ix/24, para. 135.
31 *Oudh Papers*, p. 128.
32 Pol. Letter to Bengal, 1/x/28, para. 15. See also letter dated 9/xi/25, para. 156.
33 *History of the Political and Military Transactions in India during the Administration of the Marquis of Hastings*, II, p. 410.
34 *History of British India*, II, p. 484.
35 *Oudh Papers*, p. 13.
36 Ibid., pp. 73, 131-2, 167-73.
37 Documents relating to this affair are in ibid., pp. 161-237.
38 Pol. Letters from Bengal, 31/v/26, para. 129; 27/vii/26, para. 122.
39 P.P.C., 1858, no. 125, p. 17.
40 *Oudh Papers*, p. 554.
41 Ibid., pp. 331-49, 509.
42 Ibid., p. 988.
43 Ibid., p. 853.
44 It is worth remarking that Lady Nugent, who visited Lucknow a few years before, formed the same opinion. 'I should not think', she wrote, 'that Major Baillie's manner of proceeding with [the Nawab] is good; the views of Government would, probably, be more readily carried into effect by a more conciliatory tone and less of an air of equality, indeed, almost superiority.' *Journal*, I, p. 306.
45 *Oudh Papers*, pp. 900, 920, 967, 974.
46 Bute, *Private Journal*, I, pp. 174-225; *Oudh Papers*, pp. 919-27.
47 Ibid., pp. 966-91. Baillie returned to England after his dismissal and carried on his vendetta against Hastings in London. It is said that he

threatened to impeach Hastings for his financial transactions in Lucknow, and that he was given his Directorship in the Company in order to keep him quiet. See William White, *The Prince of Oude*, pp. 52. 65.
48 *Oudh Papers*, pp. 987-8.
49 Ibid., p. 993.
50 Pol. Letters from Bengal, 3/i/17, paras. 312-19; 31/vii/23, para. 9. See also section I, above.
51 Pol. Letter from Bengal, 22/ii/28.
52 *Oudh Papers*, p. 266; Pol. Letters from Bengal. 10/ix/24, para. 134; 31/v/26, paras. 129-36.
53 Pol. Letter from Bengal, 29/ii/28, paras. 110-13.
54 Pol. Letter from Bengal, 9/x/30, para. 16.
55 *Oudh Papers*, pp. 659, 696; Pol. Letter from Bengal, 10/ix/24, para. 132.
56 *Oudh Papers*, pp. 681-4, 690-5; Pol. Letters from Bengal, 22/ii/28; 7/vii/17, para. 173; Spry, *Modern India*, II, pp. 252-3. For the character of Ghazi-ud-din, see Bute, *Private Journal*, I, p. 227; Sharar, *Guzashta Lakhnau*, pp. 51-5; Ricketts to Amherst, August 1823: I.O.L. MSS EUR/F/140, no. 59.
57 Bengal Pol. Cons., 30/ix/31, no. 3.
58 Pol. Letter from Bengal, 9/v/23. He was popularly believed to have blood on his hands. Sleeman, *Journey*, I, pp. 49-53, retails all the details.
59 Bengal Pol. Cons., 5/viii/31, no. 71.
60 Home Misc., vol. 828.
61 Pol. Letter from Bengal, 9/x/30, para. 18; Bengal Pol. Cons., 5/viii/31, nos. 5, 71.
62 Bengal Pol. Cons., 30/ix/31, no. 19.
63 Bengal Pol. Cons., 22/viii/28, nos. 11, 12; 23/x/29, no. 40; 30/ix/31, no. 3; India Pol. Cons., 23/ix/36, no. 92; Spry, *Modern India*, I, pp. 242-4.
64 Paton, *Abstract*, pp. 104-5, 108; Low to Bentinck, 7/ix/32: Home Misc., vol. 828.
65 Paton, *Abstract*, p. 109; Bengal Pol. Cons., 19/xii/33, no. 23; India Pol. Cons., 23/xi/35, no. 42; 12/ix/36, no. 73.
66 India Pol. Cons., 14/xi/38, no. 48; *Gazetteer*, I, p. liii.
67 India Pol. Cons., 20/ix/41, no. 40; India Pol. & For. Cons., 1/ii/43, no. 77.
68 India Pol. Cons., 14/xi/38, no. 48.
69 India Pol. & For. Cons., 1/ii/43, no. 77; 29/xi/45, no. 186; von Orlich, *Travels*, II, pp. 90, 106; Sharar, *Guzashta Lakhnau*, pp. 62-3; Varma, *Wajid Ali Shah*, pp. 60-2.
70 India Pol. & For. Cons., 21/xi/46, no. 87.
71 Figures given by Davidson for the three years 1842-4 (ibid.) show a progressive decline in receipts. Sleeman's figures (*Blue Book*, p. 90) show a decline over a longer period (1840-4) but seem dubious in view

Notes to pp. 72-81

of Low's assertion that the full amount due for 1841 had been received (India Pol. & For. Cons., 1/ii/43, no. 77). Sleeman's and Davidson's acutal amounts differ widely. There is no way of knowing which is nearer the truth, and any estimate is bound to be too conjectural to be of any value.

72 India Pol. Cons., 3/viii/40, no. 59.
73 Home Misc., vol. 828.
74 India Pol. Cons., 6/iii/37, no. 96.
75 *Mins. of Ev.*, 1832, sec. VI, p. 10.
76 *Oudh Papers*, p. 853.
77 India Pol. Cons., 20/ix/41, no. 40. Even during the reign of Nasir-ud--din Low had been averse to assumption, and had advocated instead deposing the King in favour of a more amenable member of the royal family. See India Pol. Cons., 6/iii/35, no. 94.
78 P.P.C., 1858, no. 125, p. 38.
79 Pol. Letter from Bengal, 9/xi/16; P.P.C., 1822, no. 415; 1834, nos. 197, 344; Philips, *The East India Company*, p. 284; Paton, *Abstract*, p. 152.
80 The government had become involved as a result of Ricketts's plea for support for the creditor, who had allegedly foregone his claim in 1825 in order to enable the King to meet the Company's request for a loan. The claim may have been spurious, and Ricketts's solicitude on the banker's behalf seemed very suspicious. See Pol. Letters from Bengal, 8/v/29; 9/x/30; 11/xi/31; Bengal Pol. Cons., 2/vii/30, no. 30; 26/viii/31, nos.19-21.
81 India Pol. Cons., 12/ix/36, no. 73; Paton, *Abstract*, pp. 153-4.
82 Secret Letter from Lord Moira, 31/viii/15: Secret Letters from Bengal, vol. 16.
83 *Oudh Papers*, pp. 952, 1027.
84 Ibid., pp. 714-15, 719.
85 Bute, *Private Journal*, II, p. 225.
86 Secret Letter from Lord Moira, 31/viii/15: Secret Letters from Bengal, vol. 16; *Oudh Papers*, p. 1031.
87 Ibid., p. 1033.
88 Ibid., p. 1035.
89 Ibid., p. 989; Marquis of Hastings's 'Summary of Events': 1832 *Report*, General Appendix II, p. 132.
90 Bengal Pol. Cons., 16/ix/25, nos. 36, 42, 47; 23/vi/26, nos. 6-8; Pol. Letter from Bengal, 27/vii/26; Paton, *Abstract*, p. 90.
91 Pol. Letter from Bengal, 3/x/29.
92 Pol. Letters from Bengal, 1/x/32; 22/viii/33; 13/iii/34; 10/vii/34; 13/xi/34; Bengal Pol. Cons., 7/i/33, nos. 2-5; 13/iii/34, no. 18.
93 Colvin, *John Russell Colvin*, p. 81.
94 Pol. Letters from Bengal, 31/xii/32; 9/v/33; Bengal Pol. Cons., 11/i/28, nos. 20, 24; Low to Bentinck, 7/ix/32: Home Misc., vol. 828; Fanny Parks, *Wanderings of a Pilgrim*, I, p. 190; Archer, *Tours in Upper India*, I, p. 6; Sleeman, *Journey*, II, pp. 137-8, 170.

95 The children of the King's deceased elder paternal uncle, Shams-ud-daula, were excluded by the Muslim law of inheritance, which, in the event of there being no children or brothers, puts the claims of surviving paternal uncles before those of cousins.
96 P.P.C., 1837-8, no. 599.
97 Auckland to Low, 25/vii/37: Home Misc, vol. 828.
98 P.P.C., 1858, no. 125.
99 Home Misc., vol. 828.
100 India Sec. Cons., 25/ix/37, nos. 1-12.
101 Home Misc., vol. 838, f. 416.
102 P.P.C., 1858, no. 125. By 13 Geo. III, c. 63, full powers of declaring war and making treaties of peace or alliance were vested in the Governor-General in Council. This power was limited (33 Geo. III, c. 52) only in cases of declaring war, or of entering into any treaty for making war, and of entering into any treaty of annexation, in which cases the prior sanction of the Court of Directors was required. The treaty of 1837 came under none of these classifications. The mere fact, therefore, of its having been disallowed by the home authorities was not sufficient to make it null. A formal instrument of abrogation by the Governor-General in Council was also required.
103 The speaker was Lord John Manners: see Ball, *History of the Indian Mutiny*, II, p. 460.
104 P.P.C., 1856, no. 102; *Blue Book*, pp. 226-7; India Pol. Cons., 12/vii/42, nos. 74, 78; 19/x/42, nos. 110, 116.
105 Figures derived from the MS records tally approximately in total with those given in the Parliamentary return, P.P.C., 1856, no. 102. But details in the latter are defective. It omits a $3\frac{1}{2}$ lakh deposit made by Ghazi-ud-din, the 30 lakh subscription of 1832, and all the 1842 loans; but it includes a 28 lakh subscription for 1831-2, of which no mention appears to exist in the records. It also includes the 50 lakh loan of 1826 twice, by counting as a second loan what was in fact merely a conversion from a temporary loan to a permanent one. There were various repayments of principal made at different times, mainly on the deaths of stipendiaries in receipt of interest, so the balance due to the King did not increase *pari passu* with the growth of the amount invested. The balance due in 1856 was, according to the Parliamentary return, some eighteen million rupees, or nearly two millions sterling.
106 Two cases at least are on record – that of William Lacey, organist of the Scottish Kirk, Calcutta, and that of John Sinclair, architect and engineer in the Company's service. See Bengal Pol. Cons., 24/iv/23, no. 18; 7/xi/23, no. 48; 12/i/27, no. 60.
107 India Pol. Cons., 15/v/37, nos. 3-5; Emily Eden, *Letters from India*, I, p. 340.

Section IV

1. Sharar, *Guzashta Lakhnau*, p. 71.
2. India Pol. & For. Cons., 11/xii/47, nos. 200, 201.
3. *Freedom Struggle*, I, p.217.
4. Lee Warner, *Life of Dalhousie*, I, p. 98.
5. Home Misc., vol. 828.
6. Cited by Mead, *The Sepoy Revolt*, p. 43.
7. Lee Warner, *Life of Dalhousie*, II, p. 317-18; Baird, *Private Letters of Dalhousie*, p. 33.
8. Baird, ibid., p. 344.
9. Sleeman, *Rambles and Recollections*, I, p. 321.
10. Ibid., I, p. 340.
11. Ibid., I, p. 227. Sleeman did not, however, favour the indiscriminate abolition of the native states, and for a somewhat cynical reason: 'If the people had not before their eyes such specimens of native rule to contrast with ours, they would think more highly than they do of that of their past Muhammadan or Hindu sovereigns and be much less disposed than they are to estimate fairly the advantages of being under ours' (ibid., I, p. 322).
12. Sleeman, *Journey*, II, p. 397.
13. Ibid., II, p. 413.
14. India Pol. & For. Cons., 19/iv/51, nos. 163, 165; 13/vi/51, nos. 145, 147; 30/iv/52, nos. 197, 210, 219-37.
15. India Pol. & For. Cons., 6/ii/52, nos. 216, 221, 226; 19/iii/52, nos. 174, 176, 177; 27/viii/52, nos. 60, 63.
16. India For. & Pol. Cons., 30/iv/52, no. 234.
17. Sleeman, *Journey*, II, p. 411.
18. Ibid., II, p. 418.
19. Ibid., I, pp. lx-lxv, lxxi.
20. *Blue Book*, pp. 165-6.
21. Ibid., p. 157.
22. Sleeman, *Journey*, II, p. 51.
23. Ibid., II, pp. 51, 60-61.
24. India Pol. & For. Cons., 21/xi/46, no. 87.
25. Outram's report, and its appendices, are to be found in the *Blue Book*.
26. Baird, *Private Letters of Dalhousie*, p. 363.
27. *Blue Book*, pp. 181-8.
28. Cited in Knighton, *The Private Life of an Eastern King*, p. 217.
29. On p. 154, for example, the author describes, in great detail and with the implication that he had been present, a tiger fight which took place before a visiting Commander-in-Chief. This can only refer to Lord Combermere's visit of 1827. Yet earlier (pp. 84-5) he talks of the Ricketts scandal (1829) and says that it all occurred before he arrived in Lucknow.
30. Most notably from Mrs Mir Hasan Ali and Major Archer.

31 *Edinburgh Review*, vol. 102: October 1855, p. 417.
32 *Blue Book*, pp. 192-219.
33 Baird, *Private Letters of Dalhousie*, p. 363.
34 *Blue Book*, pp. 234-6.
35 Baird, *Private Letters of Dalhousie*, p. 369.
36 Bengal Pol. Cons., 30/ix/31, no. 3. This view is still expressed by Indian and Pakistani writers. Sadiq, in his excellent *History of Urdu Literature*, says: 'As I see it, the sensuality of Lucknow, as it is called, is the direct result of the influence of wealth, security, and leisure on a pleasure-loving and degenerate people, who had utterly lost their martial traits and who, moreover, were encouraged by the British in their love of pleasure, the more to weaken and exploit them' (p.414). Varma, in his study of Wajid Ali Shah, writes: 'The Company and the Resident were inwardly satisfied that this should be so – that the King should be distracted from business, in order that the opportunity might arise for devouring Oudh' (p. 71).
37 Irwin, *The Garden of India*, p. 174.
38 Cited in Russell and Islam, *Ghalib: Life and Letters*, p. 154.
39 Lee Warner, *Life of Dalhousie*, II, p. 326.

Section V

1 James Tod, *Annals and Antiquities of Rajesthan,* ed. William Crooke, Oxford, 1920.
2 For a summary of both sides of the argument see Daniel Thorner, 'Feudalism in India', in Rushton Coulbourn (ed.), *Feudalism in History*. Valuable new insights have been added by Richard G. Fox, *Kin, Clan, Raja and Rule*.
3 'With his lord he lives a patriot or dies a traitor . . . It is a rare thing for a Rajput to betray his thakur, while instances of self-devotion for him are innumerable . . . Base desertion . . . is little known and known only to be execrated. Fidelity to the chief, *swamidharma*, is the climax of all virtues': Tod, *Annals and Antiquities*, I, pp. 183, 200.
4 Cited by Thorner, loc. cit., p. 140.
5 See the account of the Rautar Rajputs, in *Gazetteer*, II, pp. 421-2, for a good example of miscegenation between Brahmins and indigenous population as the producer of a new Rajput group. The same source also recounts that the ancestor of the Kalhans clan of Bara Banki, one Achal Singh, was reckoned to have been of *angrez* (English, European) stock. Such a claim does not exceed the bounds of possibility, for all sorts of ethnic oddments were undoubtedly swept up and absorbed into the Rajput class during this period of confusion.
6 *Annals and Antiquities*, II, p. 736.
7 *Oudh Papers*, pp. 248, 250, 252.
8 *Journey*, I, p. 167.

Notes to pp. 125-146

9 W. H. Russell, *My Diary in India*, II, p. 314.
10 On infanticide see Sleeman, *Journey*, I, pp. 267-8; II, pp. 28-9, 33, 37-8, 48, 60; Raikes, *Notes on the North West Provinces of India*, p. 18n. 20, 33-40.
11 *Gazetteer*, II, p. 251.
12 Ibid., II, pp. 256-7. The Muslim scholar Qureshi claims that the same features characterised Rajput rule in northern India in the pre-Muslim period. See *The Muslim Community of the Indo-Pakistan Subcontinent*, pp. 104-5.
13 Note, however, that the title of Raja, once conferred, tended to stick and be handed down even when the estate that it represented had been much divided. Thus the Tilokchandi proprietor of Murarmau in Rae Bareli District was still called Raja in 1856, even though he had by then lost all but a minute portion of the ancestral estate.
14 The same thing had happened in Rajputana. Tod wrote: 'The extent to which [subdivision of fiefs] is carried on in some of the Rajput states is ruinous to the protection and general welfare of the country. It is pursued in some parts till there is actually nothing left sufficiently large to share ... The system in these countries of minute subdivision of fiefs is called *bhayyad* or brotherhood': *Annals and Antiquities*, I, p. 202.
15 Thomas Fortescue, *Report on the Revenue System of Delhi Territory, 1820*, cited by S. C. Gupta in *Agrarian Relations and Early British Rule in India*, p. 44n.
16 *Freedom Struggle*, II, pp. 115-18; Forrest, *Selections*, III, Appendix E, p. v. Note: all the Districts mentioned in the text are those created by the post-Mutiny settlement. To use the district names in use under the Nawabi would be to introduce a needless complication, especially since the boundaries of the old administrative divisions remain uncertain.
17 He was the brother of Darshan Singh, the revenue farmer who founded an estate in Gonda District. See above, section III.
18 Cited, from the *Selected Works* (ed. Adoratsky), by Clive Dewey, 'Images of the Village Community', *Modern Asian Studies*, July 1972, p. 316n.
19 *The Popular Religion and Folklore of Northern India*, I, p. 8.
20 Ibid., I, p. 85.
21 *Chronicles of Oonao*, p. 87.
22 *Notes on the Races, Tribes and Castes Inhabiting the Province of Avadh*, p. 75.
23 The two sides of this affair will be found in Bhatnagar, *Awadh under Wajid Ali Shah*, pp. 117-39, and C. T. Metcalfe (ed.), *Two Native Narratives of the Mutiny in Delhi*, pp. 33-6.

Section VI

1 *Blue Book*, pp. 257, 261-9, 273-6.
2 The term *zemindar* had different applications in different parts of India.

The zemindars of the Ceded and Conquered Provinces were quite distinct from those of Bengal.

3 This was the conservative, romantic response to the radical critique. In Bombay the answer was found in the individual cultivator, or *ryot*, with whom the state made direct revenue engagements. This solution found more sympathy with the Utilitarians, who disparaged village joint--ownership as an inhibition to economic development and political maturity. See Clive Dewey, 'Images of the Village Community: A Study in Anglo-Indian Ideology', *Modern Asian Studies*, July 1972, pp. 291-328.

4 *Blue Book*, p. 260.
5 *Gazetteer*, I, p. lv.
6 Raikes, *Notes on the Revolt in the North Western Provinces of India*, p. 168.
7 Gubbins, *The Mutinies in Oudh*, pp. 61, 62.
8 P.P.C., 1861, no. 426, pp. 17, 19; *Freedom Struggle*, I, p. 184.
9 Ibid., I, pp. 185-6.
10 John Carbery to General Low, 30/xii/57: Home Misc., vol. 828.
11 *Freedom Struggle*, I, p. 186.
12 John Carbery to General Low, 30/xii/57: loc. cit. The estate in which Carbery had an interest was called Sammanpur and was near Salon, which was later transferred to Rae Bareli District. Sleeman describes the Raja of Bhadri as 'a fine, handsome and amiable youth, about sixteen years of age, who is now learning Persian' (*Journey*, I, p. 236). Hanumant Singh was the head of the Bisen Clan. His estate was also known as Dharupur.
13 *Freedom Struggle*, I, pp. 132, 193; II, p. 31-2; Kaye, *Sepoy War*, I, pp. 36n., 463; Gubbins, *The Mutinies in Oudh*, p. 293. He was put under house arrest about the middle of May, on suspicion of being engaged in subversive activities: see P.P.C., 1861, no 426, p. 85; fragment of a letter from Col. O'Brien, Home Misc., vol. 725, f. 554.
14 Carbery's account is fully substantiated by the report prepared by Sir Charles Wingfield (then Chief-Commissioner) in October 1859. See P.P.C., 1861, no. 426, p. 15.
15 *Papers relating to Land Tenures and Revenue Settlements in Oudh*, Appendix E.
16 Gubbins, *The Mutinies in Oudh*, p. 66.
17 P.P.C., 1861, no. 426.
18 Pol. Letters from India, 17/vii/56, 8/viii/56, 22/ix/56; P.P.C., 1861, no. 426, pp. 15-16; Jagdish Raj, *The Mutiny and British Land Policy in North India*, p. 18; *Gazetter*, I, p. 135.
19 Kaye, *Sepoy War*, III, pp. 452-3.
20 *Freedom Struggle*, I, pp. 209-30.
21 Pol. Letter from India, 22/ix/57.
22 Edwardes and Merivale, *Life of Sir Henry Lawrence*, p. 553n., Forrest, *Selections*, II, p. 3.
23 Edwardes and Merivale, *Life of Sir Henry Lawrence*, p. 557.
24 Ibid., p. 564.

25 Gubbins, *The Mutinies in Oudh*, p. 139.
26 Edwardes and Merivale, *Life of Sir Henry Lawrence*, pp. 555, 567; Innes, *Lucknow and Oude in the Mutiny*, p. 69; *Freedom Struggle*, I, p. 206; Gubbins, *The Mutinies in Oudh*, pp. 2-3.
27 Stokes, *The English Utilitarians and India*, p. 133.
28 *Freedom Struggle*, I, p. 183; P.P.L., 1859, Sess. 2, no. 74, para. 319.
29 Cited by Stokes, *The English Utilitarians and India*, p. 133.
30 The tahsildars had been the chief instrument in the ruination of the zemindari class in Benares District and had participated as buyers in the subsequent sales of land. See B. S. Cohn, 'From Indian Status to British Contract', *Journal of Economic History*, vol. XXI, 1961, pp. 613-28. A good example of the hit-and-miss methods of assessment, and of the notoriety of native officials for over-assessment, is provided by the *Gazetteer*, III, p. 571, where the Utraula estate, in Gonda District, is described as having been assessed by a native staff at Rs. 73,000. In order to allow for 'misrepresentations' the amount due was fixed at Rs. 43,965.
31 *Freedom Struggle*, I, p. 187; Carbery to Low, 30/xii/57: Home Misc., vol. 828; Gubbins, *The Mutinier in Oudh*, p. 9.
32 Edwares and Merivale, *Life of Sir Henry Lawrence*, p. 564.
33 William Edwards, *Reminiscences of a Bengal Civilian*, p. 266. The inaccessibility of European officers and the corruption of their native subordinates formed one of the most persistent themes of Indian complaint against English rule. In his tract called *Oude: Its Princes and Government Vindicated*, Masih-ud-din wrote: 'As to obtaining justice, some idea of the difficulty attending it may be formed from the fact that, in the first place, the European magistrates are very difficult of access; and secondly, that four persons at least must be bribed before the complainant has any chance of a satisfactory decision, viz: the chaprassie or peon; the sheristadar; the nazir; and the izhar nawis' (p. 163). For a particularly bitter indictment of these petty officials see *Household Words*, vol. VIII, no. 182 (17 September 1853), pp. 60-4.
34 The Oudh Irregular Force consisted of eight battalions of infantry, three regiments of cavalry and four companies of artillery. There were three battalions of Military Police, including the already existing Oudh Frontier Police. Of the soldiers discharged, only those who had served more than twenty-five years were entitled to pensions, and these were fixed at quarter-pay for up to thirty years' service, one-third-pay for up to thirty-five years' and half-pay for more than thirty-five years'. See *Blue Book*, pp. 270, 278, 304; Gubbins, *The Mutinies in Oudh*, pp. 69, 74; Hutchinson, *The Mutinies in Oudh*, pp. 10-11; Bonham, *Oudh in 1857*, pp. 11-13.
35 *Freedom Struggle*, I, p. 14.
36 N. L. Low, *Lieutenant-Colonel Gould Weston*, pp. 80-4; Hutchinson, *The Mutinies in Oudh*, pp. 55-6; Gubbins, *The Mutinies in Oudh*, p. 435n.
37 *Freedom Struggle*, II, p. 31.

38 Edwardes and Merivale, *Life of Sir Henry Lawrence*, p. 595; Forrest, *Selections*, II, p. 27.
39 Deputy-Commissioner of Unao to Secretary to Chief-Commissioner, 31/iii/58: P.P.C., 1858, no. 334.
40 *Gazetteer*, I, p. 546; II, p. 280.
41 Gubbins, *The Mutinies in Oudh*, pp. 435n., 472; *Freedom Struggle*, II, p. 16.
42 See Wingfield's account of developments in Gonda: *Annals of the Indian Rebellion*, p. 488. Montgomery describes the spontaneous submission of Raja Man Singh's erstwhile tenantry in his Administration Report for 1859: P.P.L., 1859, Sess. 2, no. 74, para. 229. In the *Gazetteer*, II, p. 515, it is noted that when the rebellion broke out the Kurmis of Nagram, in Lucknow District, invited their quondam Amethia overlords to put themselves at their head. In Rae Bareli the villagers made no opposition to the taluqdars, and remained to cultivate their fields as before: MacAndrew, *Rae Bareli Settlement Report*, p. 34.

Section VII

1 See his essay 'The Indian Army', in *Essays Military and Political Written in India*.
2 Edwardes and Merivale, *Life of Sir Henry Lawrence*, pp. 570, 571, 577.
3 Baird, *Private Letters of Dalhousie*, p. 216.
4 The Order was in fact promulgated in July 1856 by Canning, but it was Dalhousie's in conception.
5 Bengal Sec. Cons., 6/viii/13, no. 4, paras. 87-100; Kaye, *Sepoy War*, I, p. 619; *Mins. of Ev.*, 1832, sec. V, p. 2.
6 Baird, *Private Letters of Dalhousie*, p. 406.
7 *Essays Military and Political*, pp. 421-22, 427; Edwardes and Merivale, *Life of Sir Henry Lawrence*, p. 557.
8 Lee Warner, *Life of Dalhousie*, II, p. 404.
9 Forrest, *Selections*, III, Appendix, A, p. xxxii. See also Russell, *My Diary in India*, II, p. 402; A Volunteer, *Journal*, p. 19; Maude and Sherer, *Memories of the Mutiny*, I, pp. 40-1.
10 A Volunteer, *Journal*, p. 24; Ball, *History of the Indian Mutiny*, II, p. 462. Edgar Johnson (ed.), *Letters from Charles Dickens to Angela Burdett-Coutts*, p. 350.
11 North, *Journal*, p. 112. See also Maude and Sherer, *Memories of the Mutiny*, I, p. 277; II, p. 285.
12 Forrest, *Selections*, II, p. 167.
13 Ibid., II, p. 29.
14 *Annals of the Indian Rebellion*, p. 490.
15 Innes, *Lucknow and Oude in the Mutiny*, Appendix XII. Man Singh's letter is dated 20 July 1857.
16 The rebels of Sitapur flocked to the standard of Nawab Ali Khan, and his own troops took part in the battle of Chinhat. They were led by his

naib, or lieutenant, Khan Ali Khan, who had been dismissed from the post of *chakladar* of Salon during the reign of the ex-King at the insistence of Sleeman. Either Khan Ali Khan or his master appears to have been responsible for persuading the rebels to remain to besiege the Residency instead of proceeding to Delhi, as originally intended. See P.P.C., 1861, no. 426, p. 86; *Freedom Struggle*, II, p. 51; Sleeman, *Journey*, II, p. 223. Raja Jai Lal Singh was elected chief of the rebel troops in Lucknow early in July: see below, section VIII.

17 Gubbins, *The Mutinies in Oudh*, p. 169. Lawrence even sought permission to cancel the 1856 revenue settlement and conclude a new one with the taluqdars: Forrest, *Selections*, II, p. 83. Canning rejected this idea, but in September he authorised Outram to assure loyal taluqdars that they would not emerge from the Mutiny worse off than they had been at annexation: Metcalf, *The Aftermath of Revolt*, pp. 137-8.
18 *Gazetteer*, I, p. 479.
19 Gubbins, *The Mutinies in Oudh*, p. 468.
20 *Annals of the Indian Rebellion*, p. 490. See also Yeoward, *An Episode of the Rebellion and Mutiny in Oudh*, p. 19.
21 Wylie, *The English Captives in Oudh*, p. 14; *Annals of the Indian Rebellion*, pp. 456-7.
22 *Reminiscences of a Bengal Civilian*, p. 196.
23 Ibid., p. 199.
24 North, *Journal*, p. 94.
25 Ball, *History of the Indian Mutiny*, II, p. 21. See also Roberts, *Forty-One Years in India*, I, pp. 297-300.
26 *Freedom Struggle*, II, p. 464.
27 Forrest, *Selections*, III, Appendix B, p. i.
28 Ibid., II, p. 233; *Freedom Struggle*, II, p. 223; P.P.C., 1861, no. 426, p. 85.
29 Forrest, *Selections*, III, Appendix B, pp. xii-xiii.
30 *Freedom Struggle*, II, pp. 211-16; *Gazetteer*, I, p. 329.
31 *Freedom Struggle*, II, pp. 215, 216, 245; P.P.C., 1861, no. 426, p. 86; *Gazetteer*, I, pp. 32-3.
32 Edwards, *Reminiscences of a Bengal Civilian*, pp. 261, 272.
33 Digvijai Singh's motives were, however, mixed. He had been at daggers drawn with the taluqdars of Utraula and Tulsipur ever since his accession in 1836, and the fact they supported the Mutiny and induced the rebel government to decree the division of his estate between themselves undoubtedly influenced his decision to remain loyal.
34 *Freedom Struggle*, II, pp. 212, 223, 240.
35 Maude and Sherer, *Memories of the Mutiny*, I, pp. 74-6; Kaye and Malleson, *History of the Indian Mutiny*, IV, p. 223; P.P.C., 1861, no. 426, p. 85; *Freedom Struggle*, II, p. 238.
36 Wylie (ed.), *The English Captives in Oude*, pp. 15-28; *Freedom Struggle*, II, pp. 128-34.
37 *Annals of the Indian Rebellion*, pp. 723-9; Pearse, *The Hearseys*, pp. 98-117.
38 Home Misc., vol. 828.

39 *Freedom Struggle*, II, pp. 238-41.
40 A Volunteer, *Journal*, pp. 35-6.
41 Maude and Sherer, *Memories of the Mutiny*, II, p. 535.
42 Forrest, *Selections*, II, p. 228.
43 Ibid., pp. 229, 235-7.
44 Goldsmid, *James Outram*, II, p. 257.
45 He was thus described by Johnny Stanley, Canning's A.D.C., whose letters appear in Nancy Mitford (ed.), *The Stanleys of Alderley*.
46 Shadwell, *Life of Colin Campbell*, I, pp. 445, 452-3.
47 Goldsmid, *James Outram*, II, p. 262.
48 Gordon-Alexander, *Recollections*, p. 104.
49 Ibid., p. 112.
50 Forrest, *Selections*, II, p. 336.
51 Knollys, *Life of Sir Hope Grant*, I, pp. 325-9.
52 P.P.C., 1858, no. 334.
53 Ball, *History of the Indian Mutiny*, II, p. 241.
54 Forrest, *Selections*, II, p. 240; III, Appendix B, pp. vi-xvi; *Freedom Struggle*, II, pp. 230, 277-9.
55 Forrest, *Selections*, III, Appendix B, pp. ix-x.

Section VIII

1 *Freedom Struggle*, I, p. 113.
2 Edwardes and Merivale, *Life of Sir Henry Lawrence*, p. 564.
3 Gubbins, *The Mutinies in Oudh*, p. 6.
4 Pol. Letter from India, 22/ix/57, paras. 11-12; Edwardes and Merivale, *Life of Sir Henry Lawrence*, p. 558.
5 Pol. Letter from India, 22/ix/57, paras. 32-41; P.P.L., 1859, Sess. 2, no. 74, para. 176; Gubbins, *The Mutinies in Oudh*, pp. 41, 71; Rees, *Siege of Lucknow*, p. 35.
6 *Gazetteer*, II, pp. 326-7. One petitioner stated the rate to be 14 or 15 seers: see *Freedom Struggle*, I, p. 282.
7 Kaye, *Sepoy War*, II, pp. 200, 204, 205n.; Rees, *Siege of Lucknow*, pp. 29-34.
8 P.P.C., 1861, no. 426, pp. 14-21. 768 claims were allowed. These were increased to 965 after the Mutiny: see P.P.L., 1859, Sess. 2, no. 74, p. 47.
9 *Freedom Struggle*, I, pp. 196-8.
10 Ibid., I, pp. 272-8; P.P.C., 1861, no. 426, p. 20; Masih-ud-din Khan, *Oude: Its Princes and Government Vindicated*, pp. 155-7; Gubbins, *The Mutinies in Oudh*, p. 6.
11 Masih-ud-din Khan, *Oude*, pp. 155, 158; *Freedom Struggle*, I, pp. 108-9, 112-13, 124-5, 126-7, 272-7, 279-80.
12 P.P.C., 1861, no. 426, pp. 14-15, 21-2.
13 Edwardes and Merivale, *Life of Sir Henry Lawrence*, p. 564.

14 Forrest, *Selections*, II, p. 236.
15 *Freedom Struggle*, II, pp. 259, 276; Kavanagh, *How I won the Victoria Cross*, p. 151.
16 *Freedom Struggle*, II, pp. 82, 97, Appendix B, passim.
17 Ibid., II, p. 85.
18 Metcalfe (ed.), *Two Native Narratives*, pp. 142, 148, 213, 223; Muir, *Intelligence Records*, I, p. 499.
19 Metcalfe (ed.), *Two Native Narratives*, p. 69. Sen suggests (*Eighteen Fifty-Seven*, p. 210) that Birjis Qadr forebore to adopt the title of King. The suggestion seems sound, since the title would have implied both his independence of Delhi and his supersession of his father.
20 *Freedom Struggle*, I, p. 198.
21 Ibid., II, p. 80. He was also created *chakladar* of Dariabad: ibid., p. 91.
22 European writers referred to them as 'Wahhabis', but the similarities between them and the followers of the Arab reformer Abd-ul-Wahhab of Nejd were only superficial. See Qureshi, *The Muslim Community of the Indo-Pakistan Subcontinent*, pp. 194-208; Titus, *Indian Islam*, pp. 179-92; Ahmad, *Studies in Islamic Culture in the Indian Environment*, pp. 209-16; Hardy, *The Muslims of British India*, pp. 50-6. For the classic discussion on the revolutionary proclivities of the *mujahidin* see Hunter, *The Indian Musulmans* and Syed Ahmed Khan, *Review on Dr Hunter's 'Indian Musulmans'*. A more recent discussion is provided by Munir-uddin Chughtai, 'Muslim Religo-Political Movements in the Indo-Pakistan Subcontinent in the Early Half of the Nineteenth Century', *Journal of Research (Humanities)*, vol. 1, no. 1 (1966): University of the Punjab, Lahore.
23 *Freedom Struggle*, I, pp. 381-4; *Annals of the Indian Rebellion*, pp. 24-5.
24 *Freedom Struggle*, II, pp. 150-8.
25 His name appears in neither of the extant lists of the members of the council of state. See *Freedom Struggle*, I, pp. 426-7; II, p. 110.
26 Wylie, *The English Captives in Oudh*, pp. 31-2; *Freedom Struggle*, II, p. 147.
27 Ibid., I, p. 450.
28 Ibid., II, p. 256.
29 Ludlow, *British India: its Races and its History*, II, pp. 349, 369.
30 Ibid., II, p. 348.
31 It seems likely that there were European renegades among their ranks, though who these were and what their motives remain among the many mysteries of the Mutiny. See Rees, *Siege of Lucknow*, pp. 75-6, 116-17; Forbes-Mitchell, *Reminiscences*, Appendix B, passim.
32 Outram's statement in his official report to the effect that after the entry of his force six mines were found ready whose explosion would have destroyed the garrison is categorically rejected by Innes, who, as one of the chief Engineer officers, must have known what he was talking about. See *Lucknow and Oude in the Mutiny*, p. 178.
33 *Recollections of My Life*, p. 170.
34 Forrest, *Selections*, II. pp. 51-2.

35 Return of Killed and Wounded, ibid., II, p. 73. Gubbins (*The Mutinies in Oudh*, p. 354) gives the desertion figure as 230; but his other figures do not tally with the official return.
36 Cf. the returns given in Forrest, *Selections*, II, pp. 69, 73.
37 Ibid., II, p. 197; Innes, *Lucknow and Oude in the Mutiny*, pp. 148, 233; Gubbins, *The Mutinies in Oudh*, p. 261. The original error appears to have been Banks's. He reported on 10 July that the food would last 'fully six weeks' (Forrest, *Selections*, II, p. 34). It seems that Inglis accepted this estimate without further investigation.
38 Forrest, *Selections*, III, Appendix C, pp. vii-x.
39 Gubbins, *The Mutinies in Oudh*, pp. 204-5.
40 *Freedom Struggle*, II, p. 277; Goldsmid, *James Outram*, II, p. 294; Raikes, *Notes on the Revolt in the North West Provinces*, p. 104; Rees, *Siege of Lucknow*, pp. 266-8.
41 Shadwell, *Life of Colin Campbell*, II, pp. 68-90.
42 Ibid., II, p. 109.
43 Forrest, *Selections*, III, pp. 469, 471.
44 Shakespeare, *John Shakespeare of Shadwell and his Descendants*, p. 300.
45 Only the Commander-in-Chief, with strange pertinacity, refused to censure Campbell for what appears to have been an inexcusable blunder. Cf. Forrest, *Selections*, III, p. 473 with Innes, *Lucknow and Oude in the Mutiny*, p. 289, Gordon-Alexander, *Recollections*, p. 277, and Ball, *History of the Indian Mutiny*, II, p. 264.
46 P.P.C., 1860, no. 507, p. 31; 1862, no. 428, p. 2; Gordon-Alexander, *Recollections*, pp. 284-5; Goldsmid, *James Outram*, I, Appendix, passim.
47 Ball, *History of the Indian Mutiny*, II, p. 276.

Section IX

1 Ball, *History of the Indian Mutiny*, II, p. 310.
2 *Freedom Struggle*, II, p. 462.
3 Ibid., II, p. 430; Knollys, *Life of Sir Hope Grant*, II, pp. 9, 13.
4 Ball, *History of the Indian Mutiny*, II, pp. 370-2.
5 Ibid., II, p. 344; *Freedom Struggle*, II, p. 417.
6 Knollys, *Life of Sir Hope Grant*, II, pp. 9-12; Ball, *History of the Indian Mutiny*, II, pp. 345-7.
7 *Freedom Struggle*, II, pp. 418-19; Ball, *History of the Indian Mutiny*, II, p. 347.
8 *Freedom Struggle*, II, p. 441.
9 Not to be confused with Raja Beni Madho Singh of Atraulia, the brother of Raja Jai Lal Singh, who was made Nazim of Azamgarh and Jaunpur by the rebel government.
10 *Freedom Struggle*, II, p. 210.
11 Ibid., II, p. 432.
12 Ibid., II, p. 423; P.P.C., 1859, no. 110, p. 10.

13 *Freedom Struggle*, II, p. 457.
14 Ibid., II, p. 436; Forrest, *Selections*, III, Appendix E, pp. ii-iv; Russell, *My Diary in India*, II, p. 299.
15 See Ball, *History of the Indian Mutiny*, II, p. 551. Queen Victoria's Proclamation, published on 1 November 1858, declared the transference of the government of India to the British Crown and offered pardon to all not directly implicated in the murder of Europeans.
16 *Freedom Struggle*, II, p. 17.
17 Ibid., III, p. 388.
18 These were Digvijai Singh of Balrampur; Hardeo Bakhsh of Katiari; Kulraj Singh of Padhua; Kashi Parshad of Sehsendi (=Nigohan); Chandi Lal of Muraon; and Zahar Singh of Gopal Khair.
19 Ball, *History of the Indian Mutiny*, II, pp. 276-80; Goldsmid, *James Outram*, II, p. 335; Russell, *My Diary in India*, II, pp. 355, 362; P.P.C., 1858, no. 265, passim; P.P.C., 1858, no. 289, passim; P.P.C., 1859, no. 110, passim; P.P.C., 1859, no. 237, passim; P.P.L., 1859, Sess 2, no. 74, para. 232; Canning to Low, 15/ii/58: Home Misc., 828.
20 P.P.C., 1859, no. 110, pp. 5-6; P.P.C., 1858, no. 289, para. 6.
21 *Papers relating to Land Tenures and Revenue Settlements in Oudh*, Appendix E.
22 P.P.C., 1859, no. 110, pp. 9-10; *Gazetteer*, I, pp. 32-3.
23 *Freedom Struggle*, II, p. 415.
24 Ibid. II, p. 434.
25 Ibid., III, p. 384.
26 Ibid., II, pp. 436-7.
27 Ibid., II, pp. 458, 462.
28 P.P.C., 1859, no. 110, pp. 9-10; Ball, *History of the Indian Mutiny*, II, p. 372.
29 *Freedom Struggle*, II, p. 433.
30 An Urdu word of Persian origin, meaning dusty.
31 Kavanagh, *How I won the Victoria Cross*, p. 206.
32 See Forbes-Mitchell, *Reminiscences*, Appendix B, passim.
33 Gordon-Alexander, *Recollections*, pp. 337-40.
34 Ball, *History of the Indian Mutiny*, II, pp. 534-6; Russell, *My Diary in India*, II, pp. 298-305; Forrest, *Selections*, III, Appendix E, pp. ii-iv.
35 Ball, *History of the Indian Mutiny*, II, p. 537.
36 Russell, *My Diary in India*, II, pp. 313-14.
37 P.P.L., 1859, Sess. 2, no. 74, para. 302.
38 *Papers relating to Land Tenures and Revenue Settlements in Oudh*, Appendix D, passim.

Section X

1 P.P.L., 1859, Sess. 2, no. 74, para. 386.
2 P.P.C., 1861, no. 426, p. 23.

3 Oudh ceased to be the recruiting ground for the army, however. After the Mutiny, that privilege passed to the Punjab.
4 For this affair see enclosures nos. 5 and 10 to Secret Letter from India, 19/vi/57; Ball, *History of the Indian Mutiny*, I, p. 586; Kaye, *Sepoy War*, I, p. 573; III, pp. 35-41; *Freedom Struggle*, I, p. 361.
5 Ball, *History of the Indian Mutiny*, I, pp. 632-4; II, pp. 453-4; Garcin de Tassy, *Histoire de la Littérature Hindouie et Hindoustanie*, I, p. 181.
6 P.P.C., 1861, no. 426, pp. 37-9.
7 P.P.C., 1860, no. 507, p. 135.

BIBLIOGRAPHY

1 Manuscript Sources

(a) *Official records in the India Office Library and Records, London, and the National Archives of India, New Delhi*

Bengal Political Consultations
Bengal Secret Consultations
Enclosures to Secret Letters from India
Foreign Letters from India
India Political and Foreign Consultations
India Political Consultations
India Secret Consultations
Political Letters from Bengal
Political Letters from India
Political Letters to Bengal
Secret Letters from Bengal
Secret Letters from India

(b) *Private papers in the India Office Library and Records*

'A Personal Narrative of the Siege of Lucknow', by Madeleine Jackson: Photo/EUR/41.
Amherst Papers: MSS/EUR/F/140.
Correspondence of Sir John Cam Hobhouse: Home Miscellaneous Records, vols. 833, 838.
Correspondence of Sir John Low: Home Miscellaneous Records, vol. 828.
Correspondence of Sir Charles Metcalfe: Home Miscellaneous Records, vol. 738.
Mutiny Papers of Sir John Kaye: Home Miscellaneous Records, vols. 725, 726.

(c) *Unpublished theses in the Tagore Library, University of Lucknow*

'Ghazi-ud-din Haidar, the First King of Oudh', anon.
'Nasir-ud-din Haidar, King of Oudh 1827-1837', by Mohammad Ahmed Taqi.
'Two Kings of Awadh: Muhammad Ali Shah and Amjad Ali Shah', by Safi Ahmad.

2 Printed Official Documents

Benett, W. C. A., *The Final Settlement Report on the Gonda District,* Allahabad, 1878.

Forrest, G. (ed.), *Selections from the State Papers preserved in the Military Department of the Government of India,* Calcutta, 1902.

Gazetteer of the Province of Oudh, Lucknow, 1877.

MacAndrew, J. M., *Report of the Settlement Operations of Rae Bareli District,* Lucknow, 1872.

Minutes of Evidence taken before the Select Committee of the House of Commons on the Affairs of the East India Company . . . 1832, printed by Order of the Court of Directors, London, 1833.

Muir, William, *Records of the Intelligence Department of the Government of the North West Provinces of India during the Mutiny of 1857,* edited by W. Coldstream, Edinburgh, 1902.

Papers relating to Land Tenures and Revenue Settlements in Oudh, Calcutta, 1865.

Papers Respecting a Reform in the Administration of the Government of His Excellency the Nawab Vizier, printed for the Court of Proprietors of the East India Company, London, 1824.

Parliamentary Papers.

Paton, J., *Abstract of the Political Intercourse between the British Government and the Kingdom of Oude, 1764-1835,* edited by B. Prasad, Allahabad, 1944.

Report on East India Affairs from the Select Committee of the House of Commons, London, 1832.

Rizvi, S. A., and Bhargava, M. L. (eds.), *Freedom Struggle in Uttar Pradesh,* Lucknow, 1957-8.

3 Select List of Other Works

(a) *Vernacular materials*

Adib, Sayyid Masud Hasan Rizvi, *Urdu Drama aur Istej,* Lucknow, 1957 (Urdu).

Anis, Mir Babar Ali, *Intikhab-e-Marasi-e-Anis,* Allahabad, 1962 (Urdu).

Azad, Muhammad Husain, *Ab-e-Hayat,* reprint, Allahabad, 1967 (Urdu).

Dabir, Salamat Ali, *Intikhab-e-Marasi-e-Dabir,* Allahabad, 1962 (Urdu).

Durga Prasada, *Bostan-e-Awadh,* Lucknow, 1892 (corrupt Persian).

Jurat, Kalandar Bakhsh, *Kuliyat-e-Jurat,* edited by Nur-al-Hasan Naqvi, Aligarh, 1971 (Urdu).
Kamal-ud-din Haidar Husaini, *Tawarikh-e-Awadh,* Lucknow, 1879 (Urdu).
Sharar, Maulana Abd-ul-Halim, *Guzashta Lakhnau ya Mashriqi Tammadun ka Akheri Namuna,* reprint, Lucknow, 1965 (Urdu).
Varma, Paripurnanda, *Wajid Ali Shah aur Awadh Rajya ka Patan,* Lucknow, 1959 (Hindi).

(b) *Works in European languages*

Abu Talib, *History of Asaf-ud-daula,* trans. by W. Hoey, new edition, Lucknow, 1971.
Ahmad, A., *An Intellectual History of Islam in India,* Edinburgh, 1969.
Studies in Islamic Culture in the Indian Environment, Oxford, 1964.
Annals of the Indian Rebellion, Calcutta, n.d.
Archer, Major E. C., *Tours in Upper India and in Parts of the Himalaya Mountains,* London, 1833.
Asiatic Annual Register, vols. II, III, VI, Calcutta, 1800, 1801, 1804.
Bailey, T. Graham, *History of Urdu Literature,* Calcutta, 1932.
Baird, G. A. (ed.), *The Private Letters of the Marquis of Dalhousie,* London, 1911.
Ball, Charles, *History of the Indian Mutiny,* London, n.d.
Bartrum, Katherine, *A Widow's Reminiscences of the Siege of Lucknow,* London, 1858.
Basu, Purenda, *Oudh and the East India Company, 1785-1801,* Lucknow, 1943.
Benett, W. C. A., *Report on the Family History of the Chief Clans of the Roy Bareilly District,* Lucknow, 1870.
Bhatnagar, G. D., *Awadh under Wajid Ali Shah,* Benares, 1968.
Blunt, E. A. H., *The Caste System of Northern India,* Madras, 1931.
Bonham, J., *Oudh in 1857,* London, 1928.
Boulger, Demetrius, *Lord William Bentinck,* Oxford, 1892.
Brodkin, E. I., 'The Struggle for Succession: Rebels and Loyalists in the Indian Mutiny of 1857', *Modern Asian Studies,* vol. 6, part 3, Cambridge, July 1972.
Brown, C. J., 'The Coins of the Kings of Awadh', *Journal and Proceedings of the Asiatic Society of Bengal,* vol. VIII, no. 6, Calcutta, 1912.
Brown, Percy, *Indian Architecture (the Islamic Period),* reprint, Bombay, n.d.
Browne, E. G., *A Literary History of Persia,* Cambridge, 1928.

Bute, Marchioness of (ed.), *The Private Journal of the Marquis of Hastings*, London, 1858.
Butter, D., *Outline of the Topography and Statistics of the Southern Districts of Oudh and of the Cantonment of Sultanpur Oudh*, Calcutta, 1839.
Campbell, George, *Modern India, A Sketch of the System of Civil Government*, London, 1852.
Carnegy, Patrick, *Notes on the Races, Tribes and Castes Inhabiting the Province of Avadh*, Lucknow, 1868.
Clint, L., 'A Tale by Inshah Allah Khan', *Journal of the Asiatic Society of Bengal*, Calcutta, 1852.
Cohn, B. S., 'From Indian Status to British Contract', *Journal of Economic History*, vol. XXI, New York, 1961.
Colvin, Auckland, *John Russell Colvin*, Oxford, 1895.
Coulbourn, Rushton (ed.), *Feudalism in History*, Princeton, 1956.
Crooke, William, *The North West Provinces of India*, London, 1897.
The Popular Religion and Folklore of Northern India, London, 1896.
Davidson, C. J. C., *Diary of Travels and Adventures in Upper India*, London, 1843.
Davies, C. Collin, *Warren Hastings and Oudh*, London, 1939.
Deare, A., *A Tour through the Upper Provinces of Hindoostan*, London, 1823.
Dewey, Clive, 'Images of the Village Community: A Study in Anglo-Indian Ideology', *Modern Asian Studies*, vol. 6, part 3, Cambridge, July 1972.
Diskalker, D. B., 'The Foundation of an Observatory at Lucknow', *Journal of the United Provinces Historical Society*, Lucknow, July 1937.
Eden, the Hon. Emily, *Letters from India, Edited by her Niece*, London, 1872.
Up the Country, London, 1866.
Edinburgh Review, vol. 102 (1855).
Edwardes, H. B. and Merivale, H., *The Life of Sir Henry Lawrence*, London, 1872.
Edwards, William, *Reminiscences of a Bengal Civilian*, London, 1866.
Elliot, C. A., *Chronicles of Oonao*, Allahabad, 1862.
English, Barbara, *John Company's Last War*, London, 1971.
Fayrer, Joseph, *Recollections of My Life*, Edinburgh, 1900.
Fergusson, James, *History of Indian and Eastern Architecture*, edited by James Burgess and R. Rene Spiers, London, 1910.
Forbes-Mitchell, William, *Reminiscences of the Great Mutiny*, London, 1893.
Forrest, Sir George, *History of the Indian Mutiny*, Edinburgh, 1904.
Fox, Richard G., *Kin, Clan Raja and Rule*, Berkely, 1971.

Frykenburg. R. E (ed.), *Land Control and Social Structure in Indian History*, Wisconsin, 1969.
Garcin de Tassy, Joseph, *Histoire de la Littérature Hindouie et Hindoustanie*, 2nd edition, Paris, 1870.
Gibb, H. A. R., *Muhammadanism*, Oxford, 1953.
Gilchrist, J. B., *The Stranger's Infallible East Indian Guide or Hindoostanie Multum in Parvo*, London, 1820.
Goldsmid, F. J., *James Outram, a Biography*, London, 1881.
Gordon-Alexander, W., *Recollections of a Highland Subaltern under Sir Colin Campbell*, London, 1898.
Grant, Sir James, *Incidents in the Sepoy War, 1857-58*, Edinburgh, 1873.
Groom, W. T., *With Havelock from Allahabad to Lucknow*, London, 1894.
Gubbins, Martin, *An Account of the Mutinies in Oudh and of the Siege of the Lucknow Residency*, 2nd edition, London, 1858.
Gupta, P. C., *Nana Sahib and the Rising at Cawnpore*, Oxford, 1963.
Gupta, S. C., *Agrarian Relations and Early British Rule in India*, London, 1963.
Habib, Irfan, *The Agrarian System of the Mughal Empire*, London, 1963.
Hardy, P., *The Muslims of British India*, Cambridge, 1972.
Hare, Augustus, (ed.), *The Story of Two Noble Lives*, London, 1893.
Havell, E. B., *Indian Architecture*, London, 1927.
Hay, Sidney, *Historic Lucknow*, Lucknow, 1939.
Heber, Reginald, *Narrative of a Journey through the Upper Provinces of India*, 4th edition, London, 1829.
Hill, S. C., *The Life of Claude Martin*, Calcutta, 1901.
Hoey, W. (trans.), *Memoirs of Delhi and Faizabad*, Allahabad, 1887.
Hollister, J. N., *The Shia of India*, London, 1953.
Holmes, T. R. E., *A History of the Indian Mutiny*, 4th edition, London, 1891.
Household Words, vol. VIII, London, 1853.
Hunter, W. W., *The Indian Musulmans: Are They Bound in Conscience to Rebel against the Queen?*, London, 1871.
Hutchinson, G., *A Narrative of the Mutinies in Oudh*, London, 1859.
Ikram, S. M., *History of Muslim Civilization in India and Pakistan*, Lahore, n.d.
Innes, J. J. M., *Lucknow and Oude in the Mutiny*, London, 1895.
Irwin, H. C., *The Garden of India or Chapters in Oudh History and Affairs*, London, 1880.
Jafar Sharif, *Islam in India or the Qanun-e-Islam*, trans. by G. A. Herklots, edited by William Crooke, Oxford, 1921.

Kavanagh, T. Henry, *How I won the Victoria Cross*, London, 1860.
Kaye, J. W., *History of the Sepoy War in India*, 7th edition, London, 1875.
and Malleson, G. B., *History of the Indian Mutiny*, cabinet edition, London, 1889.
Keene, H. G., *Here and There: Memories Indian and Other*, London, 1906.
Knighton, William, *The Private Life of an Eastern King*, edited by B. S. Smith, Oxford, 1921.
Knollys, Henry, *The Life of General Sir Hope Grant with Selections from his Correspondence*, London, 1894.
Lambrick, H. T., *John Jacob of Jacobabad*, London, 1960.
Law, Sir Algernon, *India Under Lord Ellenborough*, London, 1926.
Lawrence, H. M., *Essays Military and Political Written in India*, London, 1859.
Lee Warner, William, *The Life of the Marquis of Dalhousie*, London, 1904.
Low, C. R., *The Life and Correspondence of Field Marshal Sir George Pollock*, London, 1873.
Low, N. L., *Lieutenant-Colonel Gould Weston of Hunterston*, Selkirk, 1914 (privately printed).
Low, Ursula, *Fifty Years with John Company*, London, 1936.
Lucas, Samuel, *Dacoitee in Excelsis or the Spoliation of Oude by the East India Company*, new edition, Lucknow, 1971.
Ludlow, J. M., *British India: its Races and its History*, Cambridge, 1858.
Mackay, J. *From London to Lucknow*, London, 1860.
Maclagan, Michael, *Clemency Canning*, London, 1962.
Maine, H. S., *Village Communities in the East and West*, New York, 1876.
Majendie, V. D., *Up Among the Pandies*, London, 1859.
Majumdar, R. C., *The Sepoy Mutiny and the Revolt of 1857*, 2nd edition, Calcutta, 1963.
Martin, R. Montgomery, *The Despatches, Minutes and Correspondence of the Marquess Wellesley*, London, 1836.
The Indian Empire, London, n.d.
Masih-ud-din Khan, *Oude: Its Princes and Government Vindicated*, edited by S. Ahmad, Meerut, 1969.
Maude, F. C., *Memories of the Mutiny, with which is incorporated the Personal Narrative of John Walter Sherer*, London, 1894.
Mead, Henry, *The Sepoy Revolt*, London, 1857.
Metcalf, Thomas R., *The Aftermath of Revolt*, Princeton, 1965.

Metcalfe, C. T. (ed.), *Two Native Narratives of the Mutiny in Delhi*, London, 1890.
Metcalfe, Henry, *The Chronicle of Private Henry Metcalfe*, edited by F. Tuker, London, 1953.
Mir Hasan Ali, Mrs, *Observations on the Musulmans of India*, 2nd edition, edited by William Crooke, London, 1917.
Mitford, Nancy (ed.), *The Stanleys of Alderley: Their Letters 1851-65*, new edition, London, 1968.
Moore, R. J., *Sir Charles Wood's Indian Policy*, Manchester, 1966.
Moreland, W. H., *The Agrarian System of Moslem India*, Cambridge, 1929.
Morison, J. L., *Lawrence of Lucknow*, London, 1934.
Mundy, G. C. *Pen and Pencil Sketches*, 3rd edition, London, 1832.
Munir-ud-din Chughtai, 'Muslim Religio-Political Movements in the Indo-Pakistan subcontinent in the Early Half of the Nineteenth Century', *Journal of Research (Humanities)* vol. 1 no. 1 (1966): University of the Punjab, Lahore.
Nilsson, Sten, *European Architecture in India 1750-1850*, London, 1968.
North, Major, *Journal of an English Officer in India*, London, 1858.
Nugent, Maria, *A Journal from the Year 1811 to the Year 1815*, London, 1839.
Orlich, L. von, *Travels in India*, translated by H. Evans Lloyd, London, 1845.
Palmer, J. A. B., *The Mutiny Outbreak in Meerut in 1857*, Cambridge, 1966.
Parks, Fanny, *Wanderings of a Pilgrim in Search of the Picturesque*, London, 1850.
Pearse, Hugh, *The Hearseys: Five Generations of an Anglo-Indian Family*, Edinburgh, 1905.
Philips, C. H., *The East India Company*, Manchester, 1940.
Pollock, J. C., *Way to Glory: The Life of Havelock of Lucknow*, London, 1957.
Price, William, *A New Grammar of the Hindoostani Language to which are added Selections from the Best Authors*, London, 1828.
Prinsep, Henry T., *History of the Political and Military Transactions in India during the Administration of the Marquis of Hastings*, London, 1825.
Pryme, J. T. and Bayne, A., *Memorials of the Thackeray Family*, London, 1879 (privately printed).
Qureshi, I. H., *The Muslim Community of the Indo-Pakistan Subcontinent*, The Hague, 1962.

Raikes, Charles, *Notes on the North Western Provinces of India*, London, 1852.
  Notes on the Revolt in the North West Provinces of India, London, 1858.
Raj, Jagdish, *The Mutiny and British Land Policy in North India*, London, 1965.
Rees, L. E. R., *A Personal Narrative of the Siege of Lucknow*, 2nd edition, London, 1858.
Reeves, P. D., *Sleeman in Oudh: An Abridgement of W. H. Sleeman's 'A Journey through the Kingdom of Oude in 1849-50'*, Cambridge, 1971.
Ritchie, Gerald (ed.), *The Ritchies in India*, London, 1920.
Rizvi, S. N. Haidar, 'Music in Muslim India', *Islamic Culture*, vol. XV, no. 3, Hyderabad, July, 1941.
Roberts, Emma, *Scenes and Characteristics of Hindustan*, London, 1837.
Roberts, Frederick, Earl of Kandahar, *Forty-One Years in India*, London, 1897.
  Letters Written During the Indian Mutiny, London, 1924.
Robertson, H. D., *District Duties During the Revolt in the North West Provinces of India*, London, 1859.
Rosen, Freidrich, *Die Indarsabha des Amanat*, Leipzig, 1892.
Ruggles, John, *Recollections of a Lucknow Veteran*, London, 1906.
Russell, Ralph and Islam, Kurshidul, *Ghalib: Life and Letters*, London, 1969.
  Three Mughal Poets, London, 1969.
Russell, William Howard, *My Diary in India in the Year 1857-58*, London, 1860.
Sadiq, Muhammad, *A History of Urdu Literature*, London, 1964.
Sen, S. N., *Eighteen Fifty-Seven*, Delhi, 1957.
Shadwell, L., *Life of Colin Campbell, Lord Clyde*, London, 1881.
Shakespeare, John, *John Shakespeare of Shadwell and his Descendants, 1619-1931*, Newcastle, 1931 (privately printed).
Shore, F. J., *Notes on Indian Affairs*, London, 1837.
Sleeman, W. H., *A Journey through the Kingdom of Oude in 1849-50*, London, 1858.
  Rambles and Recollections of an Indian Official, 2nd edition, edited by V. A. Smith, London, 1893.
Smith, R. Bosworth, *Life of Lord Lawrence*, 3rd edition, London, 1883.
Smith, Vincent A., *A History of Fine Art in India and Ceylon*, 3rd edition, Bombay, n.d.
Soltykoff, Prince A., *Voyage dans l'Inde*, 2nd edition, Paris, 1851.
Spry, H. H., *Modern India*, London, 1837.
Stocqueler, J. H. (ed.), *Memoirs and Correspondence of Major-General Sir William Nott*, London, 1854.

Stokes, Eric, *The English Utilitarians and India,* Oxford, 1959.
Syed Ahmed Khan, *Review on Dr Hunter's 'Indian Musulmans',* Benares, 1872.
Tarikh-e-Badshah Begum, translated by Muhammad Taqi Ahmad, Allahabad, 1938.
Tennant, W., *Indian Recreations,* London, 1804.
Thornton, Edward, *The History of the British Empire in India,* London, 1843.
Titus, Murray T., *Indian Islam, a Religious History of Islam in India,* London, 1930.
Tod, James, *Annals and Antiquities of Rajesthan,* edited by William Crooke, Oxford, 1920.
Trevelyan, G. O., *Life and Letters of Lord Macaulay,* London, 1876.
Valentia, George, Viscount, *Voyages and Travels to India, Ceylon, the Red Sea, Abyssinia and Egypt,* London, 1809.
Volunteer, A [pseud.], *My Journal or What I Saw and Did between 9th June and 25th November 1857,* Calcutta, 1858.
White, William, *The Prince of Oude,* London, 1838.
Wilson, H. H., *The History of British India,* London, 1845.
Wylie, W. (ed.), *The English Captives in Oude,* Calcutta, 1858.
Yeoward, George, *An Episode of the Rebellion and Mutiny in Oudh of 1857 and 1858,* Lucknow, 1876.
Zimmer, Heinrich, *Philosophies of India,* edited by Joseph Campbell, New York, 1951.

Index

Adventurers, European and Eurasian, 26-7, 29-31
Afghanistan, 5
Afghans, 48, 234, 242
Afghan War, First, 76, 81, 85
Aga Mir, 39-40, 45, 65, 66-7, 78-9, 80, 267 n. 18
Agra, 12, 255
Ahban clan, 126, 131, 132, 161
Ahmad Ullah Shaj, *see* Maulvi of Faizabad, the
Ajmir, 122
Ajodhya, 18, 140, 142
Akbar, Mughal Emperor, 13, 92
Akbarpur, 162
Akhtar, 89
Alambagh, 194, 198, 201, 202, 222, 225, 229
Alexander the Great, 265 n. 10
Aligarh, 255
Ali Naqi Khan, 91, 92, 151, 211
Allahabad, 8, 151, 171, 172, 173, 176, 180, 182, 187, 203, 206, 214, 244, 248
Amanat, 23, 265 n. 19
amani system, 67, 69, 92, 103
Amethi, 130, 184, 190, 235, 237, 244, 278 n. 42
Amherst, Earl of, 80
amils, 50
Aminabad, 15, 194, 256
amins, 61
Amin-ud-daula, 71, 91
Amjad Ali Shah, King, 11, 51, 70, 71, 211
Amman, 265 n. 14
Andaman Islands, 247
Anderson, Mr, 209
Anis, 21
Arabia, 26

architecture, Lucknow school of, 11-14, 31-2
Asaf-ud-daula, Nawab, 8, 11, 13, 14-15, 16, 20, 22, 23, 26, 27, 33, 50, 52, 61, 267 n. 12, 17
Asghar Ali, perfumier, 16
Athens, 1
attar, 15
Attila, 122
Auckland, Earl of, 72, 76, 81-5, 86
Aurangzeb, Mughal Emperor, 5, 19
Auxiliary Force, *see* Oudh Auxiliary Force
Awadh, *see* Oudh
Azamgarh, 171, 189
 Nazim of, 201

Babu Madho Parshad, 189
Babu Ram Bakhsh, taluqdar, 161, 202, 237, 245, 247
Bachgoti clan, 126, 132
bagh-o-bahar 265 n. 14
Bahraich, 171, 172
Bahraich District, 153, 160, 172, 183, 187, 235, 240
Bahu Begam, 35, 38
Baillie, John, Colonel, 38, 46, 50, 60-4, 66, 67, 78-9, 144, 269-70 n. 47
Bais clan, 126, 129, 236
Baiswara, 133, 187, 235, 244
Bakhtawar Singh, 133
Balrampur, 184, 190, 252
Banda Husain, 191
Bandhalgoti clan, 128
Bani bridge, 181
Bangarmau, 202
bankers, *see* Chandan Lal, Das brothers, Shah Behari Lal
Banki, 246

Index

Banks, Major, 152, 219, 222
Bansi, 184
barber, of King of Oudh, see Derusett, George
Bareilly, 8, 233
Bari, 234, 240
Barker, Brigadier, 244
Barlowe, Captain, 143
Baroda, 7
Barrackpore, 167
Barrow, Colonel, 152
Bashiratganj, 181, 192
Baundi, 153, 235
Begam Kothi, 32, 194, 227
Bell, Dr, 99-100
Benares, 8, 18, 44, 171, 172, 180, 182, 206, 248
Bengal, 5, 6, 7, 144, 146
Beni Madho, Rana, 130, 235-6, 241, 244-7
Beni Madho, Nazim, 201, 282 n. 9
Bentham, Jeremy, 86
Bentinck, Lord William, 33, 36, 44, 46-7, 72, 76, 86, 87, 148
Berhampore, 167
Bhadri, 151, 276 n. 12
Bhagavad Gita, 142
Bhagwan Bakhsh, 237
bhakti, 142
Bhands, 18
Bhoor, 191
Bihar, 7, 165, 183
Bijapur, 13, 19
Birjis Qadr, 210-11, 214, 281 n. 19
Birch, Colonel, 170
Bird, R. M., 147, 148
Bird, Robert, Captain, 98–9
birts, 130
Birwa, 244
Bisen clan, 126, 128, 276 n. 12
Bishambarpur, 162
Biswan, 240
Bithauli, 234, 235
Bithur, 179, 182
Blackstone, William, 86, 145
Board of Control, 43-44, 46, 73, 75, 84, 108
Bodhgaya, 141
Boileau, Lieut., 172
Bokhara, 16
Bombay, 175, 176
Bombay Presidency, 7

Bonham, Lieut., 172
Brahmaputra, the, 190
brahman, 139
Brahmins, 120, 121, 123, 124, 139, 168, 188
Brajbasha, 16
Brandon, Mr., 99-101, 110
bridges, of Lucknow, 11, 228-9, 254, 256
brothels, of Lucknow, 22-3, 92, 256
Brougham, Lord, 84
'Brown Bess' (musket), 178
Buddha, 140, 141
Buddhism, 138, 140
Buland Darwaza, 13
Bundelkhand, 122
Burke, Edmund, 87
Burma, 145, 176, 192
Burmese War, First, 80
  Second, 87, 93, 104
Burnes, Lieut., 187

Cambridge, Duke of, 197
Campbell, Sir Colin (later Lord Clyde), 196-8, 222, 224-30, 233-4, 238, 242-6, 282 n. 45
Campbell, William, Brigadier, 229
canal, in Lucknow, 12, 194, 223, 265 n. 12
Canning, Charlotte, Viscountess, 193
Canning, Earl, 110, 153, 156, 158, 166, 176, 179, 181, 188, 195, 196, 201, 205, 208, 224, 238-9, 251, 253, 279 n. 17
Cape of Good Hope, 198
Carbery, John, 151-2, 276 n. 12
Carnatic, 75
Carnegy, Patrick, 143
caste, 120-1
Cawnpore, see Kanpur
Ceded and Conquered Provinces, 48, 77, 144, 146, 147-8, 259, 260
Central Drugs Research Institute, 256
Central Star, The, 110
Ceylon, 142, 176, 192
Chanda, 202
Chandan Lal, banker, 132
Chandi Lal, 283 n. 18
chakladars, 50, 51, 54, 208
Charbagh, 194, 223, 254
Charda, 235
Chattar Manzil, 11, 32, 194, 195, 200, 207, 216, 227, 228, 229, 256
Chattris, 121, 126

Index

China, 192
China trade, 76, 87, 206
Chinhat, 174, 188, 278 n. 16
Chowk Bazaar, 11, 15, 22, 256
Christian, George, 153-5, 159, 171
Chunar, 8
Clarke, Lieut., 172
Clive, Robert, 81, 165
Cochin, 7
Colvin Taluqdars' College, 252
Combermere, Lord, 44, 273 n. 29
Constantia, 32, 198, 256. *See also* La Martinière
Constantinople, 1, 13
Coorg, 72
Cornish regiment, 217, 218
Cornwallis, Earl of, 47, 61, 78, 146-7
courtesans, 22-3
Court of Indra, The, 23
Crooke, William, 140
cungi, 206
Currie, 99

Dabir, 21
Dacoitee in Excelsis, 102
Dalhousie, Marquis of, 36, 87, 89, 92-6, 98, 99, 101, 102, 104, 107-11, 115, 116, 156, 166-7, 168, 197
Dariabad, 161, 171, 184, 281 n. 21
Darshan Singh, revenue contractor, 56
Das brothers, bankers, 75-6
Daulat Khana 11, 256
Davidson, T. R., 71
debts, of Oudh government, 74-6
Deccan, 7
Delhi: architecture of, 12, 255; decline of, 11, 16, 17; and the Indian Mutiny, 161, 169, 170, 172, 176, 198, 201, 210, 214, 224, 248; Kings of, 7, 10, 192, 210; Sultans of, 5, 17, 123, 129, 264 n. 1
Deoband, 255
Deogarh, 123
Dera, 132, 157, 184, 240
Derusett, Charles, 30, 31
Derusett, George, 30-1, 86, 99
Derusett, William, 30
Devi Bakhsh Singh, Raja, 162, 235
dharma, 113
Dharupur, 184, 186, 276 n. 12
Dhaurahra, 184, 191
Dhaurwa, 189, 241

Dhundiakhera, 161, 202, 237, 245, 247
Dickens, Charles, 179
Digvijay Singh, Raja of Balrampur, 184, 186, 190, 252, 279 n. 33, 283, n. 18
Digvijay Singh, Raja of Mahona, 237-8, 247
Digvijay Sing, Raja of Murarmau, 184
Dikhit clan, 126
Dilkusha château, 1, 32, 33, 198, 201, 225, 231, 254, 257
Dinapur, 181, 184
Doab, 48
Domnis, 18
Dorin, 108
Dravidians, 121, 138-9

East India Company: armies of, 41, 93-4, 120, 124, 160, 165, 175; finances of, 76; relations of with Oudh, 8, 9, 23-9, Section 11, *passim,* Section 111, *passim Edinburgh Review,* 108.
Edmonstone, N. B., 79
Edwards, William, 159, 187, 189
Ellenborough, Earl of, 70, 73
Enfield rifle, 167, 178
Englishman, The, 107
Esanagar, 191
Eurasians, 26, 28, 29, 41
Evangelicalism, 72-3, 88, 111-2

Faizabad, 11, 17, 37, 38, 119, 143, 161, 171, 203, 211, 212, 226, 233
Faizabad District, 130, 151, 155, 183-4, 185, 189, 210, 241
Faizabad Division, 150, 152, 156, 158
Farakhabad, 192, 243
Farhad, 26
Farhangi Mahal, 16, 19
Farhatbakhsh palace, 11, 33, 82, 194, 200, 216, 256
fasana-e-ajaib, 265 n. 14
Fayrer, Joseph, 169, 218
Fatehgarh, 56, 69, 102, 190
Fatehpur, 177, 178
Fatehpur Chaurassi, 202
Fatehpur Sikhri, 13
Firoz Shah, 234, 244
Five Pillars of Islam, 18
Five Pure Ones, 19
Forbes, W. A., 157
forts, 130
Franks, General, 202, 225

Index

French, the, in India, 6

Gahlot clan, 126
Ganges, river, 12, 56, 170, 175, 180, 182, 187, 190, 192, 202, 244, 261
Garden of India, The, 114
Gardner, James, 29
Gardner, William, 29, 266 n. 28
Gattie, Mr., hairdresser, 86
Gaur clan, 126
General Service Order, 167
Ghalib, 115
ghazals, 25, 26
Ghazipur, 8
Ghazi-ud-din Haidar, King, 9, 10, 14, 16, 33, 39, 51, 61, 63, 78, 80
Ghazni, 123
Ghor, 123, 129
Ghulam Singh, Raja, 235, 244
Gogra, river, 128, 172, 240, 243, 244, 245
Golconda, 19
Goldney, Philip, Colonel, 150-2, 155
Gomti, river, 1, 11, 12, 194, 198, 201, 223, 226, 229
Gonda, 128, 132, 162, 171-2, 247
Gonda District, 130, 161, 187, 235, 240, 277 n. 30
Gonda-Bahraich, *chakla*, 57, 114
Gonne, W., 191
Gopal Khair, 283 n. 18
gopis, 91
Gorakhpur, 48, 140, 188, 189, 192, 201-2, 203
Gordon-Alexander, Lieut., 199-200
gots, 121
Grand Trunk Road, 177
Grant, Charles, 75-6
Grant, Member of Council, 108
Grant, Hope, General, 234, 235, 240
Gray, Brigadier, 168
guarrantee system, 37-41
Gubbins, Martin, 149-50, 152-8, 173-4, 183, 208, 220, 221
Gujarat, 17
Gujars, 122, 161
Gulab Singh, 186
Gurkhas, 168, 189, 231. *See also* Nepalese
Gwalior, 36, 64, 97, 124
Gwalior Contingent, 183, 201, 202, 225

Haidari Khan, 21
Hall, Colonel, 243, 244
Hanumangarhi, 143, 189
Hanumant Singh, Raja, 151, 184, 190, 276 n. 12
Haraura, 184
Hardeo Bakhsh, Raja, 159, 184, 186, 189, 252, 283 n. 18
Hardinge, Viscount, 9, 92
Hardoi District, 128, 134, 159, 161, 184, 243, 244
Harris, the Rev., 218
Hastings, Marquis of, 6, 8, 9, 29, 63-4, 67, 75, 78, 86, 114
Hastings, Warren, 8, 44, 60, 81, 267 n.12
Havelock, Henry, Brigadier, 176-8, 180-2, 188, 189, 192-5, 197, 198, 201, 216, 218, 219, 220
Hazratganj, 15, 194, 223, 227, 228
Hazrat Mahal, Begam, 210-11, 213, 222-3, 229, 234, 236, 245-7
Hearsey, Hyder Jung, 29
Hearsey, John, 191
Heber, Reginald, 27, 36, 124
Hegel, 139
Herat, 16
Herbert, Captain, 29, 266 n. 30
Highlanders, 93rd, 199, 221
Highlanders, 78th, 178, 194
Hinduism, 139-43
Hobhouse, John Cam, 84-5
Hugo, Victor, 24
Huns, 122
Hasainabad Imambara, 14
Husainabad quarter, 254
huzur tahsil, 54
Hyderabad, 7, 60, 65, 76, 87, 94, 124, 255

Iqbal-ud-daula, 84
imams, 19-20
imambaras, 20
Imperialism, British, 215
indar sabha, 23, 265 n. 19
Inder Narayan, Residency Treasurer, 46
India Act (1784), 43
Indian Mutiny: British interpretation of, 251; causes of, 165-8; general character of, 175-6, 192, 213-4; outbreak of, 161, 167, 168, 171
Indo-Europeans, 121, 138-9. *See also* Eurasians
Infanticide, 71, 125
Inglis, Brigadier, 218-9

Index

Insha, 24, 265 n.14
Irwin, H. C., 114
Islam, 18-20, 141-43; movement for regeneration of, 212. *See also* Wahhabis

Jackson, Coverley, 154-5, 156, 206, 207
Jacob, John, 166
jagirs, 49
jagirdars 207
Jahangir, Mughal prince, 9
Jai Lal Singh, Raja, 185, 210-11, 213, 222, 234, 245, 247, 279 n. 16, 282 n. 9
Jainism, 138
Jama Masjid (Delhi), 12
Jama Masjid (Lucknow), 14, 31-2
Jan Sahib, 25
Janwar clan, 126, 127
Jaunpur, 17, 129, 171, 172, 201, 236
Jaunpur District, 189, 190
Jats, 242
Jessop, engineer, 11
Jhansi, Rani of, 192
jihad, 212
Jung Bahadur, Maharajah, 235, 228, 232, 234, 247
Jurat, 25
Jussa Singh, 202
Jyoti Singh, 235

Kabul, 16, 230
Kaimahra, 130
Kaisarbagh, *see* Qaisarbagh
Kaiwan Jah, 81
Kalakankar, 151, 184, 190
Kalhans clan, 128, 274 n. 5
Kalinjar, 122, 123
Kamal-ud-din, 9
Kanauj, 122, 123
Kanhpuria clan, 126, 161, 237, 182, 244
Kanpur, 55, 56, 78, 99, 100, 110, 170, 173-4, 180, 187, 192, 196, 201, 220, 243, 255; massacre at, 178-9, 214
Kapila, 140
Karbala, battle of, 19
karbalas, 20, 21
Kashi Parshad, taluqdar, 283 n. 18
Kathaks, 17
Katiari, 159, 184, 189, 252
Kathmandu, 46
Kavanagh, Henry, 198
Kaye, Sir John, 148
Khairabad, Amil of, 241

Khairabad Division, 155, 158
Khajuri, 124
Khalji dynasty, 17
khalsa, 49
Khan Ali Khan, 279 n.16
Khan Bahadur Khan, 234
Khanjan Sing, taluqdar, 131-2
Khanzadas, 126, 143
kharif crop, 136
Khasrau, 17
Kheri District, 125, 130, 131, 161, 171, 183, 184, 191, 240, 243
Khusrau Parviz, 265 n.10
Kim, 1
Kipling, Rudyard, 1
Knighton, William, 108
Krishna, 142
ksatriyas, 121, 122
Kulraj Singh, taluqdar, 283 n.18
Kurshid Manzil, 32, 169, 200, 210, 223, 256
Kurmis, 278 n.42

Lacey, William and Mrs., 266 n. 19, 272 n. 106
Lahore, 122
Laila, 26
Lal Madho Sing, Raja, 184, 235, 237, 244
Lal Partab Sing, 151, 190
La Martinière, 32, 198, 208, 220, 221, 227, 256
lapse, doctrine of, 94
Lawrence, Sir Henry, 145, 155-7, 166, 168-70, 172, 173-5, 186, 192, 201, 205, 206, 207, 208-9, 220, 279 n. 17
Lawrence, Sir John, 176
Leckie, Dr., 23
liberalism, 72-4, 86-8, 107, 111-2
library, of Kings of Oudh, 16, 208
Liverpool, Earl of, 44
loans, by Oudh government to East India Company, 37-40, 77-85, 207, 272 n.105
Locke, John, 58, 86, 145
Lockett, Captain, 34, 43, 45
Loni Singh, Raja, 132, 184, 187, 190, 243, 247
Low, John, Colonel, 33, 36, 40, 50, 51, 55, 56, 62, 67-70, 72, 74, 82-4, 94, 101, 270-1 n. 71

Index

Lucas, Samuel, 102
Lucknow: cultural life of, 10-32; description of, 1-2; effects of annexation in, 205-9; history of, 11; Mutiny in, 69-70, 172-5, 209 ff; recapture of, 224-32; post-Mutiny development of, 254-7
Lucknow District, 130, 133, 153, 161, 237, 241, 278 n. 42
Lucknow Division, 152, 158
Ludlow, J. M., 214-5
Lyndhurst, Lord, 84

Macaulay, T. B., 60, 86, 87
Mackenzie, Holt, 147
McLeod, Captain, 32, 63
Machhi Bhawan, 11, 168, 175, 254
Maddock, Thomas, 45-7, 54, 67, 113
Madho Singh, Raja, 190
Madras, 175, 176, 192
Madras Fusiliers, 194
Madras Presidency, 7
Mahdauna, 130, 133, 143, 151, 184, 203, 240, 252
Mahmudabad, 130, 185
Maholi, 132
Mahrattas, 5, 6, 48, 49
Mahratta War, Second, 86
Maine, Sir Henry, 134
Majnun, 26
Malihabad, 161
Mallapur, 184
Malthus, Thomas 147
Mammu Khan, 211, 222, 229, 245, 247
Manners, Lord John, 272 n. 103
Man Singh, Raja, 143, 151, 184, 185, 186, 188, 190, 199, 203, 240, 252, 276 n. 13
Mario, singer, 266 n. 19
marsiya (pl.*marasi*), 20-2
Martin, Claude, 30
Marx, Karl, 137-8
Masih-ud-din, 277 n. 33
masnavi, 25, 26
Matera, 184
Maujadubanspur, 185
Maulvi of Faizabad, the, 211-4, 222-3, 229-30, 233-4
Mauranwan, 132
maya, 139
Meerut, 161, 167, 169, 176
Mehdi Ali Khan, *hakim*, 66-9, 78, 81, 102

Mehdi Hasan, Nazim, 202
Metcalfe, Sir Charles, 76, 81, 147
Mianganj, 202
Mill, James, 73, 86, 87
Minto, Earl of, 62, 144
Mir, 22, 24, 25, 26
Mir Dard, 22
Mir Hasan, 26
Mir Zamir, 21
Mithauli, 126, 130, 132, 184, 187, 190, 223, 243, 247
Moharram, 20, 265 n. 15
Moira, Earl of, *see* Hastings, Marquis of
Mongolians, 121
Montgomery, Robert, 234, 239, 251
mosques, *see* Jama Masjid
Moti Mahal palace, 194, 195, 200, 223, 256
muafi, 49
Mughal Emperors, 4, 5, 6, 7, 10, 17, 48, 210, 214, 264 n. 1
Muhamdi, 125, 171, 184, 234
Muhammad Ali Shah, King, 51, 62, 69, 70, 81, 82, 84, 85, 211
Muhammad Husain, Nazim, 201-2
mujahidin, 212
mujtahidin, 19, 281 n. 22
mukti, 142
Multan, 211
Mundy, George, 29
Munna Jan, 81-2
Muraon, 283 n. 18
Murarmau, 184, 240
Muriaon cantonments, 34, 168, 170
Musabagh, 229
Mus-hafi, 26
mushairas, 16
music, in Lucknow, 17-8, 265-6 n. 19
Muslim invasions of India, 123, 126
Mysore, 7, 72
Mysore War, Third, 78

Nain, 161, 237
Nagpur, 7, 124
Nagram, 278 n. 42
Nana Sahib, 179, 192
nankar, 131
Nanpara, 183
Napier, General, 230
Napier, Sir Charles, 73, 151, 166, 193
Narpat Singh, taluqdar, 243
Nasikh, 25-6

Index

Nasir-ud-din Haidar, King, 10, 12, 22, 27-8, 30, 31, 33, 39, 51, 52, 55, 65, 68-9, 81, 82, 97, 265 n. 19
Nasratpur, 202
Nawab Ali Khan, 185, 278 n. 16
Nawabganj, 172, 234
nazims, 52, 54, 208
Neill, General, 180, 181, 182, 195
Nepal and Nepalese, 188, 189, 190, 191, 201, 202, 225, 228, 232, 240, 246-7. *See also* Gurkhas, Jung Bahadur
Nepal War, 78, 86
Nigohan, 130, 133, 283 n. 18
nizamats, 52, 268 n. 10
non-Regulation Provinces, 206
non-Regulation system, 145
North, Major, 180, 187
Northwestern Provinces, 148, 153, 157-8, 182, 254-5
Nott, Sir William, 36, 70, 71
Nugent, Maria, Lady, 269 n. 44
Nugent, Sir George, 167

observatory, 9, 30
Oel, 130, 183
Ommaney, Mr, 209
opium, 206
Orissa, 7
Oude: Its Princes and Government Vindicated, 277 n. 33
Oudh Auxiliary Force, 83, 85
Oudh Frontier Police 277 n. 34
Oudh Irregular Force, 160, 168, 170, 171, 172, 235, 277 n. 34
Oudh Military Police 160, 170, 172, 242
Oudh, native state: annexation of 108-16; army of, 28, 64-5, 72, 105, 260; colonization of, 123, 134; crime in, 105, 106; economy of, 49-57, 74-6, 104-5, 136; Muslim conquest of, 128; religion in, 138-43; revenue system of, 49-50, 51-7, 67, 69, 131-4; royal family of, 2-3, 7; rural society of, 120-37; topography of, 119
Oudh, Province of: administration of, Sect. VI *passim*; Indian Mutiny in, 167ff, Sect. IX, *passim*; revenue settlements of, 148-60, 238-40, 241-42
Outram, James, Colonel, 104-6, 109-10, 148, 154, 168, 192-6, 197, 201, 208, 209, 216, 218, 219, 220, 226-9, 238-9, 279 n. 17, 281 n. 32

Padshahbagh, 227
Padshah Begam, 81-2
Pakistan, 255
Pali, 234
Palmer, Miss, 220
Palwar clan, 189
pan, 20
panchayats, 135
Pande family, of Gonda, 132, 162
parganas, 131
Parihar clan, 126
Parks, Fanny, 102
Partabgarh District, 56, 129, 130, 151, 155, 184, 186, 191, 235
Pasis, 188
Pathan Behar, 161
Pathoangarh, 184
Patna, 212
Paton, Lieut., 39, 42, 74, 76, 77
pattidars, 148
patwaris, 152, 158
Pawayan, 235
pensioners, at the Court of Lucknow, 37-8, 207
Persia, 5, 19, 26, 81, 176, 186, 192, 265 n. 10
Persian language, 16-7, 25-6
poetry: Delhi school of, 22, 24, 25, 26; Lucknow school of, 21-6
Pollock, Sir George, 70, 71
Prendergast, Mr, 75
presents from natives, 43-4
Prinsep, Henry, 60
Private Life of an Eastern King, The, 107-8, 273 n. 29
Probyn, Mr, 187
Punjab, 5, 6, 87, 93, 94, 105, 122, 144, 145, 155, 166, 183, 212, 284 n. 3
Punjabi, 16
Punjabis, 176. *See also* Sikhs
Puranas, 138

qabz, 52-3
Qadam Rasul, 205, 227
Qaisarbagh, 11, 32, 91, 194, 200, 201, 208, 210, 223, 227, 228, 231, 256
qanungos, 152, 158
qasida, 26
queen mother of Oudh, 109, 253

rabi harvest, 137
Rae Bareli, 212

Index

Rae Bareli District, 124, 129, 130, 153, 161, 187, 236, 237, 241, 275 n. 13, 278 n. 42
Raghbar Dyal, 114
Raghubansi clan, 126
rahas, 23, 91, 265 n. 19
Raikwar clan, 121, 126, 127, 243
raj, 127, 131
Raja, title of, 121, 127, 131, 275 n. 13
Rajkumar lineage, 126, 132, 189, 241
Rajputana, 7, 12, 36, 122
Rajputs, 120-6, 142-3, 168, 188, 274 n. 5
Rajwar lineage, 126
Ramayana, 142
Rampur, 130, 151
Rampur Khasia, 235, 244
Ram Sahai, taluqdar, 184
Rangin, 85
rani kethi ki kahani, 265 n. 14
Rapti river, 246
Raushan-ud-daula, 69
Rautar clan, 274 n. 4
Ravana, 141
Red Fort (Delhi), 7
Reform Ministry, 73
Regulating Act (1773), 43
Regulation Provinces, 206
rekhti, 25
religious conflict, 20, 143
Renaud, Major, 177-8
Rennie, John, 265 n. 11
rent theory, 147, 157
Residency, Lucknow: first relief of, 192-6; second relief of, 196-201; siege of, 170, 174-5, 211, 214-22
Residents, British, in Lucknow, 8, 28, 34-47, 60-8
revenue settlements, British, 145-8, 157-9. *See also* Oudh, Province of, revenue settlements of
Ricardo, David, 147
Ricketts, Mordaunt, 34, 36, 44-7, 80, 271 n. 80
Roberts, Abraham, 29, 266 n. 27
Roberts, Emma, 2
Roberts, Frederick, Lieut., 199, 266 n. 27
Roberts, W., 29
Rohilkhand, 48, 233, 234, 235
Rohillas, 8
Roshannagar, 161
rubai, 26

Rudamau, 243
Rudauli, 143
Ruia, 243
Rumi Darwaza, 13, 256
Russell, William Howard, 1, 2, 103, 223, 225
Russia, 81
Rustam Shah, Raja, 157, 184, 189, 240
ryots, 120, 276 n. 3

Saadat Ali Khan, Nawab, 8, 11, 31, 38, 46, 48, 50, 52, 54, 56, 61, 63, 66, 78, 258; tomb of, 32, 257
Saadat Khan, Nawab, 4, 19, 22
Sabbala, 138
Sadiq, Muhammad, 274 n. 36
Safdar Jung, 11, 22; tomb of, 12
Sakyamuni (the Buddha), 140, 141
Salon, 151, 152, 171
Sammanpur, 276 n. 12
Sandila, 233, 244
Sanskrit, 121
Sarur, 265 n. 14
sati, 71
Sauda, 22, 26
saut-e-mubarik, 89
Sayyid Ahmad of Rae Bareli, 212
Sayyids, 20
Sayyid Salar Masaud, 128
Sehsendi, *see* Nigohan
Sekrora, 171, 246
Sengur clan, 126
sepoys, 6, 160, 165-7, 209, 224, 237, 246; petitions of 41-3, 167. *See also* East India Company, armies of
Shah Behari Lal, banker, 76, 268 n. 12
Shahganj, 184, 240
Shah Jahan, Mughal Emperor, 12, 19.
Shahjahanpur, 129, 234, 235, 243
Shams-ud-daula, 272 n. 95
Shah Wali Ullah, 212
Shankarpur, 130, 236, 244
Sharf-ud-daula, 69, 71, 211, 222, 230
Sharqi dynasty, 129, 236
Sherer, John, 177-8
Shiism, 18-21, 143, 213
Shirin, 26
Shiva, 140
Shiv Ratan Sing, 161
shoes, etiquette concerning, 9
Shore, Sir John, 8, 261
Shuja-ud-daula, Nawab, 17, 22, 30, 37

Sikandarbagh, 13, 198-9, 227, 228
Sikhs, 5, 168, 176, 199, 212, 225, 228, 231, 242
Sinclair, John, 272 n. 106
Sind, 5, 6, 73, 67, 145, 151, 155, 166, 193
Singapore, 176, 192, 198
Singha Chauda, 130, 133, 162
sir, 134
Sita, 142
Sitapur, 170, 171
Sitapur District, 130, 132, 185, 240, 278 n. 16
sitar, 17
Sleeman, William, Major, 35, 43, 53, 56, 96-107, 124, 125, 148, 270-1 n. 71, 273 n. 11
Smith, Adam, 86
Soltykoff, Prince, 35
Sombansis, 125, 126
soz-khwanan, 21
Strachey, Richard, 64
Subsidiary Force, *see* Oudh, native state
subsidiary system, 6, 7, 56-60, 65, 71-2, 67, 115
sufis, 17, 141
Sulaiman Qadr, 210
Sultanpur, 171, 202, 236; Nazim of, 192, 202; Raja of, 130, 189
Sultanpur District, 56, 132, 155, 157, 184, 235
Sunni sect, 18
Suraj Narayan, 140
suttee, *see sati*

tah bazari, 206
tahsildars, 158, 277 n. 30
Tahsin Ali Khan, 38-9, 267 n. 17
Taj Mahal, 12
taluqas, 133
taluqdars, 53, 56, 57, 71, 103, 133, 146, 148-57, 251-2; attitude of during the Indian Mutiny, 183-92, 203, 223, 224, 235-48, 251
Tantras, 139
Taraul, 186
telegraph, electric, 175
Thackeray, Edmund, 228
Thomason, James, 143, 148
thuggee, 96
titles, of Kings of Oudh, 10
Tiloi, 241
Tilok Chand 129, 236

Tilokchandi lineage, 129
Tod, James, 122-3,124
Transoxiana, 26, 264 n. 1
Treaty, Anglo-Oudh: of 1772, 8; of 1775, 8, 28; of 1798, 8, 259, 261; of 1801, 48, 49, 62, 63, 72, 77, 83, 95, 107, 115, 258-62; of 1825, 39, 80; of 1837, 82-5, 95, 272 n. 102
Troup, Brigadier, 243, 244
Tulsidasa, 142
Tulsipur, 153, 161, 237, 247, 279 n. 33
Turks, 5, 264 n. 1
Twelvers, the, 19
Travancore, 7
Tytler, Robert, Colonel, 180, 187

Udresh Singh, Raja, 189, 241
Unao, 181
Unao District, 126, 132, 134, 153, 161, 184, 187, 202, 237, 240, 245
United Provinces, 255
United Services Club, 256
Upanishads, 139
Urdu, language and literature, 16-7
Utilitarians, 86, 87, 276 n. 30
Utraula, 161, 277 n. 30, 279 n. 33
Uttar Pradesh, 255

vaisyas, 121
Valentia, George, Viscount, 27
Varma, Paripurnanda, 274 n. 36
varna, 121
Vedas, 138-9
Vernon Smith, 108, 115
Victoria, Queen, 110, 253
village communities, 41, 53, 103, 127-8, 129, 131, 133-6, 146, 147, 148, 187, 202, 239-40, 275 n. 14. *See also* zemindars
Vishnu, 142
Vindhya mountains, 123
Vizier Ali Khan, 267 n. 17

Wahhabis, 212, 281 n. 22
Wajid Ali Shah, King, 16, 22, 89-92, 95, 109-10, 205, 207, 208, 210, 211, 252-4, 266 n. 19
Walpole, General, 233, 243
Wanderings of a Pilgrim in Search of the Picturesque, 102
Wasi Ali Khan, 100, 101

Wazir Ali, Nawab, 8, 14
Wellesley, Marquess, 6, 48, 258
Wellesley, the Hon. Henry, 258
Wetherall, Brigadier, 244
Wheeler, Brigadier, 109, 173, 178
White Huns, 122
Wilcox, Colonel, 266, n. 30
William IV, 46
Willis, Captain, 194
Wilson, Colonel, 196
Wilson, Horace, 60
Wingfield, Charles, 153, 172, 183, 188, 203
Wroughton, Colonel, 190, 201

yoga, 138
Yusuf, 26

Zahar Singh, 283 n. 18
Zahur-ul-hasan, 190
Zaman Shah, 48
zemindars: in Benares, 277, n. 30; in Bengal, 146-7, 275-6 n. 2; in Oudh, 42, 56, 67, 71, 127, 131, 159, 162; attitude during the Mutiny, 186-92, 202, 233
zemindaris, 131, 133, 134, 153
zillas, 61
Zulaiqa, 26